ISBN 978-0-332-39093-2
PIBN 11225108

1 MONTH OF
FREE
READING

at
www.ForgottenBooks.com

By purchasing this book you are eligible for one month membership to ForgottenBooks.com, giving you unlimited access to our entire collection of over 1,000,000 titles via our web site and mobile apps.

To claim your free month visit:
www.forgottenbooks.com/free1225108

English
Français
Deutsche
Italiano
Español
Português

www.forgottenbooks.com

Mythology Photography **Fiction**
Fishing Christianity **Art** Cooking
Essays Buddhism Freemasonry
Medicine **Biology** Music **Ancient**
Egypt Evolution Carpentry Physics
Dance Geology **Mathematics** Fitness
Shakespeare **Folklore** Yoga Marketing
Confidence Immortality Biographies
Poetry **Psychology** Witchcraft
Electronics Chemistry History **Law**
Accounting **Philosophy** Anthropology
Alchemy Drama Quantum Mechanics
Atheism Sexual Health **Ancient History**
Entrepreneurship Languages Sport
Paleontology Needlework Islam
Metaphysics Investment Archaeology
Parenting Statistics Criminology
Motivational

OR, A

THIRD PART

OF THE

ENQUIRY

AFTER

HAPPINESS.

BY

RICHARD LUCAS, *D. D.*
Late Prebendary of *Westminster.*

Therefore leaving the principles of the doctrine of Christ, let us go on to perfection, Heb. vi. 1.

The FIFTH EDITION.

LONDON:
Printed for W. INNYS and R. MANBY, at the West-End of St. *Paul's.* MDCCXXXV.

T O

Whitelocke Bulstrode,

O F T H E

INNER TEMPLE, Esquire.

I Here present you, my dear Friend, with a discourse, wherein I labour to advance the great and true ends of life, the glory of God, and the perfection and happiness of man. I cannot, I confess, pretend to have come up to the dignity of my subject; yet I have done what I could, and have attempted it with my utmost force. I know you too well to imagine you fond of an ad-

A 2 dress

The Epiſtle Dedicatory.

dreſs of this publick nature : you
love the real and ſolid ſatisfactions,
not the pomp and ſhew, thoſe ſplen-
did incumbrances of life : your rational and virtuous pleaſures burn
like a gentle and chearful flame,
without noiſe or blaze. However, I
cannot but be confident, that you'll
pardon the liberty which I here take,
when I have told you, that the making the beſt acknowldgement I
could to one, who has given me ſo
many proofs of a generous and paſ-
ſionate friendſhip, was a pleaſure too
great to be reſiſted. I am,

Dear Sir,

Unfeignedly Yours,

R. LUCAS.

THE
CONTENTS.

SECT. I.
Of Religious Perfection *in general.*

A 3   *duced*

The CONTENTS.

SECT

The CONTENTS.

SECT. II.

The CONTENTS.

SECT. III.

Of the Impediments of Perfection.

THE

THE
INTRODUCTION.

firſt, I endeavour to remove thoſe objections which repreſent all enquiries and attempts after true happineſs in this life, either as fantaſtick or unneceſſary; or, which
is as bad, vain and to no purpoſe: and, after I have aſſerted the *value* and *poſſibility* of
happineſs, I do in general point out the
true reaſons of our ill ſucceſs and diſap-
pointment in purſuit of it. In the *ſecond*,
I ſtate the true notion of *human life*, inſiſt
upon the ſeveral kinds of it, and ſhew what
qualifications and virtues the *active* and *contemplative* life demand; and then conſider
how life may be prolonged and improved,
in this *third*, I proſecute the ſame deſign,
which I had in the two former; the promoting human happineſs. For *life, perfection*, and *happineſs* have a cloſe and inſepa-
rable

rable dependance on one another. For as *life*, which is the rational exercife and employment of our powers and faculties, does naturally advance on, and terminate in *Perfection*; fo *Perfection*, which is nothing elfe but the maturity of human virtues, does naturally end in that reft and peace, that tranquillity, ferenity, and joy of mind, which we call *Happinefs.* Now *Perfection*, in an abftracted and metaphyfical notion of it, is a ftate that admits neither of acceffion nor diminution. But talking of it practically, and in a manner accommodated to the nature of things, the *Perfection* of man confifts in fuch endowments and attaiments as man is generally capable of in this life. And becaufe man may be confidered either in relation to *this*, or to *another* world, therefore *human Perfection* may, I think, naturally enough be divided into *religious* and *fecular*. By *fecular*, I mean that which regards our intereft in this life: by *religious*, that which fecures it in eternity. The one more directly and immediately aims at the favour of man; the other at the favour of God: the one purfues that happinefs, whatever it be, that is to be found in outward and worldly advantages: the other, that which flows from virtue and a good confcience. 'Tis eafy now to difcern, which of thefe two kinds of *Perfection* is the more defirable; the one

purifies

purifies and exalts our nature, the other po-
lifhes and varnifhes it; the one makes a
compleat gentleman, the other a true Chriftian; the fuccefs of the one is precarious,
that of the other certain, having no dependance on time or chance, the humour or
fancy of man ; the pleafure of the one, is
fhort and fuperficial ; that of the other,
great and lafting ; the *world* admires the
one, and *God* approves the other. To be
throughly perfuaded of *this*, is a good ftep
towards true wifdom, as being that, which
will enable man to fteer the whole courfe
of life aright. But while I prefer the one,
I do not prefcribe the neglect or contempt
of the other; fo far am I from it, that I
am of opinion, that fecular *Perfection* has
very often fome influence upon our fpiritual
ftate, as well as its ufe and advantage in
reference to our temporal one : that the moft
admired accomplifhments of a fecular life,
are fo far from being inconfiftent with religion, that they naturally fpring from it,
and thrive and flourifh moft when they are
influenced and cultivated by it ; and judging that it might be of fome fervice to the
world to inform and convince them of *this*,
I had it fometimes in my thoughts to have
treated here as well of fecular as religious
Perfection: but doubting how well this
might fuit with my function, and how far
the beft obfervations I could make on this

fubject

fubject might fall fhort of anfwering t
expectation of men of worldly parts a
experience, I laid afide the defign. He
then, I confine my meditations wholly
Religious Perfection; I examine the natu
of it, both in general, and in particula
not only ftating the true notion of it, b
alfo defcending to the feveral branches ar
parts of it; I free it from thofe miftak
and difputes that perplex and incumber i
I lay down the motives to it, and prefcrit
the ways of obtaining it.

After this fhort account of my defign
the next thing I am to do, is to prevent,
I can, thofe prejudices which may eith
wholly fruftrate, or at leaft very much hin
der and diminifh the fuccefs and influence
it. Some are apt to ftartle at the ver
mention of Perfection; they have enter
tained fuch humble thoughts, not only o
human nature, but, as it feems, of divin
grace too and evangelical righteoufnef
that all talk of Perfection feems to then
like the preaching a new gofpel, and an ob
truding upon the world a fantaftick fchem
of proud and pretending morality. Bu
this fear will foon vanifh, when I tel
fuch; that I difcourfe of the *Perfection* o
men, not *angels*: and, that I treat *this*, no
like a *monk*, or a fublime and fubtle *fchoo*
man, but like one, who have been dail
converfant with the doubts and fcruples
witl

with the fears and frailties of human nature, and departing fouls. I do not pretend to blefs the world with the difcovery
of *new* truths. If at any time I place *old*
ones in a better light; if I wipe off the
duft, which difpute and time, and the corruption of manners, has here and there fcat-
tered upon them, 'tis the utmoft I aim at.

But how numerous, will fome fay, are
the controverfies that have in every age
perplexed this fubject? *Grace* and *nature*,
perfection and *fin*, *merit*, *fupererogation*, &c.
thefe are themes that have exercifed and
embroiled the Church of Chrift, almoft
through all the feveral ages of it down to
this day: and with how little advantage
to the honour of Chriftianity, and the intereft of virtue, have the brighteft parts,
and the deepeft learning been here employed? To *this*, all I have to fay, is, I write
practically, and confult the intereft of fouls,
not *parties*. I cannot but fee, and that with
trouble and regret, how much Chriftianity
has in almoft all times fuffered by thofe nice
and fubtle, by thofe obftinate and paffionate difputes, with which writers have even
oppreffed and ftifled the moft *practical* fub-
jects; and do moft earneftly defire to fee the
fpirit of *Polemical* divinity caft out of the
Church of Chrift, and *that* of a *practical*
and *experimental one* eftablifhed in the room
of it. Tho' therefore, I have confidered
those

thofe controverfies which concern my fu[l]
je&t, it was with no other defign, than [i]
guard and fortify my reader againft the
influence of feveral errors, with which the
abound. I decline all ufelefs fpeculation
and labour wholly to reftore religion to· i
native ftrength and beauty; fo that I thin[k]
this obje&tion will not touch me, who d[o]
not propofe to write a *learned*, but a *ufefi*
book.

If any man be apprehenfive, that'tis im
poffible to affert the do&trine of *Perfection*
without looking a little too favourably to
wards *Pelagianifm* or *Enthufiafm*, or fome
thing of this kind; I do here affure fuch [a]
one, that I advance no *Perfection* that raife[s]
men above the ufe or need of *means*, or in
vites them to negle&t the *word*, *prayer*, o[r]
Sacraments, or is raifed on any other foundation than the *gofpel* of *Chrift*. I revive
not *Pelagianifm*, nor clafh with St *Auftin* [:]
I need not thofe conceffions which he make[s]
Cœleftius in the clofe of his book *de Per-
fectione Juftitiæ*. I am perfuaded that the
ftrength of *nature* is too flight a foundation
to build *Perfection* on: I contend for *freedom* from no other fin than *actual*, *voluntary*, and *deliberate* : and let concupifcence,
or any unavoidable diftemper, or diforder
of our nature, be what it will, all that I
aim at here is, the *reducing*, not *extirpating*
it. And finally, how earneftly foever I
                                                    exhort

exhort to *Perfection*, I can very well content my self with St. *Auftin's notion of it,* namely, that it is nothing elfe, but *a daily progrefs towards that pure and unfpotted holinefs, which we fhall attain to in another life.*

Thus, I think, I have fufficiently guarded this following difcourfe againft the mifapprehenfions and jealoufies of all, who have any ferious concern for religion, how much foever they may be fwayed by fome particular opinions. But after all, I do not expect that it fhould meet with a very obliging reception from a great part of the world. Many there are, who will ever openly rally and ridicule all attempts of this kind: and there are others, who will fecretly flight and inwardly defpife them, as the vain and fond projects of well-meaning indeed, but very weak and unexperienced mortals. But this moves me little; thefe men are generally too much ftrangers to *fincerity*, to be competent judges of *Perfection:* nor do I wonder, if the corrupt and vicious part of mankind be infected with as much malice and envy againft extraordinary goodnefs, as fome are againft power and greatnefs. The confcioufnefs of much bafenefs and corruption in one's felf, is apt to make one ftrive to bring down all men to the fame level, and to believe that there is nothing of *Perfection* in the world, but only a groundlefs or hypocritical pretenfion to it.

it. This is an opinion that ill men gree
ly embrace, becaufe it gives them fo
kind of peace, fecurity, and confidenc
whereas the contrary opinion, as it wou
be apt to make them afhamed of their *p
fent* ftate, fo would it make them fear
and apprehenfive of their *future* one.
write not therefore to fuch as thefe, n
can be much concerned what cenfure th
pafs on a defign, againft which they ha
an inveterate and obftinate averfion.

The method I obferve in this treatife i
in the *firft fection*, I confider *Perfection* mo
generally : in the *fecond*, the feveral pai
of it ; and in the *laft*, the *obftacles* and *imp
diments* of our attaining it. In the two fi
fections, I always firft fix and explain tl
notion of that ftate of virtue which I di
courfe of. Next I proceed to the *fruits*
advantages of it ; and in the laft place pr
fcribe the *method* by which it may be a
tained.

SECT. I.

Of Religious Perfection *in general.*

CHAP. I.

Perfection *a confirmed habit of holiness. This notion conformable to reason and scripture. The nature of an habit considered, according to four properties of it.*

OST disputes and controversies arise from false and mistaken notions of the matter under debate; and *so* I could shew it has happened here. Therefore, to prevent mistakes, and cut off all occasions of *contention* (which serves only to defeat the influence and success of practical discourses) I think it necessary to begin here with a plain account *what* it is I mean by *Religious Perfection.*

Religion is nothing else, but the purifying and refining nature by grace, the raising and exalting our faculties and capacities by wisdom and virtue. *Religious Perfec-*

B
tion,

tion, therefore, is nothing elſe but the me
ral accompliſhment of human nature, ſuc
a maturity of virtue as man in this lif
is capable of; *Converſion* begins, *Perfectic*
conſummates the habit of righteouſneſs
in the one, religion is, as it were, in it
infancy; in the other, in its ſtrength an
manhood; ſo that *Perfection*, in ſhort,
nothing elſe, but a ripe and ſettled *hab*
of true holineſs. According to this not
on of religious *Perfection*, he is a *perfec*
man, whoſe *mind* is pure and vigorous, an
his *body* tame and obſequious; whoſ
faith is firm and ſteady, his *love* arden
and exalted, and his *hope* full of aſſu
rance; whoſe *religion* has in it that ardou
and conſtancy, and his *ſoul* that tranquil
lity and pleaſure, which beſpeaks him
child of the *light*, and of the *day, a par*
taker of the Divine Nature, and raiſe
above the corruption which is in the wor
through luſt.

This account of religious *Perfection*
ſo natural and eaſy, that I fancy no ma
will demand a *proof* of it; nor ſhould I g
about one, were it not to ſerve ſome *fur*
ther ends than the mere confirmation of i
It has manifeſtly the countenance both
reaſon and *ſcripture;* and how contradict
ry ſoever ſome ancient and latter ſchem
of *Perfection* ſeem to be, or really are,
one another; yet do they all agree in effe

in what I have laid down. If we appeal to *Reason*, no man can doubt, but that an *habit* of virtue has much more of excellence and merit in it, than single accidental *acts*, or uncertain fits and passions; since an *habit* is not only the source and spring of the noblest actions and the most elevated passions, but it renders us more regular and steady, more uniform and constant in every thing that is good. As to good natural *dispositions*, they have little of strength, little of perfection in them, till they be raised and improved into *habits*: and for our *natural faculties*, they are nothing else, but the *capacities* of good or evil; they are undetermined to the one or other, till they are fixed and influenced by *moral* principles. It remains then, that religious *Perfection* must consist in an *habit* of righteousness. And to prevent all impertinent scruples and cavils, I add a *confirmed* and well established one.

That this is the scripture notion of *Perfection*, is manifest; *First*, From the use of this word in scripture. *Secondly*, From the characters and descriptions of the best and highest state which any ever actually attained, or to which we are invited and exhorted.

1. From the use of the word: wherever we find any mention of *Perfection* in *scripture*, if we examine the place well,

we

we fhall find nothing more intended, t
uprightnefs and *integrity*, an unblame:
and unreproveable life, a ftate well
vanced in knowledge and virtue.   I
upright and *perfeƈt* are ufed as terms e
valent, *Job* i. *And that man was per*
and upright, fearing God and efchewin
vil; and *Pfalm* xxxvii. 37. *Mark the per*
man and behold the upright man, for the
of that man is peace. Thus again, w
God exhorts *Abraham* to *Perfeƈtion*, (
xvii. 1 *I am the Almighty God ; walk*
fore me and be thou perfeƈt, all that he
horts him to, is a fteady *obedience* to all
commandments, proceeding from a liv
fear of, and faith in him ; and this is the
neral ufe of this word *Perfeƈt* through
the *Old Teftament,* namely to fignify a
cere and juft man, that feareth God, ;
efcheweth evil, and is well fixed and e:
blifhed in his duty.   In the *New Teftam*
Perfeƈtion fignifies the fame thing whicl
does in the *Old*; that is, univerfal rigl
oufnefs, and ftrength, and growth in
Thus the *perfeƈt* man, 2 *Tim.* iii. 17
one who is *throughly furnifhed to every*
work. Thus St. *Paul* tells us, *Col.* iv. 12. t
Epaphras laboured fervently in prayers
the Coloffians, that they might ftand per
and compleat in all the will of God. In *Ja*
i. 4. the *perfeƈt* man is one, *who is ent*
lacking nothing, i. e. one who is advancec
a *ma*

a *maturity* of virtue through patience and experience, and is fortified and eſtabliſhed in faith, love, and hope. In *this* ſenſe of the word *Perfect* St. *Peter* prays for thoſe to whom he writes his epiſtle, 1 *Pet.* v. 10. *But the God of all grace, who called us into his eternal glory by Chriſt Jeſus, after that ye have ſuffered a while, make you perfect, ſtabliſh, ſtrengthen, ſettle you.* When St. *Paul* exhorts the *Hebrews* to go on to *Perfection, Heb.* vi. he means nothing by it, but that ſtate of manhood which conſiſts in a well ſettled *habit* of wiſdom and goodneſs. This is plain, *firſt,* from *ver.* 11, 12. of this *chapter,* where he himſelf more fully explains his own meaning; *and we deſire that every one of you do ſhew the ſame diligence, to the full aſſurance of hope* unto the *end; that ye be not ſlothful, but followers of them who through faith and patience inherit the promiſe. Next,* from the latter end of the 5th *chapter;* where we diſcern *what* gave occaſion to this exhortation; *there* diſtinguiſhing *Chriſtians* into two claſſes, *babes* and *ſtrong men,* i. e. *perfect* and *imperfect,* he deſcribes *both* at large thus: *For when for the time ye ought to be teachers, ye have need that one teach you again which be the firſt principles of the oracles of God, and are become ſuch as have need of milk, and not of ſtrong meat; for every one that uſeth milk is unſkilful in the word of righteouſneſs; for he*

is

*is a babe; but strong meat belongeth to them
that are of full age, even those who by reason
of use have their senses exercised to discern both
good and evil.* And 'tho' here the apostle
seems more immediately to regard the
perfection of *knowledge*; yet the *perfection*
of *righteousness* must never, in the language of the *scripture*, be separated from
it. Much the same remark must I add
concerning the *integrity* of righteousness,
and the Christians progress or advance in
it. *Tho'* the *scripture*, when it speaks of
Perfection, doth sometimes more directly
refer to the one, and sometimes to the
other; *yet* we must ever suppose that they
do mutually imply and include *one another*;
since otherwise the notion of *Perfection*
would be extremely maimed and incom-
pleat. I will insist therefore no longer on
the use of the words *Perfect* and *Perfection* in *scripture:* but as a further proof that
my notion of *Perfection* is truly *scriptural,*
I will shew,

2. That the utmost *height,* to which the
scripture exhorts us, is nothing more than
a steady *habit* of holiness; that the brigh-
test *characters* it gives of the *perfect man,*
the loveliest *descriptions* it makes us of the
perfectest state, are all made up of the *natural* and confessed *properties* of a ripe *habit.* There is no controversy that I know
of, about the *nature* of a *habit,* every
man's

man's experience inftruAs him in the whole philofophy of it; we are all agreed, that it is a kind of *fecond nature,* that it makes us exert our felves with defire and earneftnefs, with fatisfaAion and pleafure; that it renders us fixed in our choice, and conftant in our aAions, and almoft as a-verfe to thofe things which are repugnant to it, as we are to thofe which are dif-tafteful and difagreeable to our nature. And that, in a word, it fo entirely and abfolutely poffeffes the man, that the pow-er of it is not to be refifted, nor the em-pire of it to be fhaken off; nor can it be removed and extirpated without the great-eft labour and difficulty imginable. All this is a confefs'd and almoft palpable truth in *habits of fin:* and there is no reafon why we fhould not afcribe the fame force and efficacy to *habits of virtue;* efpecially if we confider that the ftrength, eafinefs, and pleafure which belong *naturally to thefe ha-bits,* receive no fmall *acceffion* from the *fu-pernatural* energy and vigour of the *Holy Spirit.* I will therefore in a few words fhew how that *ftate of righteoufnefs* which the *fcripture* invites us to, as our *Perfecti-on,* directly, anfwers this account I have given of an *habit.*

Is *habit* in *general* a fecond nature? This ftate of righteoufnefs is in fcripture cal-led *the new man,* Ephef. iv. 24. *the new*

creature,

creature, 2 Cor. v. 17. *the Divine Nature,*
2 *Pet.* i. 4. Does it confequently *rule* and
govern man? Hear how St. *Paul* expreffes
this power of the *habit* of holinefs in himfelf, *Gal.* ii. 20. *I am crucified with
Chrift; neverthelefs I live, yet not I, but
Chrift liveth in me; and the life which I
now live in the flefh, I live by the faith of
the Son of God, who loved me, and gave
himfelf for me.* This is a conftant effect of
habits, and is equally difcernible in thofe of
vice and *virtue,* that they *fway* and *govern*
the man they poffefs; *Rom.* vi. 16. *Know
ye not, that to whom ye yield your felves fervants to obey, his fervants ye are to whom ye
obey; whether of fin unto death, or of obedience unto righteoufnefs?*

Shall I go on to a more diftinct and particular confideration of the properties of
an habit? The *firft* is, a great *averfion* for
thofe things which are *contrary* to it, or
obftruct us in the exercife of it. And this
is directly the difpofition of the *perfect*
man towards *temptations* and *fins;* he is
now afhamed of thofe things, which before
he gloried in; he is filled with an holy indignation againft thofe things, which before
he took pleafure in; and what before he
courted with fondnefs and paffion, he
now fhuns with fear and vigilance. In
brief, the *fcripture* defcribes fuch an one as
poffeffed with an utter hatred and abhorrence

rence of every evil way, and as an irreconcileable enemy to every thing that is an enemy to his virtue and his God. Thus Pſal. cxix. 163. *I hate and abhor lying, but thy law do I love*; and *verſe* 128. *Therefore I eſteem all thy precepts concerning all things to be right, and I hate every falſe way.* And this is a genuine and natural effect of integrity or uprightneſs of heart; whence 'tis the obſervation of our *Saviour,* Matt. vi. 24. *No man can ſerve two maſters; for either he will hate the one, and love the other; or elſe he will hold to the one, and deſpiſe the other.* And indeed every-where a hatred, a perfect hatred of evil, is accounted as a neceſſary conſequence of the love of God; *Pſal.* xxxvii. 10. *Ye that love the Lord, hate evil:* and therefore the *Pſalmiſt* reſolves to practiſe himſelf what he preſcribes to others; *Pſal.* ci. 2, 3. *I will behave my ſelf wiſely in a perfect way: O when wilt thou come unto me? I will walk within my houſe with a perfect heart: I will ſet no wicked thing before mine eyes: I hate the work of them that turn aſide, it ſhall not cleave to me.* And how can this be otherwiſe? the love of God muſt neceſſarily imply an abhorrence of evil; and that *habit,* which confirms and increaſes the one, muſt confirm and increaſe the other too.

2. The *next* property of an *habit* is, that the *actions* which flow from it are

(if

(if we meet not with violent oppofition)
performed with *eafe* and *pleafure:* what
is *natural,* is pleafant and eafy, and *habit* is a *fecond nature.* When the love of
virtue, and the hatred of vice, have once
rooted themfelves in the foul, what can
be more natural than to follow after the
one, and fhun the other? fince this is no
more than embracing and enjoying what
we love, and turning our backs on what
we deteft. This therefore is one conftant
character of *Perfection* in *fcripture: delight* and *pleafure* are every-where faid to
accompany the practice of virtue, when
it is once grown up to ftrength and maturity: *The ways of wifdom are ways of pleafantnefs, and all her paths are peace,* Prov.
iii. 17. *Perfect love cafteth out fear,* 1 Joh.
iv. 18. And to him that loves, *the commandments of God are not grievous,* 1 Joh.
v. 3. Hence it is, that *the good man's delight is in the law of the Lord,* and that *he
meditates therein day and night,* Pfal. i. 2.
Nor does he delight lefs in *action* than *meditation,* but grows in *grace* as much as
knowledge; and abounds daily more and
more in *good works,* as he increafes in the
comfort of the *Holy Ghoft.* Confonant to
this property of *Perfection* it is, that in
Pfalm xix, and cxix, and elfewhere frequently, we hear the *Pfalmift* expreffing a
kind of inconceivable joy, and tranfport
in

in the meditation and practice of the commands of God. So the first Christians, who spent their lives in devotion, faith, and charity, are said, *Acts* ii. 46. to have *eaten their meat with gladness and singleness of heart.* And 'tis a delightful description we have of the apostles, 2 *Cor* vi. 10. *As sorrowful, yet alway rejoicing ; as poor, yet making many rich; as having nothing, yet possessing all things.*

3. *Vigour* and *activity*, or much *earnestness* and *application* of mind, is a *third* property of an *habit.* 'Tis impossible not to be intent upon those things for which we have even an *habitual* passion, if this *expression* may be allow'd me ; an inclination, which has gathered strength and authority from custom, will exert itself with some warmth and briskness. Now certainly there is nothing more frequently required of, or attributed to the *perfect* man in *scripture*, than *zeal* and *fervency* of spirit in the ways of God; and no wonder; for when actions flow at once from principles and custom; when they spring from love, and are attended by pleasure, and are incited and quickened by faith and hope too; how can it be, but that we should repeat them with some eagerness, and feel an holy impatience as often as we are hindered or disappointed ? and as the nature of the thing shews, that thus it

ought

ought to be, so are there innumerable instances in the *Old Teſtament* and the *New*,
which make it evident that thus it *was*.
Shall I mention the example of our *Lord*,
who went about doing good, Acts x. 38 ?
shall I propoſe the labours and travels of
St. *Paul?* theſe patterns it may be will be
judged by ſome too bright and dazling a
light for us to look on, or at leaſt too perfect for us to copy after; and yet St. *John*
tells us, that *he, who ſays he abides in him,
ought himſelf alſo ſo to walk, even as he
walked,* 1 John ii. 6. And we are exhorted
to *be followers of the apoſtles, as they were of
Chriſt.* But if the fervency of *Chriſt* and
St. *Paul* ſeemed to have ſoared out of the
reach of our imitation, we have *inferior*
inſtances enough, to prove the zeal and
fruitfulneſs of *habitual* goodneſs. Thus
David ſays of himſelf, *Pſal.* cxix. 10. *With
my whole heart have I ſought thee.* And *Jo-
ſiah,* 2 *Kings* xxiii. 25. is ſaid to have *turned
to the Lord with all his ſoul, and with all his
might.* How fervent was *Anna,* who *de-
parted not from the temple, but ſerved God
with faſtings and prayers night and day,* Luke
ii. 37 ? How charitable *Tabitha,* who *was
full of good works and alms-deeds which ſhe
did,* Acts ix. 36? where ſhall I place
Cornelius? with what words ſhall I ſet out
his virtues? with *what* but thoſe of the
Holy Ghoſt, Acts x. 2. *He was a devout*
man,

man, and one that feared God with all his
house, which gave much alms to the people,
and prayed to God alway. But peradventure
some may imagine, that there is something
singular and extraordinary in these eminent persons, which we must never hope
to equal; but must be content to follow
them at a vast distance. Well, let this
be so; what have we to say to whole
churches animated by the same spirit of
zeal? what are we to think of the *churches*
of *Macedonia,* whose *charity* St. *Paul* thus
magnifies, 2 Cor. viii. 2, 3. *In a great trial of
affliction, the abundance of their joy and their
deep poverty abounded to the riches of their
liberality. For to their power I bear record,
yea, and beyond their power, they were willing
of themselves.* And St. *Paul* declares himself *persuaded* of the *Romans, that they
were full of goodness, filled with all knowledge,* Rom. xv. 14. And of the *Corinthi-
ans* he testifies, *that they were inriched in
every thing, and came behind in no gift.*
1 Cor. i. 5, 6. *That they did abound in all
things, in faith, in diligence,* &c. 2 Cor. viii. 7.
I will stop here; 'tis in vain to heap up
more instances: I have said enough to
shew, that *vigour* and *fervency* in the service of God, is no miraculous gift, no extraordinary prerogative of some peculiar
favourite of heaven, but the natural and
inseparable *property* of a well-confirmed *habit* of holiness.   Lastly;

Lastly ; Is *constancy* and *steadiness* the property of an *habit?* it is an undoubted property of *perfection* too. In *scripture* good men are every-where represented *as standing fast in the faith*; *stedfast and unmoveable in the works of God*; *holding fast their integrity:* in one word, as constantly following after righteousness, and maintaining a good conscience towards God and man. And so natural is this to one *habitually* good, that St. *John* affirms of such a one, *that he cannot sin*; 1 John iii. 9. *Whosoever is born of God, doth not commit sin, for his seed remaineth in him, and he cannot sin, because he is born of God.* Accordingly, *Job* is said *to have feared God, and eschewed evil*; which must be understood of the constant course of his life. *Zachary* and *Elizabeth* are said to be *righteous, walking in all the commandments of God blameless*, Luke i. 6. *Enoch, Noah, David*, and other excellent persons, who are pronounced by God *righteous*, and *just*, and *perfect*, are said in *scripture, to walk with God, to serve him with a perfect heart with a full purpose of heart to cleave to him*, and the like. And this is that *constancy* which *Christians* are often exhorted to ; *watch ye, stand fast in the faith, quit ye like men, be strong*, 1 Cor. xvi. 13. And of which the first followers of our *Lord* left us such remarkable *examples*. The *disciples* are
said

said to have been continually in the temple *blessing and praising God,* Luke xxiv. And the *first Christians* are said to *have continued stedfastly in the apostles doctrine and fellowship, and in breaking of bread, and in prayers,* Acts ii. 42.

Thus I think I have sufficiently cleared my notion of *Perfection* from *scripture*: nor need I multiply more texts, to prove what I think no man can doubt of, unless he mistake the main design and end of the *gospel*; which is to raise and exalt us to a steady *habit* of holiness: *The end of the commandment,* saith St. *Paul,* 1 Tim. i. 5. *is charity out of a pure heart, and of a good conscience, and of faith unfeigned.* This is the utmost *Perfection* man is capable of, to have his mind enlightened, and his heart purified; and to be informed, acted, and influenced by faith and love, as by a vital principle: and all this is essential to *habitual* goodness.

If any one desire *further* light or satisfaction in this matter, let him read the eighth *chapter* to the *Romans,* and he will soon acknowledge, that he there finds the substance of what I have hitherto advanced. *There,* though the *word* itself be not found, the *thing* called *Perfection* is described in all the strength and beauty, in all the pleasure and advantages of it: there the disciple of *Jesus* is represented

as

as one, *who walks not after the flesh, but after the spirit*; as one, *whom the law of the spirit of life in Christ Jesus has set free from the law of sin and death*; one, who ὃ φρονῶ, *does not mind or relish the things of the flesh, but the things of the spirit*; one, *in whom the spirit of Christ dwells*: he does not stand at the door, and knock; he does not make a transient visit; but here he reigns, and rules, and inhabits: one finally, *in whom the body is dead because of sin, but the spirit is life because of righteousness.* And the result of all this is the joy and confidence, the security and transport that becomes the child of God. *Ye have not received the spirit of bondage again to fear, but ye have received the spirit of adoption, whereby we cry Abba, Father. The spirit itself beareth witness with our spirit, that we are the children of God; and if children, then heirs, heirs of God, and joint-heirs with Christ.* And now 'tis no wonder, if the *perfect* man *long for the revelation of the glory of the sons of God*; if he cry out in rapture, *If God be for me, who can be against me? who shall lay any thing to the charge of God's elect? who shall separate me from the love of Christ?* and so on. If any one would see the *perfect* man described in *fewer* words, he needs but cast his eye on *Rom.* vi. 22. *But now being made free from sin, and become servants to God, ye have your fruit unto holiness, and the end everlasting life.* C H A P.

CHAP. II.

This notion of Perfection countenanced by all parties, however different in their expressions. Some short reflections upon what the Pelagians, *the* Papists, *the* Quakers, *and the* mystical *writers, have said concerning* Perfection.

AFTER I have shewed that this notion of *Perfection* is warranted by *reason* and *scripture*; I see not why I should be very solicitous whether it do or do not clash with the *opinions* of men. But the truth is, if we examine not so much the *expressions* and *words*, as the *sense* and *meaning* of all *parties* about this matter, we shall find them well enough *agreed* in it at the bottom. And 'tis no wonder, if (notwithstanding several incidental *disputes*) they should yet agree in the *main:* since the experience of mankind does easily teach us *what* sort of *Perfection* human *nature* is capable of; and what can, or cannot actually be attained by *man*. The *Pelagians* did not contend for an *angelical Perfection*, nor St. *Austin* deny *such* a one as was truly *suitable to man:* the *one* could not be so far a stranger to *human nature*, as to exempt it in reality from those errors and defects which the best of men complain of,

C and

and labour againſt. Nor was St. *Auſtin* ſo
little acquainted with the *power of the goſpel,* and of the *ſpirit,* as not to be well
enough aſſured that man might be *habitually good,* and that ſuch were influenced
and acted by a firm faith, and a fervent
love, and well-grounded hope. The *diſpute* between them then, concerning *Perfection,* did not conſiſt in *this,* whether
men might be *habitually* good? This was
in reality *acknowledged* on *both* ſides: nor,
whether the beſt men were ſubject to defects? For *this* too *both* ſides could not
but be ſenſible of: but in theſe *two things*
eſpecially; *Firſt, What* was to be attributed to *grace, what* to *nature?* and this
relates not to the *definition* or *eſſence* of
Perfection, but to the *ſource* and *origin*
of it. *Secondly,* Whether thoſe *irregular*
motions, defects, and errors, to which
the beſt men were ſubject, were to
be accounted *ſins,* or not? neither the one
ſide nor the other then, as far as I can diſcern, did in truth miſtake the nature of
human Perfection : each placed it in *habitual* righteouſneſs ; the one contended for
no *more,* nor did the other contend for *leſs,*
in the *perfect* man. And when the *one* aſſerted him free from *ſin,* he did not aſſert
him free from *defects :* And while the
other would not allow the beſt man to be
without *ſin,* they did not by *ſin* under-
                                    ſtand

stand any thing elſe, but ſuch *diſorders*, *oppoſitions* to, or *deviations* from the law of *God*, as the *Pelagian* himſelf muſt needs own to be in the *perfect* man. The diſpute then was not, *what* man might or might not attain to? for both ſides agreed him capable of the ſame *habitual* righteouſneſs; both ſides allowed him ſubject to the ſame *frailties:* but *one* ſide would have theſe *frailties* accounted *ſins*, and the *other* would *not*.

Numerous indeed have been the controverſies between the *popiſh* and *reformed churches*, about *precept* and *counſel*, *mortal* and *venial* ſin, the *poſſibility* of fulfilling the law of *God*, the *merit* of good works, and ſuch like. But after all, if we enquire what that *height* of *virtue* is to which the beſt of men may arrive; what thoſe *frailties* and *infirmities* are, to which they are ſubject; 'twere, I think, eaſy to ſhew, that the wiſe and good are on all hands *agreed* about this. Nor does it much concern my preſent purpoſe, in what ſenſe, or on what account *Papiſts* think ſome ſins venial, and *Proteſtants* deny them to be ſo; ſince neither the one nor the other exempt the *perfect* man from *infirmities*, nor aſſert any other *height* of *Perfection*, than what conſiſts in a conſummate and well-eſtabliſhed *habit* of virtue. Some men may, and do talk very extravagantly;

but

but it is very hard to imagine that fober
and pious men fhould run in with them.
Such, when they talk of *fulfilling* the law
of *God,* and keeping his commandments,
muft furely underftand this of the law
of *God* in a *gracious* and *equitable* fenfe:
And this is no more than what the *fcripture* afferts of every fincere *Chriftian.*
When they talk of I know not what tranfcendent *Perfection* in *monkery,* they muft
furely mean nothing more, than that poverty, chaftity, and obedience, are *heroick*
inftances of faith and love, of poverty of
fpirit, and purity of heart; and that an *Af-
cetick* difcipline is the moft compendious
and effectual way to a confummate *habit* of
righteoufnefs. *Finally,* By the diftinction
of *precept* and *counfel,* fuch can never intend furely more than this, that we are obliged to *fome* things under pain of damnation; to *others,* by the hopes of greater degrees of glory: for 'tis not eafy for me to
comprehend, that any man, whofe judgment is not enflaved to the dictates of his
party, fhould deny *either* of thefe *two* truths.
1. That whatever is neither forbidden nor
commanded by any law of *God,* is *indifferent.* 2. That no man can do more than
love the *Lord* his *God* with all his heart,
with all his foul, and with all his might,
and his neighbour as himfelf. I fay, there
is no degree or inftance of *obedience,* that
                                        is

is not compriz'd within the *latitude* and *perfection* of thefe words. But whatever fome of the *Church* of *Rome*, or it may be the greater part of it may think; this, 'tis plain, was the fenfe of the *ancients.* St. *Auftin* (a) could never underftand any merit or excellence in thofe things that were matter of counfel, not precept, unlefs they flowed from, and had regard to the love of God and our neighbour. And *Caffian*'s (b) excellent *Monks* refolved all the value of fuch things to confift in their tendency to promote apoftolical purity and charity. And *Gregory Nazianzen* (c) thought it very extravagant, to pretend to be *perfecter* than the *rule*, and *exacter* than the *law.*

The *Quakers* have made much noife and ftir about the doctrine of *Perfection*, and have reflected very feverely on others, as fubverting the great defign of our redemp- tion (which is deliverance from fin) and upholding the kingdom of darknefs: but with what *juftice*, will eafily appear when I have reprefented their *fenfe*, which I will do very *impartially*, and in as few

C 3   and

(a) *Quæ-cunq; non jubentur, fed fpecia-li confilio monentur, tum recte fiunt, cum referuntur ad diligen-dum Deum, & proxi-mum prop-ter Deum,* Aug. Ench. *cap.* 121.

(b) *Ac pro-inde ea quibus qua-litates fta-tutas vide-mus, & tempora; & quæ fic obfervata fanctifi-cant, ut o-miffa non pulluant. Media effe manifeftum eft, ut pu-ta nuptias, agriculturam, divitias, folitudinis remotionem,* &c. Caffian. Colla. Patr. *Talem igitur definitionem fupra Jejunii,* &c. *Nec in ipfo fpei noftræ terminum defigamus, fed ut per ipfum ad puritatem cordis & apoftolicam charitatem pervenire poffimus;* ibid.

(c) Μηδὲ τῦ νόμυ νομιμότερος, μηδὲ λαμπρότερος τῦ Φωτὸς, μηδὲ τῦ κανόν⊙ εὐθύτερ⊙, μηδὲ τῆ ἐντολῆς ὑψηλότερ⊙. Greg. Nazian.

(d) A Key opening, &c.

and plain words as I can. Mr. *W. P.* (d tells us, *That they are so far infallible an*[a] *perfect, as they are led by the Spirit.* This is indeed *true,* but 'tis mere *trifling :* for *this* is an *infallibility* and *perfection* which no man denies, who believes in the *Holy Ghost*; since whoever follows *his* guidance must be in the right, unless the *Holy Ghost* himself be in the wrong. He urges, 'tis true, a great number of *scriptures* to *shew* (they are his own words) *that a state of Perfection from sin (tho' not in fulness of wisdom and glory) is attainable in this life* ; but this is too dark and short a hint to infer the sense of his *party* from it.   Mr. *Ed. Burroughs* (e) is

(e) Principles of Truth, &c.

more full : *We believe* (saith he) *that the saints upon earth may receive forgiveness of sins, and may be perfectly freed from the body of sin and death, and in Christ may be perfect and without sin, and may have victory over all temptations, by faith in Jesus Christ. And we believe every saint, that is called of God, ought to press after Perfection, and to overcome the devil and all his temptations upon earth : and we believe, they that faithfully wait for it, shall obtain it, and shall be presented without sin in the image of the father; and such walk not after the flesh, but after the Spirit, and are in covenant with God, and their sins are blotted out, and remembered*

bered

bered no more; for they cease to commit
sin, being born of the seed of God. If by
sin here, he means, as he seems to do, *de-*
liberate or *presumptuous* sin; I do not think
any established *Church*, whether *Protes-*
tant or *Popish*, teaches otherwise. Mr.
Barclay (*f*) goes very *methodically* to (*f*) *Apol.*
work, and *first* sets down the state of the *Thes.* 8.
question; *then* confutes *those* that differ
from him; answers their objections out of
scripture; and, *lastly*, establishes his own
doctrine. As to the *Perfection* which he
asserts, he lets us know, that it is to be
derived from the *Spirit* of *Christ*; that it
consists not in an impossibility of sinning,
but a possibility of not sinning; and that
this *perfect* man is capable of daily growth
and improvement. When to this I have
added, that he speaks all along of *that*
which we call *wilful sin*, as appears from
his description of *it*; for he calls it *ini-*
quity, *wickedness*, *impurity*, the *service* of
Satan, and attributes such effects to it as
belong not at all to what we call *sins* of
infirmity; when, I say, *this* is added to
render the sense *clear*, I can readily sub-
scribe to him: for, I know no such doctrines in our *Church* as those which he
there opposes; namely, that the *regene-*
rate are to live in *sin*, and that their *good*
works are *impure* and *sinful*. But then, he
either mistakes the main point in debate,

or

or prudently declines : for the queftion is not, whether good men may live in *mortal* or *wilful fin*, but whether good men are not fubject to *frailties* and *infirmities*, which are indeed *fins*, tho' not *imputable* under the covenant of *grace* ? Whether the *Quakers* are not in this point *Pelagians*, I do not now enquire ; becaufe if they be, they are already confidered. Two things there are in Mr. *Barclay*'s ftate of the queftion, which I cannot fo well approve of ; the *one* is, that he expreffes himfelf fo injudicioufly about the growth and improvement of his *perfect* man, that he feems to forget the difference the *fcriptures* make between *babes* and full *grown* men in *Chrift*, and to place Perfection fo low in reference to *pofitive* righteoufnefs or virtue, as if it confifted in *negative* only or ceafing from fin. The *other* is, that tho' he does not peremptorily *affirm* a ftate of *impeccability* attainable in this life ; yet he feems inclinable to *believe* it, and imagines it countenanced by 1 *John* iii. 9. But he ought to have confidered, that whatever *impeccability* may be inferred from that *text*, it is attributed, not to fome extraordinary perfons, but to all, whofoever they be, that are born of *God* ; but this is out of my way. All that I am to obferve upon the whole is, that thefe men place *Perfection* efpecially in refraining

refraining from *sin :* I advance *higher,* and place it in a well-settled *habit* of righteoufnefs. And I believe they will be as little diffatisfied with me for this, as I am with them, for afferting the perfect man freed from fin. For, as Mr. *Barclay* expreffes himfelf, I think he has in reality no adverfaries but *Antinomians* and *Ranters.*

As to that Perfection which is magnified by *myftical* writers, fome of them have only darkened and obfcured the plain fenfe of the *gofpel,* by figurative and unintelligible terms. *Thofe* of them, which write with more life and heat than other men ordinarily do, recommend nothing but that *holinefs* which begins in the *fear,* and is confummate in the *love* of God ; which enlightens the mind, purifies the heart, and fixes and unites man to his foveraign good, that is, *God:* and I am fure I fhall not differ with *thefe.*

There are, I confefs, almoft innumerable fayings of the *fathers,* which fufficiently teftify how little friends they were to *Perfection,* in fuch a notion of it as is too generally embraced in the Church of *Rome.* The *primitive* fpirit breathed nothing but *humility :* it was a profeffed enemy to all felf-confidence and arrogance, to fupererogation and merit; and it invited men earneftly to reflect upon the

fins

fins and *flips* of life, and on that *oppofition*
which the law of the *body* maintains a-
gainft the law of the *mind*, in some degree or other, in the *beft* men. This confideration forced the *bifhop* of *Condome* to
that plain and honeft *confeffion*; *Itaque
Juftitia noftra, licet per charitatis infufio-
nem fit vera*, &c. *Tho' our righteoufnefs,
becaufe of that love which the Spirit fheds
abroad in our heart, be fincere and real*;
*yet it is not abfolute and confummate, be-
caufe of the oppofition of concupifcenfe: fo
that it is an indifpenfable duty of Chriftianity, to be perpetually bewailing the errors of
life*: *Wherefore we are obliged humbly to
confefs with St.* Auftin, *that our righteoufnefs in this life confifts rather in the pardon
of our fins, than in the perfection of our
virtues.* All this is undoubtedly true, but
concerns not me: I never dream of any
man's paffing the courfe of life *without
fin*: nor do I contend for fuch a *Perfection* as St. *Auftin* calls *abfolute*, which will
admit of no increafe, and is exempt from
defects and errors. Tho' on the *other*
hand, I confefs, I cannot but think, fome
carry this matter too far; and while they
labour to abate the *pride* and *confidence* of
man, give too much encouragement to
negligence and *prefumption*. I cannot fee
how frequent relapfes into *deliberate* acts
of wickednefs can confift with a well-fet-
tled

tled and eſtabliſhed *habit* of goodneſs. The heat of diſpute in ſome, and a ſort of *implicite* faith for their *authority* in others, has produced many *unwary expreſſions,* and I doubt very *unſound* and pernicious *notions* about this matter.

CHAP. III.

*Several inferences deduced from the true no-
tion of Perfection. With a plain method
how perſons may judge of their preſent
ſtate. The difference between the extraordinary primitive converſions, and thoſe
which may be expected in our days, with
a remark about* infuſed *habits.*

HAVING in the *two former* chapters fixed the notion of religious *Perfec-
tion,* and proved it conſonant to *reaſon* and *ſcripture;* and not ſo only, but alſo made it appear, that it is countenanced by the unanimous *conſent* of *all,* who have ever handled this ſubject: I have nothing now to do, but by way of *inference* to repreſent the *advantages* we may reap from it.

1. It is from hence plain, that *Perfection* muſt not be placed in fantaſtick ſpeculations or voluntary obſervances, but in the ſolid and uſeful *virtues* of the goſpel; in
the

the works of faith, the labour of love, and the patience of hope; in the purity and humility of a child of light; in the conftancy and magnanimity which becomes one who has brought the body into fub- jection, and has fet his affections on things above. *This* ftate of *Perfection* is well enough defcribed by the rule of St. *Bennet. Ergo his omnibus humilitatis gradibus afcenfis, monachus mox ad charitatem,* &c. *The monk, having paffed through thefe feveral ftages of humility or mortification, will arrive at that love of God which cafteth out fear; by which he will be enabled to perform all things with eafe and pleafure, and, as it were, naturally, which before he performed with reluctancy and dread; being now moved and acted, not by the terrors of hell, but by a delight in goodnefs, and the force of an excellent habit : both which, Chrift by his Spirit vouchfafes to increafe and exalt in his fervants now cleanfed and purged from all fin and vice.*

2. This notion of *Perfection* proves all men to lie under an obligation to it : for as all are *capable* of an *habit* of holinefs ; fo is it the duty of all to *endeavour* after it. If *Perfection* were indeed an *angelical* ftate ; if it did confift in an exemption from all defects and infirmities, and in fuch an elevation of virtue, to which nothing can be added; *then,* I confefs, all *difcourfes*

courses of it, and much more all *attempts* after it, would be vain, and infolent too. *If* again, it did confift in fome *heroick* pitch of virtue, which fhould appear to have fome-thing fo *fingular* in it, as fhould make it look more like a *miracle* than a *duty*, it were *then* to be expected but once in an *age* from fome *extraordinary* perfon, called to it by peculiar *infpiration* and extraor-dinary *gifts*. But if *Chriftian Perfection* be, as I have proved, only a well confirmed *habit* in goodnefs ; if it differ from *fince-rity* only, when *fincerity* is in its *weaknefs* and *infancy*, not when *grown* up ; then 'tis plain, that *every Chriftian* lies under an *ob-ligation* to *it*. Accordingly the *fcripture* exhorts all *to perfect holinefs in the fear of God, to go on to Perfection,* Heb. vi. and it affigns this as one great end of the infti-tution of a ftanding *miniftry* in the *churches* of *Chrift*, namely, *the perfecting the faints, the edifying the body of Chrift ; till we all come in the unity of the faith, and of the knowledge of the Son of God, unto a perfect man, unto the meafure of the ftature of the fulnefs of Chrift,* Ephef. iv. 12, 13. And hence it is, that we find the *apoftles* purfuing this great end, by their *prayers* and *labours*, earneft-ly contending and endeavouring to prefent all Chriftians *perfect* before *God*, 1 Theff. iii. 10. *Night and day prying exceedingly, that we might fee your face, and might perfect*
                                        that

that which is lacking in your faith, Colof. i. 28. *When we preach, warning every man, and teaching every man in all wisdom, that we may present every man perfect in Christ Jesus,* see 1 *Pet.* v. 10. *Colof.* iv. 13. Nay further, the *scripture* frequently puts us in mind, that they are in a state of *danger,* who do not *proceed* and *grow* in grace, and press on towards *Perfection.* Now all this is very eafily accountable, taking *Perfection* for a well settled *habit* of holiness; but on no *other* notion of it.

3. This account of *Perfection* removes *those scruples* which are often started about the *degrees* of holiness and *measures* of duty, and are wont to disturb the peace, clog the vigour, and damp the alacrity of many well-meaning and good people. Nay, many of acute parts and good learning are often puzzled about this matter: some teaching, that man is not bound to do his best; others on the quite contrary, that he is so far bound to it, that he is always obliged to *pursue* the most *perfect duty,* to *chuse* the most *perfect* means, and to exert the *utmost* of that *strength,* and act according to the *utmost* of that *capacity* with which God has endowed him. Now all these things, when we come to apply these *general* doctrines to *particular* instances, and a vast variety of *circumstances,* have so much *latitude,* ambiguity,

and

and uncertainty in them, that men of *tender* confciences, and *defective* underſtandings, reap nothing from fuch highflown *indefinite* diſcourſes, but *doubts* and *ſcruples*. It requires a ſtrong and penetrating judgment to reſolve what is the utmoſt *extent* of our power and capacity; what the *beſt* mean, and what the *moſt perfect* duty, when *many* preſent themſelves to us, and all *variouſly* circumſtantiated. But now, as I have ſtated matters, we are bound indeed to purſue and labour after *growth* and *improvement* in the love of God, and charity towards our neighbour, in purity, humility, and the like. And this we ſhall certainly do, if we be *ſincere*; in other matters we are left to our *prudence*, and if the error of our *choice* proceed only from an error in *judgment*, and a *corruption* in our *hearts*, we are *ſafe* enough.

4. 'Tis very eaſy to *diſcern* now *where* we ſtand in reference to *Perfection*; how *remote* we are from it, or how *near* to it. For the *nature* of an *habit* being plain and intelligible, the *effects* and *properties* of it obvious to the meaneſt capacity, 'tis *eaſy* to determine, upon an impartial *examination*, whether we be *habitually* good or not, or what *approaches* we have made towards it. And becauſe this is a matter of no ſmall *importance*, and men are generally
back-

backward enough to advance too far into
such *reflections* and *applications*, as may
breed any *disturbance* to their *peace*, or any
diminution of their good *opinion* for *themselves*, tho' neither the one nor the other be
too well grounded; I shall not think my
time misspent, if I here take this task upon
me; and endeavour by several *particular*
deductions, to lay every man's *state* as plainly
open to his *view* as I can.

1. Then, from the notion I have given
of *Perfection*, it appears, that *if* a man's
life be very *uneven*, unconstant, and
contradictory to itself; if he be to day a
saint, and to morrow a *sinner*; if he yield
to day to the motives of the *gospel* and im-
pulses of the *spirit*, and to morrow to the
sollicitations of the *flesh* and temptations
of the *world*, he is far from being *perfect*;
so far, that there is not ground enough to
conclude him a *sincere* or *real*, tho' *imperfect*,
convert. The only certain proof of *regeneration* is victory; *he that is born of God,
overcometh the world,* 1 John v. 4. *faith,*
tho' it be *true*, is not presently *saving* and
justifying, till it have subdued the *will* and
captivated the heart, *i. e.* till we begin to
live by *faith*; which is evident from *that*
corn in the *parable*, which tho' it shot
up, yet had it not *depth* of earth, nor
root enough, and therefore was *withered*
up, and brought forth *no* fruit. Regret
and

and sorrow for sin is an excellent passion; but till it has subdued our corruptions, changed our affections, and purified our hearts, 'tis not that *saving* repentance in the apostle, 2 *Cor.* vii. 10. *Godly sorrow worketh repentance, not to be repented of.* We may have sudden heats and passions for virtue; but if they be too short-liv'd to implant it in us, this is *not* that *charity* or *love* which animates and impregnates the new creature mentioned, *Gal.* v. 6. *faith working by love.* Lastly, We may have good purposes, intentions, nay, resolutions; but if these prove too weak to obtain a *conquest* over our *corruptions*, if they prove too weak to resist the *temptations* we are wont to fall by, 'tis plain that they are not such as can demonstrate us *righteous*, or entitle us to a *crown*, which is promised to him that *overcometh.* And here I cannot but remark, to how little purpose *controversies* have been multiplied about the *justification* of man. 'Tis *one* thing for *God* to *justify us*, *i. e.* to *pardon* our *sins*, and account us *righteous*, and *his* children; and *another* for us to *know*, or be *assured*, that he does so. If we enquire after the *former*, 'tis plain to me, that no man can be *accounted* righteous by *God*, till he really *is* so: and when the man is *sanctified* throughout in spirit, soul, and body; then is he certainly *justified*, and

D   not

not till then. And this I think is confessed
by all, except *Antinomians* ; and whatever
difference there is amongst *Christians* in this
matter, it lies in the forms and variety
of *expression*. They, that contend earnestly
for the necessity of *good works*, do not, I
suppose, imagine, that the *works* are holy, before the *heart* is so ; for, as is the
fountain, such will be its *streams* ; as is
the *tree*, such will be its *fruits*. What
absurdity then is there in admitting that
men are justified before they bring forth
good works ; if they cannot bring forth
good works, till they be sanctified and
changed ? on the other hand, they who contend so earnestly for *justification* by *faith*
without *works*, do not only suppose that
the man is throughly changed, by the *infu-
sion of habitual grace* ; but also that this grace,
as soon as it has opportunity, will exert and
express itself in *good works* : and they do
readily acknowledge that the *faith* which
does *not* work by *love*, is an *historical* un-
animated *faith*. And if so, how natural is it
to comprise in that holiness, which *justi-
fies*, not only the change of the *heart*, but
of the *actions* ? but here I think it is well
worth the considering, whether that thorough *change* in the *nature* of a sinner,
which is called *holiness*, be now effected
at *once* and in a *moment*, and not rather
gradually and in *time* ? for this may give
some

some light to the doctrine of *justification*, and draw us off from speculations and theories to more useful and practical thoughts and discourses about it. 'Tis true, in the *primitive* times, when the conviction of a sinner was wrought by a dazling light, by surprizing miracles, by exuberant influxes of the *spirit*, and the concurrence of many extraordinary things, *sanctification* (as in the *goaler* and his *family*, Acts xvi.) might be *begun* and *finished* in the *same* hour. But I doubt it is *rarely* so with us at *this* day; our vices are not so suddenly subdued, nor our virtues so suddenly implanted. *Our* convictions, in the beginning of conversion, are seldom so full and clear as *theirs*: and, if we may judge by the *effects*, 'tis but seldom that the principle of a new life is infused in the *same* plenty and power it appears to have been in *them*. And if so, then these things will follow; 1. Though in the first *plantation* of the *gospel* men being converted, as it were, in a *moment*, ingrafted by *baptism* into *Christ*, and receiving the *Holy Ghost*, the *earnest* of their *justification* or acceptance with *God*, and their future *glory*: we may very well say of them, that they were not only *justified*, but also *knew* themselves to be so, *before* they had brought forth any other *fruit* of righteousness, than what was implied in

D 2

the

the *dedication* of themselves to *Christ* by
that solemn rite of *baptism* : but at *this*
day, when conversion is not effected in
the same manner ; when faith and good
works do mutually cherish one another ;
when righteousness is not brought forth
into victory, but by *long* labour and travel ; I see not why *faith* and *good works*
may not be pronounced *jointly* and *antecedently* necessary to our *justification.* 2. The
doctrine of *infused habits* has been much
ridiculed and exposed as absurd, by some
men ; and, I must confess, if it be *essential* to a *habit*, to be acquired by length of
time and repetition of the same acts,
then an *infused habit* is a very *odd* expref-
sion : but why *God* cannot produce in us
those strong dispositions to virtue in a
moment, which are *naturally* produced by
time ; or why *we* may not ascribe as much
efficacy to *infused grace*, as philosophers
are wont to do to *repeated acts,* I cannot see?
nor can I see, why such *dispositions,* when
infused, may not be called *habits,* if they
have all the *properties* and *effects* of an
habit. And that such excellent dispositions *were* on a sudden wrought in the minds
of Christians in the beginning of Christianity, is too plain from the history of
those times to need a proof. But whether
such changes are ordinarily effected so suddenly at *this* day, we have much reason to
doubt ;

doubt; nay, I think it appears from what I have said, there is fufficient reafon to *deny* it. And, if fo, the *infufion* of *habits* cannot be fo properly infifted on *now* as *then*; and *we* may be more fubject to make *unwarrantable* inferences from the doctrine of *infufed habits,* than *they* were in thofe bright and *miraculous* days. 3. As our *progrefs* to *fanctification* muft be *flower* than formerly, as it muft be *longer* before the grace that is infufed, fo far mafter our corruption and dilate and diffufe itfelf through our whole nature, as that we may juftly be denominated *holy* and *righteous* from the prevalence of this holy principle : fo, by a neceffary confequence, our *juftification* muft commence *later.* But, after all, I know not why we fhould be fo inquifitive after the *time* of our *juftification* by *God.* The *comfort* of a Chriftian does not refult immediately from *God's juftifying* him, but from *his knowing* that he does fo. And if this be the thing we are now fearching after, namely, what rational *affurance* we can have of our *juftification*, and when, as indeed it is; then, though I do not pretend to determine, that man *is* not, or *may* not be juftified or accounted righteous by *God*, upon a thorough change of mind or foul, before this change *difcovers* itfelf in a feries of *victories* over thofe *temptations* by which he was led *captive* before; yet I affert,

firft,

first, that the true and solid proof of the *sanctification* of the *heart,* is *sanctity* of life. *Next,* when I talk of *victory,* I suppose man *engaged,* I suppose him *encountered* by *temptations* and *enemies;* and *then* I affirm, that the *faith,* which is not strong enough to *conquer,* is not strong enough to *justify.* If any man demand, may not that faith, which is foiled to *day,* conquer to *morrow?* I answer, I must leave this to *God:* I can pronounce nothing of the *sincerity* of the heart, but by the outward *deportment* and *success.* And if this be the proper way of judging of a man's sincerity, I am sure I may with much more confidence affirm, that nothing less than *victory* can be a clear argument of *Perfection.* My business therefore shall ever be to be *Holy,* and then I am *sure* I shall be *justified.* If *I be* Holy, *God,* who cannot err, will certainly *account* me so; and if I *cease* to *be* so, *God* must *cease* to *account* me so. And this is all which I design by this long paragraph: that is, to render Men more careful and diligent in making their calling and election sure, and to prevent presumption and groundless confidence. And that nothing that I have here *said* may be perverted to a *contrary* purpose; that no man, from some passionate resolutions or sudden changes of his own mind, may be tempted to conclude too *hastily* of his being

justified,

justified, as if the change wrought in him were equal to that commonly effected in the *first* converts of *Christianity*; I think it not amiss to put such a one in mind, that even *these* were not justified, unless they did *profess Christ* with the *mouth,* as well as *believe* in him with the *heart*; and that this *publick* profession of Christianity in *those* days was equivalent to *many* good works in *these*.

2*dly,* He, that feels in himself little or no fervency of spirit, little or no hunger and thirst after righteousness, has reason to suspect, that his *regularity* is little more than common *decency* and *civility,* and to doubt, left his *religion* be nothing else but *custom* or common *prudence.* I see not *how* so much *indifference* and *sluggishness* can consist with a firm *belief* and *expectation* of a *crown,* with a sincere *love* of God and *righteousness.* But if we may suppose such a one restrained from evil, and preserved in the way of duty, after a sort, by the *fear* of God, and a *desire* of *heaven*; yet certainly this can be but the *infancy* of the *new creature* at most : and the best advice, that can be given such a one, is surely that of St. *Peter,* that *by adding one degree of virtue to another, he would use all diligence to make his calling and election sure,* 2 Pet. i. 10.

3*dly,* If a man's religion produce very few good works, or such only as put him

to little travel or expence, we may conclude that this man is not *perfect*; his
charity is too weak, too narrow to be that
of an *exalted* Christian: the best that we
can think of such a one is, that he is yet
taken up in the *discipline* of *mortification*,
that he is *contending* with his *lusts* and *paf-
sions*, which are not yet so far reduced, so
far subdued and brought under, as to leave
him in a state of *liberty* and *peace*, and in
a capacity of *extending* and *enlarging* his
charity. This remark, that the *inconfi-
derableness* of our good works is reason
enough to question, not only one's *Perfection* but *sincerity*, holds good in *such* ca-
ses only, where neither *opportunity* nor
capacity of higher and nobler performances
is wanting. I dare not pronounce, that no
man can be a *Christian*, unless he be fit to
be a *martyr*: 'tis true, the *lowest* degree of
sincerity must imply a purpose and *resolution* of universal *obedience*, in defiance of
all temptations; but yet *that* grace, for
ought I can prove to the contrary, may be
sufficient to *save* a man, that is sufficient
to master the difficulties *he* is to encounter
with, altho' he should not be able to grapple
with the distempers and tryals to which
the body and the state of *another* man may
be subject. Surely the wisdom and the
faithfulness of God can be no further concerned, than to qualify any one for the discharge

charge of *thofe* duties which he thinks fit to
call him to: and if the difcharge of fuch
duties be not a fufficient proof of our fincerity, we can never have any, but muft be
always held in fufpence and torture about
our future ftate. I fee no reafon to queftion, but that the difciples of our Lord were
in a ftate of *grace* before the *refurrection,*
and the following *Pentecoft:* and yet I
think I have plain reafon to believe, that
they were not fit to be *martyrs* and *confeffors*
till then; the *grace* they had *before* might,
I doubt it not, have enabled them to live
virtuoufly amidft *common* and *ordinary* temptations: but it was neceffary, that they
fhould be endowed with *power* from on
high, before they could be fit to encounter
thofe *fiery trials,* to which the *preaching* of
the *gofpel* was to expofe them. To this
furely our Mafter refers, when he tells the
Pharifees, That the children of the bride-
chamber were not to faft while the bridegroom
was with them: when he tells *his* difciples,
I have many things to fay, but you cannot bear
them yet: when he asked the fons of *Zebe-*
dee, are ye able to drink of the cup that I fhall
drink of, and to be baptized with the baptifm
that I am baptized with? Matth. xx. 21.
If this be true divinity, as I am (I had almoft faid) confident it is; then I am confident, that which requires very *unaccount-*
able tefts of a man's *fincerity,* is very *ex-*
travagant,

travagant. For example, when men talk at this rate, that a sincere Christian should have such an *abhorrence* for *sin*, as to fear *guilt* more than its *punishment* : such a *love* of *God*, as rather than offend him, to be content to precipitate and plunge himself into the jaws, not of *death*, like the martyrs, but of *hell* it self.

4thly, If the duties of religion be very *troublesome* and *uneasy* to a man, we may from hence conclude, that he is not *perfect* : for tho' the *beginning* of wisdom and virtue be generally *harsh* and *severe* to the *fool* and *sinner*, yet to him that has *conquered*, the yoke of Christ is *easy*, and his burthen *light*; *to him that is filled with the love of God, his commandments are not grievous*; hence is that observation of the son of *Sirach*, Ecclus. iv. 17, 18. *For at the first she will walk with him by crooked ways, and bring fear and dread upon him, and torment him with her discipline, until she may trust his soul, and try him by her laws ; then will she return the straight way unto him, and comfort him, and shew him her secrets.* The reason of this assertion is palpable; it is the nature of an *habit* to render *difficult* things *easy*, *harsh* things *pleasant*, to *fix* a *floating* and *uncertain* humour, to nurse and ripen a weak and tender *disposition* into *nature*. And 'tis as reasonable to expect these effects in *religious*, as in any *other* sorts of *habits*.

Lastly,

Lastly, He who does not find *religion* full of *pleasure,* who does not *glory* in *God,* and *rejoice* in our *Lord Jesus,* he who is not filled with an humble *assurance* of the *divine favour,* and a joyful *expectation* of immortality and *glory,* does yet *want* something; he is yet *defective,* with respect either to the *brightness* of *illumination,* the *absoluteness* of *liberty,* or the *ardor* of *love*; he may be a *good* man, and have gone a *great* way in his Christian *race*; but there is something still behind to *compleat* and *perfect* him; some *error* or other creates him groundless *scruples*; some *incumbrance* or *impediment* or other, whether an *infelicity* of temper, or the *incommodiousness* of his circumstances, or a little too warm an application towards *something* of the world, *retards* his *vigour,* and *abates* his *affections.*

I have now finished all that I can think necessary to form a general *idea* of religious *Perfection:* for I have not only given a plain *definition* or *description* of it, and *confirmed* and *fortified* that description by *reason* and *scripture,* and the *concurrent sense* of *all sides* and *parties*; but here also by various *inferences,* deduced from the *general* notion of *Perfection,* precluded all groundless *pretensions to it,* and enabled men to see how *far they are removed* and *distant* from it, or how *near they approach* it.

it. The *next* thing I am to do, according to the method I have proposed, is, to consider the *fruits* and *advantages* of *Perfection.* A consideration which will furnish us with many great, and, I hope, effectual *incitements* or *motives* to it ; and demonstrate its *subserviency* to our *happiness.*

CHAP. IV.

A general account of the blessed fruits *and* advantages *of Religious Perfection. Which is reduced to these four heads.* 1. *As it advances the honour of the true and living* God, *and of his* Son Jesus, *in the world.* 2. *As it promotes the good of mankind. These two treated of in the chapter of zeal.* 3. *As it produces in the perfect man a full assurance of eternal happiness and glory.* 4. *As it puts him in possession of true happiness in this life. These two last,* assurance, *and present* happiness *or* pleasure, *handled in this chapter. Where the pleasures of the sinner and of the perfect Christian are compared.*

OF the *two former* I shall say nothing *here*; designing to insist upon them more particularly in the *following* section,

under

under the *head* of *zeal*, where I shall be
obliged by my *method* to consider the *fruit*
of it ; only I cannot *here* forbear *remark-
ing*, that *Perfection*, while it promotes the
honour of *God* and the good of *man*, does
at the same time promote our *own happiness* too ; since it must on this account most
effectually recommend us to the love of the
one and the *other ; Them that honour me,*
saith God, *I will honour*, 1 Sam. ii. 30.
And our Saviour observes, that even *Pub-
licans and sinners love those who love them,*
Matth. v. 46. Accordingly St. *Luke* tells
us of Christ, *Luke* ii. 52. *That Jesus increased in wisdom and stature, and in favour
with God and man*; and of those eminently
devout and charitable souls, *Acts* ii. *that
they had favour with all the people ;* so re-
sistless a charm is the beauty and loveliness of perfect charity, even in the most
depraved and corrupt times. And what
a *blessing* now, what a *comfort*, what a
pleasure is it, to be the favourite of *God*
and *man !*

The *third* and *fourth* I will *now* discourse
of, and that the more *largely*, because as
to *assurance*, it is the *foundation* of that
pleasure, which is the richest *ingredient* of
human *happiness* in *this* life. And, *as to
our present happiness*, which is the *fourth*
fruit of *Perfection*, it is the very *thing* for
the sake of which I have *engaged* in my
present

present subject.   And therefore it is very
fit that I should render the tendency of
Perfection to procure our *present happiness*
very conspicuous. Beginning therefore with
assurance, I will assert the *possibility* of attaining it in *this* life; not by embroiling
my self in the brakes of several nice and
subtle *speculations* with which this subject
is over-grown; but by laying down in a
practical manner, the *grounds* on which *affurance* depends; by which we shall be able
at once to discern the truth of the *doctrine*
of *assurance*, and its *dependance* upon *Perfection.*

Now *assurance* may relate to the time
present, or to *come:* for the resolution of *two*
questions, gives the mind a perfect *ease*
about this matter.   The *first* is, am I *assu-*
red that I am at *present* in a state of grace?
The *second*, am I *assured* that I shall *conti-*
nue so to my life's *end?*   To begin with
the *first:* the answer of this enquiry depends on *three* grounds.

First, A divine *revelation*, which declares in general, *who* shall be *saved*; namely, they *who believe* and *repent*.   Nor does
any *sect* doubt, but that *repentance towards*
God, and faith in our Lord Jesus Christ,
as St. *Paul* speaks, are the indispensable
conditions of life.   'Tis true, the notion of
repentance is miserably *perverted* by *some*;
and that of *faith* by *others:* But what re-
                                    medy

medy is there againſt the luſts and paſſions of men? The *ſcripture* does not only *re-quire* repentance and faith; but it *explains* and *deſcribes* the nature of *both*, by ſuch conſpicuous and infallible *characters*, that no man *can* be miſtaken in theſe *two* points, *but* his error muſt be owing to ſome criminal *prejudices* or *inclinations* that biaſs and pervert him. *Good* men have ever been *agreed* in theſe matters: and catholick *tradition* is no-where more *uncontroulable* than here: the general doc-trine of all *ages* hath been, and in *this* ſtill is, that by *repentance* we are to underſtand a *new nature* and *new life :* and by *faith*, when diſtinguiſhed from *repentance* (as it ſometimes is in *ſcripture*) a *reliance* upon the *mercy* of God through the *merits* and *interceſſion* of *Jeſus*, and *atonement* of *his* blood. *Heaven* lies open to all that per-form theſe *conditions*; every page of the *goſpel* atteſts this; *this* is the ſubſtance of *Chriſt's* commiſſion to his *apoſtles*, that they ſhould preach *repentance* and *remiſ-ſion* of ſins through his name amongſt *all* nations. And this is one bleſſed advan-tage, which *revealed* religion has above *natural* ; that it contains an expreſs *decla-ration* of the Divine Will, concerning the *pardon* of all ſins whatſoever upon theſe *terms.* *Natural* religion indeed teaches us, that *God is merciful;* but it

teaches

teaches us, that he is *juſt* too; and it can
never *aſſure* us, what *bounds God* will ſet
to the exerciſe of the *one* or the *other*; and
when juſtice, and *when* mercy ſhall take
place : *what* ſins *are*, and *what* are not capable of the benefit of ſacrifice and repentance. And this *uncertainty*, conſider-
ing the ſins of the beſt life, was ever naturally apt to beget deſpondencies, melancholy, and ſometimes a ſuperſtitious
dread of *God.*

The *ſecond* ground of aſſurance, as it
relates to our preſent ſtate, is an *application* of the conditions of life laid down in
the goſpel to a man's own *particular* caſe,
thus; *they* that *believe* and *repent* ſhall
be *ſaved*; *I believe* and *repent*, therefore
I ſhall be *ſaved.* Now that a man upon
an *examination* of himſelf, may be throughly *aſſured* that he *does* believe and repent,
is evident from *ſcripture*, which does not
only *exhort* us to enter upon this *examination*, but alſo aſſerts, that *aſſurance, joy*
and *peace*, are the natural *fruits* of it: but
*let a man examine himſelf, and ſo let him eat
of that bread, and drink of that cup,* 1 Cor.
xi. 28. *Examine your ſelves whether you be in
the faith; prove your own ſelves: know ye not
your own ſelves, how that Jeſus Chriſt is in
you, except ye be reprobates?* 2 Cor. xv. 5.
*But ſanctify the Lord God in your hearts; and
be ready always to give an anſwer to every man*
                                        that

that asketh you a reason of the hope that is in you, with meekness and fear, 1 Pet. iii. 13. *And hereby we do know that we know him, if we keep his commandments,* 1 John ii. 3. *Beloved, if our hearts condemn us not,* then *have we confidence towards God,* 1 John iii. 2. 'Tis true, men do often *deceive* themselves, and entertain a more favourable opinion of their state than they ought. But *whence* proceeds this? Even from too *partial* or *superficial* reflections on themselves, or *none* at all. And therefore the apostle teaches us plainly, that the only way to correct this error, is a *sincere* and *diligent* search into our selves : *for if a man think himself to be something when he is nothing, he deceiveth himself : but let every man prove his own work, and then shall he have rejoicing in himself alone, and not in another,* Gal. vi. 34. But it is *objected* against all this, that the *heart* of man is so *deceitful,* that it is a very dificult matter to make a thorough *discovery* of it. We often *think* our selves *sincere,* when the success of the next *temptation* gives us just reason to call this *sincerity* into *question* ; such is the contradictious *composition* of our nature, that we often act *contrary* to our inward *convictions,* and frequently fail in the *execution* of those *designs,* in the *performance* of those *resolutions,* which we have *thought* very well *grounded* ; and this being not to be charged upon the insuffi-

E ciency

ciency of God's *grace*, but the levity or in-
sincerity of our own *hearts*, *how* can we
safely frame any *right* opinion of our *selves*
from those *affections* and *purposes*, which
are so little to be *relied* upon ? To this I
answer. *First*, We are not to conclude any
thing concerning our *progress* or *perfection*
too *hastily* ; we are not to determine of the
final *issue* of a *war* by the *success* of *one* or
two engagements; but our *hopes* and *assu-
rances* are to advance slowly and gradually
in *proportion* to the *abatement* of the *enemy's*
force, and the *increase* of our *own* ; so that
we may have *time* enough to *examine* and
prove our own hearts. *Secondly*, A *sincere*
Christian, but especially one of a *mature*
virtue, may easily *discern* his spiritual state,
by the inward *movings* and *actings* of the
soul, if he *attend* to them : for it is impossible that such a one should be *ignorant*,
what *impressions* divine *truths* make upon
him ? Is it possible he should be *ignorant*,
whether his *faith* stands *firm* against the
shock of all *carnal* objections; whether he
earnestly desire to please *God*, as loving
him above all things; whether he thirst
after the consolation and joy of the *Spirit*,
more than after that of *sensible* things ? Is it
possible the soul should *bewail* its *heavi-
ness* and *driness*, which the best are liable
to at some season or other ? Is it possible
that the soul should be *carried* upwards
                                    frequent-

frequently on the wings of *faith* and *love*, that it fhould maintain a familiar and conftant *converfation* with *heaven*, that it fhould *long* to be *delivered* from this *world* of trouble, and this *body* of *death*, and to *enter* into the *regions* of peace, of life, and righteoufnefs? Is it poffible, I fay, that *thefe* fhould be the *affeCtions*, the *longings* and *earnings* of the foul; and yet that the *good* man, the *perfeCt* man, who often *enters* into his *clofet*, and *communes* with his own *heart*, fhould be *ignorant* of them? It *cannot* be. In a *word*, can the reluCtances of the *body*, and the allurements of the *world*, be difarmed, weakened, and reduced? Can the hunger and thirft after *righteoufnefs* be very eager, the relifh of *fpiritual* pleafure brisk and delightful, and the contempt of *worldly* things be really and thoroughly fettled, and yet the man be *infenfible* of all this? It *cannot* be. But if we feel *thefe* affeCtions in us, we may fafely conclude, that we *are partakers of the Divine Nature*; that *we have efcaped the corruption that is in the world through luft*; and that *the new creature* is at leaft growing up into a *perfeCt man, to the meafure of the ftature of the fulnefs of Chrift.* Thirdly, The fureft *teft* of a ftate of grace, is our *abounding* in good works: *you fhall know the tree by its fruit*, is our *Mafter*'s own rule, and it can never deceive us: *He that doth righteoufnefs is born of God.* If then we be frequent and fervent in our *devotion* towards *God* ; if we be modeft and grateful in the *fuccefes,* patient and refigned, calm and ferene under the *crofes* and *troubles* of life ; if we be not only *punctual,* but *honourable* in our dealings ; if we be *vigorous* and *generous* in the exercifes of *charity* ; if we be not only juft and true, but meek, gentle and obliging in our *words*; if we retrench not only the *finful,* but *fomething* from the *innocent* liberties and gratifications of *fenfe,* to give our felves more *intirely* up to the duties and pleafures of *faith* : if finally, we never be afhamed of virtue, nor flatter, compliment, nor wink at vice; if we be ready to meet with *death* with comfort, and retain *life* with fome degree of indifference: if *thefe* things, I fay, be in us, we have *little* reafon to *doubt* of the *goodnefs* of our *ftate* : for *good works* being the natural fruit of *grace,* it is impoffible we fhould abound in the *one* without being poffeffed with the *other.* One would think now, that there fhould be nothing further needful to eftablifh the *confolation* of a *Chriftian* ; and yet *God,* out of regard, no doubt, to the vaft *importance* and happy *influence* of *affurance,* has furnifhed us with *another* ground of it, which is,

The

The 3*d* and *laſt*, namely, the teſtimony of the *Spirit*. This Spirit, as it *aſſiſts* us in our *examination*, ſo it *ratifies* and *confirms* our ſentence by its *ſuffrage*, *fortifying* our *aſſurance*, and *increaſing* our *joy*. All this the *ſcripture* expreſly teaches us ; for the Spirit is called, *The earneſt of our inheri-tance, the ſeal of our redemption*, Eph. i. 13, 14. Eph. iv. 30, 31. 2 Cor. ii. 10. 2 Cor. v. And tho' it be not improbable, but that theſe, and ſuch like places, may relate more *immediately* to the *ſpirit* of *promiſe* which was conſpicuous in *miracles*, and ſeems to have accompanied *all* that be-lieved in the *infancy* of the *Church*, accor-ding to thoſe words of our Saviour, *And theſe ſigns ſhall follow them that believe* ; *in my name they ſhall caſt out devils*, &c. *Mark* xvi. 17. Yet there are texts enough which aſſure us, that the Spirit of God ſhould be imparted to believers through all ſucceed-ing ages, and that this ſhould be one effect of it to comfort us, and be a pledge to us of the divine favour : thus, Rom. xv. 13. *Now the God of hope fill you with all joy and peace in believing, that ye may a-bound in hope through the power of the Holy Ghoſt.* And Rom. viii. 15, 16. *For ye have not received the ſpirit of bondage again to fear* ; *but ye have received the ſpirit of adoption, whereby we cry Abba Father* ; *the Spirit itſelf beareth witneſs with our ſpirit, that we*

E 3   *are*

are the children of God ; and if children, then heirs, heirs of God, and joint heirs with *Chrift.* If it be here demanded *what* this *teftimony of* the *Spirit* is: I anfwer, 'tis a powerful *energy* of *the* bleffed Spirit, *fhed-ding abroad* and increafing *the love of God in our hearts,* Rom v. *Tribulation worketh pa-tience, patience experience, and experience hope, and hope makes not afhamed ; becaufe the love of God is fhed abroad in our hearts by the Holy Ghoft which is given unto us. This is* the *fpirit* of *adoption,* the fpirit of *obfigna-tion,* the fpirit of *glory,* and the fpirit of *love ;* happy is he who is partaker of it, he has attained the maturity of *Perfection* and *pleafure.* I can fcarce forbear going in with fome of the *fathers,* who thought that fuch as thefe could never finally fall. I can fcarce forbear applying to fuch, thofe words, *Rev.* xx. 6. *Bleffed and holy is he that hath part in the firft refurrection ; on fuch the fecond death hath no power.* Thus far I have confidered *affurance* as it relates to the *prefent* time. But,

2. *Affurance* may regard the *time to come ;* and it conduces very little lefs to the *peace* and *pleafure* of a *Chriftian* to be *affured* that he fhall *perfevere* in a good ftate, than that he is *now* in *one.* Let us therefore in the *next* place examine what *grounds* the *perfect* man may have for fuch a perfuafion : Now thefe are likewife *three.*

Firft,

First, The propension and *favour* of God for the *perfect* man:
Secondly, The *sufficiency* of divine *assistance.* And,
Thirdly, The *conscience* of his own *integrity.*

1. The *favour* of God. I need not go about to prove that God will be ever ready to *assist* the *perfect* man; I need not prove that *his eyes are always upon the righteous, and that his ears are always open to their prayers;* that *they* are the dear objects of his *delight* and *love: reason* and *scripture* both do abundantly *attest* this, and the repeated *promises* of God to *good* men, encourage them to *hope* from God whatever beloved *children* may from a tender and kind *father.* Is not *this* enough then to inspire the *perfect* man with great and confident *hopes?* He knows, not only, that God is an *immutable God,* free from all levity and inconstancy; and therefore, that nothing less than presumption and obstinacy, habitual neglect or wickedness, can tempt him to recall his gifts, or repent him of his favours: he knows not only that God is *faithful, and will not suffer him to be tempted above what he is able*; but he knows also, that he has a powerful *Intercessor* at the *right-hand* of God, an *Advocate with the Father,* who cannot but

E 4 pre-

prevail. Nor is this all yet; he has a great *many* things that *plead* for him with *God :* there are his *tears* which are *bottled* up ; there are his *prayers* and *alms* which are gone up for a *memorial* before God; there is a *book of remembrance* written, wherein all his pious diſcourſes are regiſtred; and God is faithful, and cannot forget his *works* and *labour of love.* The *Spirit* of *God* will not ſoon *quit* the *boſom* that it ſo long *reſided* in; it will not ſuffer itſelf to be *divided* from that perſon, with whom it had entred into ſo cloſe an *union,* that it ſeemed as it were inanimated or incorporated with him, and become eſſential to his Being : whence it is that the *ſpirit* is ſaid *to be grieved* when he is forced and compelled to retire.

2. The *ſecond* ground of *aſſurance* for the *time to come,* is the *ſufficiency* of *divine aſſiſtance.* The good man is well *aſſured,* that God will never refuſe the protection of his *Providence,* or the aid of his *Spirit :* and *what* can be too *difficult* for *ſuch a one?* *Providence* can prevent a temptation, or remove it; the *Spirit* can ſupport him under it, and enable him to vanquiſh it; nay, it can enable him to extract new *ſtrength* and *vigour* from it; *my grace is ſufficient for thee,* 2 Cor. xii. 9. the truth of which aſſertion has been illuſtriouſly proved by the victories of *martyrs* and *confeſſors,* who

trium-

triumphed over the united force of *men* and
devils. Tho' then the *confcience* of human
frailty may awaken in the beft of men
fear and *caution,* the *affurance* of *divine
affiftance* cannot but beget in them an holy *confidence* ; the fnares and temptations
of the *world,* the fubtilty and vigilance
of the *devil* may juftly create a *follicitude* in the beft of men ; but when they
confider themfelves encompaffed with the
divine favour, they can have no reafon to
defpond.

3. The *confcience* of his own *integrity* is
a *third* ground of a good man's *confidence* ;
he knows that nothing but *crying* provocations can *quench* the fpirit, and oblige *God* to *defert* him ; and he has reafon
to hope, that *this* is that he *cannot* be *guilty*
of. He is fure, that *prefumptuous* wickednefs is not only repugnant to his *principles* ; but to the very bent of his *nature,*
to all the *inclinations* and *paffions* of his
foul : I fpeak here of the *perfect* man ; can
he ever wilfully difhonour and difobey *God,*
who loves him above all things, and has
done fo *long?* Can he forfake, and betray
his *Saviour,* who has long rejoiced and gloried in him ; who has been long accuftomed
to look upon all the glories and fatisfactions
of this life, as dung and drofs in comparifon of him ? Can *he,* in one word, ever
be feduced to renounce and hate *religion,*
who

who has had so long an *experience* of the beauty, and of the pleasure of it? *Good habits*, when they are grown up to *perfection* and *maturity*, seem to me as *natural* as 'tis possible *evil* ones should be : and if so, 'tis no less difficult to extirpate the *one* than the *other*. And I think I have the *scripture* on my side in this opinion : Does the *prophet Jeremy* demand, *Can the Ethiopian change his skin, or the leopard his spots? then may you that are accustomed to do evil, learn to do well*, Jer. xiii. 23. St. *John* on the other hand does affirm, *whosoever is born of God, doth not commit sin ; for his seed remaineth in him ; and he cannot sin, because he is born of God*, 1 John iii. 9. *Whosoever abideth in him, sinneth not*, v. 6. *These* are the grounds of *assurance* with respect of the *time to come*. As to personal and peremptory *predestination* to life and glory, 'tis at least a *controverted* point, and therefore *unfit* to be laid as the *foundation* of *assurance*. But suppose it were granted, I see not which way it can affect our present enquiry, since the wisest amongst those who stickle *for it*, advise *all* to govern themselves by the *general* promises and threats of the *gospel* ; to look upon the fruits of *righteousness* as the only solid *proof* of a *state* of grace ; and if they be under the dominion of any *sin*, not to presume upon personal *election*, but to
look

look upon themselves as in a state of *damnation*, till they be recovered out of it by *repentance*. Thus far all sides agree; and this I think is abundantly enough; for here we have room enough for *joy* and *peace*, and for *caution* too; room enough for *confidence*, and for *watchfulness* too: the *Romanists* indeed, will not allow us to be certain of salvation, *certitudine fidei cui non potest subesse falsum*, with such a *certainty* as that with which we entertain an article of *faith*, in which there is no room for *error*; i. e. we are not so *sure* that we are in the *favour* of *God*, as we are, or may be, that there *is a God*: We are not so *sure*, that we have a title to the *merits* of *Christ*, as we are, or may be, that *Jesus is the Christ*. Now if this assertion be confined to that *assurance* which regards the *time to come*, as it generally is; and do not deny *assurance* in *general*, but only certain *degrees* or *measures* of it; then there is nothing very *absurd* or *intolerable* in it. For a *less assurance* than that which this doctrine excludes, will be *sufficient* to secure the *pleasure* and *tranquillity* of the *perfect* man. But if this assertion be designed against *that* assurance which regards our *present* state; then I think it is not *found*, nor agreeable, either to *reason*, *scripture*, or *experience*. For *first*, the question being about a matter

of

of *fact*, 'tis in vain to argue *that cannot be*, which does appear manifeftly to *have been :* and certainly they who rejoiced in *Chrift* with *joy unfpeakable, and full of glory*, were as fully *perfwaded*, that they were in a ftate ot *grace* and *falvation*, as they were that *Jefus* was *rifen* from the dead. *Secondly*, 'tis *one* thing to balance the *ftrength* and *degrees* of *affurance* ; another to balance the *reafons* of it. For it is very poffible that *affurance* may be ftronger, where the *reafon* of it may not be fo clear and evident as where the *affurance* is lefs. Thus for *example* ; the evidence of *fenfe* feems to moft learned men to be ftronger than that of *faith :* and yet through the affiftance of the *fpirit*, a man may embrace a truth that depends upon *revelation*, with as much *confidence* and *certainty* as one depending upon *fenfe*. And fo it may be in the cafe of *affurance :* the *Spirit* of God may by its concurrence raife our *affurance* as high as he pleafes ; although the *reafon* on which it be built, fhould not be *divine* and *infallible*, but merely *moral*, and fubject at leaft to a *poffibility* of error. But *thirdly*, why fhould not the *certainty* I have concerning my *prefent ftate*, be as divine and infallible, as that I have concerning an *article* of *faith?* if the *premifes* be infallible, why fhould not the *conclufion?* he, that *believes*

and

and repents is in a state of grace, is a divine and infallible proposition: and why may not this other, *I believe and repent,* be equally infallible, though not equally divine? *what* faith and repentance is, is *revealed*; and therefore there is no room for my being here *mistaken* : besides, I am *assisted* and *guided* in the trial of myself by the *Spirit* of *God.* So that the truth of this proposition, *I believe and repent,* depends *partly* upon the evidence of *sense*; and I may be as *sure* of it, as of what I *do* or leave *undone: partly* upon the evidence of *inward sensation,* or my *consciousness* of my own thoughts; and I may be as sure of it as I can be of what *I love* or *hate, rejoice* or *grieve* for: and lastly, it depends upon the evidence of the *Spirit* of *God,* which *assists* me in the *examination* of myself according to those characters of faith and repentance, which he hath himself revealed. And when I *conclude* from the two former propositions, that *I am in a state of grace, he* confirms and ratifies my *inference.* And now, let any one tell me, what kind of *certainty* that is, that can be greater than *this?* I have taken this pains to set the doctrine of *assurance* in a clear light, because it is the great spring of the *perfect* man's *comfort* and *pleasure,* and source of his *strength* and *joy.* And this puts me in mind of that
other

other fruit of Perfection, which in the beginning of this *chapter* I promised to insist on, which is,

Its subserviency to our happiness in this life.

That *happiness* increases in proportion with *Perfection*, cannot be denied; unless we will at the same time deny the happiness of a man, to exceed *that* of an infant, or the happiness of an angel *that* of man. Now *this* truth being of a very great *importance*, and serving singly instead of a thousand *motives* to *Perfection*, I will consider it impartially, and as closely as I can. *Happiness* and *pleasure*, are generally thought to be only two words for the same thing: nor is this very remote from truth; for let but *pleasure* be solid and lasting, and I cannot see what more is wanting to make man *happy*. The best way therefore to determine how much *Perfection* contributes to our *happiness*, is to examine how much it contributes to our *pleasure.*

If, with the *Epicurean*, we think *indolence* our supreme *happiness*, and define *pleasure* by the *absence of pain*; then I am sure the *perfect* man will have the best claim to it. *He* surely is freest from the mistakes and errors, from the passions and

follies,

follies, that embroil human life: he creates no evil to himself, nor provokes any unneceffary danger. His *virtue* effectually *does that,* which *atheifm* attempts in vain; difpels the terror of an invifible power: he needs not drown the voice of confcience by wine, or noife, or the toil of life; it fpeaks nothing to him, but what is kind and obliging; it is his comforter, not his perfecutor: and as to this world, he reaps that fatisfaction and tranquillity from the *moderation* of his affections; which *ambition* and *avarice* do in vain promife themfelves from *preferments,* or the *increafe* of *wealth.* If therefore there were *any* ftate on this fide heaven exempt from *evil,* it muft be *that* of the *perfect* man. But he knows the world too well to flatter himfelf with the expectation of *indolence,* or an *undifturbed tranquillity* here *below*; and is as far from being *deluded* by vain *hopes,* as from being fcared by vain *fears,* or tortur'd and diftended by vain *defires.* He *knows* the world has its *evils,* and that they cannot wholly be *avoided*; he *knows* it, and dares *behold* them with open eyes, *furvey* their force, and *feel* and *try* their edge. And then, when he has collected his *own* ftrength, and called in the *aid* of heaven, he *fhrinks* not, nor *defponds*; but *meets* evil with that *courage,* and *bears* it with that *evennefs* of mind, that *he* feems, even in his

affli-

affliction, nearer to *indolence,* than the *fool* and *finner* in his *profperity.* So that I cannot forbear profefling, there appears fo much *beauty,* fo much *lovelinefs* in the deportment of the *perfect* man, with refpect to the *evils* of *life,* that for *that* reafon alone, were there no *other,* I fhould admire and prefer his *virtue* above any *poffeffion* or *enjoyment* of life. Give me leave to *compare* the faint and finner on this occafion; and but very briefly: *The wife man's eyes,* faith *Solomon,* Ecclef. ii. 14. *are in his head; but the fool walketh in darknefs.* The wife man fees that he has enemies, I mean evils; and therefore he informs himfelf well of their ftrength, obferves their motion, and prepares for the encounter: but ignorance and ftupidity is the greateft blefling of the finner's life; and his moft admired quality is not to be apprehenfive of evil, till it crufh him with its weight. But if the finner be not *fool* enough to arrive at this degree of *brutality;* then as foon as the report of the moft diftant evil, or the moft inconfiderable, reaches his ear, *how* it fills his imagination, how it fhakes his heart, and how it embitters his pleafures! and to what poor and defpicable arts, to what bafe and difhonourable fhifts does his *fear* force him? when on the fame occafion we difcover nothing in the *perfect* man, but a beautiful mixture of

humi-

humility and faith, devotion and confidence or assurance in God ; *He is not afraid of evil tidings ; his heart is fixed, trusting in the Lord,* Psal. cxii. a frame of spirit, which, to those who have opportunity and sense to observe it, renders him both more *beloved* and *revered. Lastly,* If we consider the *wicked* and the *good* man, actually under the weight and pressure of *evil,* how much *unlike* is the state of the *one* in reality to *that* of the *other,* even while the *outward* circumstances are the same ? what chearfulness, what courage, what resignation, what hopes adorn the *one !* what instruction to all, what satisfaction to his friends and relations does his deportment afford! and how does it inspire and warm the breasts of those that converse with him, with an esteem for, and love of *goodness,* and *himself !* what charm, what delight is there in those gracious speeches, that proceed at this time out of a good man's mouth ! *I know that my Redeemer liveth : the Lord giveth, and the Lord taketh away, and blessed be the name of the Lord : thou of very faithfulness hast caused me to be afflicted : God is the strength of my heart, and my portion for ever :* and such like. And how often does he pour out his heart in secret before God ! how often does he reflect on the gracious and wise ends of divine chastisement! and

F   how

how often does he, with defire and thirft,
meditate on that fulnefs of joy which expects him in the prefence of God! but
let us caft our eye now on the *voluptuary*,
on the *ambitious*, on the *covetous*, or
any *other* fort of *finner*, under difgrace,
poverty, ficknefs, or any fuch calamity;
what a mean and defpicable figure does
fuch a one make! what impatience, what
defpondency, what guilt, what pufillanimity does every *word*, every *action* betray! or it may be, his infolence is turned
into crouching and fawning; his rudenefs and violence, into artifice and cun-
ning; and his irreligion, into fuperftition.
Various indeed are the *humours*, and very
different the *carriage* of thefe unhappy
men in the day of *tryal*; but all is but *mifery* in a *different* drefs; *guilt* and *bafenefs*
under a *different* appearance. Here I might
further remark, that *that* faith which produces *patience* in *adverfity*, produces likewife *fecurity* and *confidence* in *profperity*.
I will lay me down (may every good man
fay in the words of the *Pfalmift*) *and fleep,
and rife again, for thou, Lord, fhalt make me
dwell in fafety.* And furely the *one* is as ferviceable to the eafe of human life as the
other. But I think I have faid enough to
fhew, that if *pleafure* be fuppofed to imply no more than *indolence*, the *perfect*
man has without controverfy a far *greater*.
fhare

fhare of it than any *other* can pretend to.

But let us take *pleafure* to be, not a mere *calm*, but a gentle *breeze* ; not to confift in mere *reft* and *quiet*, but a delightful *motion*; not in the mere *tranquillity* of the mind, but in the *tranfport* of it, or fomething *nearly* approaching it. *Perfection*, I am confident, will fuffer nothing by this change of the notion of *pleafure.* How many *pleafures* has the *wife* man, which depend not on *fortune*, but *himfelf*, (I mean his diligence and integrity) and to which the *finner* is an utter *ftranger!* what pleafure, what triumph is equal to that of the *perfect* man, when he *glories* in God, and makes his *boaft* of him all day long? when he *rejoyces* in the Lord with joy *unfpeakable and full of glory?* when being *filled* with all the *fulnefs* of God, *tranfported* by a vital fenfe of *divine* love, and *ftrengthened* and *exalted* by the mighty energy of the *fpirit* of *adoption*, he maintains a *fellowfhip with the Father, and with his Son Jefus?* All communion with God, confifts in this joy of *love* and *affurance*, and has a tafte of *heaven* in it. Let the moft *fortunate*, and the *wifeft Epicurean* too, ranfack all the ftore-houfes and treafures of *nature* ; let him mufter together all his legions of *pleafure*, and let him, if he can, confolidate and incorporate them all; and after

all,

all, being put into the fcale againft *this*
alone, they will prove lighter than vanity
itfelf. To be the care, the delight, the
love of an *Almighty God,* to be dear to
him who is the *origin* and *fountain* of all
Perfections ; Lord, what reft, what confidence, what joy, what extafy, do thefe
thoughts breed! how fublime, how lof-
ty, how delightful and ravifhing are thofe
expreffions of St. *John!* 1 Epift. iii. 1, 2.
Behold, what manner of love the Father has
beftowed upon us, that we fhould be called the
fons of God! therefore the world knoweth us
not, becaufe it knew him not. Beloved, now are
we the fons of God, and it doth not yet appear
what we fhall be ; but we know, that when he
fhall appear, we fhall be like him, for we fhall
fee him as he is. And thofe again of the
Pfalmift, I am continually with thee ; *thou doft*
hold me by my right hand : thou fhalt guide me
with thy counfel, and afterwards receive me
into glory, Pfal. lxxiii. 23, 24. But I will
defcend to *cooler* and *humbler* pleafures. It is
no fmall happinefs to the *perfect* man,
that he is *himfelf* a proper object of his
own *complacency.* He can reflect on the
truth and juftice, the courage and conftancy, the meeknefs and charity of his
foul, with much *gratitude* towards *God,*
and *contentment* in *himfelf.* And *this* furely he may do with good *reafon :* For
the *Perfections* of the *mind* are as juftly
to

to be preferred before thofe of the *body*, as thofe of the *body* before the gifts of *fortune*. Nor is it a matter of *fmall* importance to be *pleafed* with one's *felf* : for grant any one but *this*, and he can never be very *uneafy*, or very *miferable*. But *without* this there are very few things which will not difturb and difcompofe; and the moft obliging accidents of life will have no relifh in them. 'Tis true, *folly* and *vanity* does fometimes create a *felf-complacency* in the finner; why, even *then*, 'tis a *pleafing error*. But there is as much difference between the *juft* and *rational* complacency of a *wife* man in himfelf, and the *miftaken* one of a *fool*, as there is between the falfe and fleeting fancies of a dream, and the folid fatisfactions of the day. This will be very manifeft upon the *flighteft* view we can take of *thofe* actions, which are the true *reafon* of the good man's *fatisfaction* in himfelf, and render his confcience a continual *feaft* to him.

It is commonly faid, that *virtue* is its *own* reward : and though it muft be acknowledged, this is a *reward* which is not fufficient in *all* cafes, nor great enough to vanquifh *fome* forts of *temptations*; yet there is a great deal of *truth* and *weight* in this faying. For a ftate of virtue is like a ftate of health or peace, of ftrength and beauty; and therefore defirable on its *own*

ac-

account. And if *pleasure*, properly speaking, be nothing elfe but the *agreeable exercife of the powers of nature about their proper objects*; and if it be *then* abfolute and compleat, when thefe *powers* are *raifed*, and the *exercife* of them is *free* and *undifturbed*, then certainly *virtue*, which is nothing elfe but the *perfect* action of a *perfect* nature, as far as the *one* and the *other* may be admitted in th's ftate of *mortality*, muft be a very confiderable *pleafure*. Acts of wifdom and charity, the contemplation of truth, and the love of goodnefs, muft be the moft *natural* and *delightful* exercife of the *mind* of man : and becaufe *truth* and *goodnefs* are *infinite* and *omniprefent*, and nothing can hinder the *perfect* man from *contemplating* the one, and *loving* the other; therefore does he in his degree and meafure participate of his *felf-fufficiency*, as he does of *other* Perfections of *God*; and enjoys within *himfelf* an inexhauftible fpring of *delight*. How many, how various are the exercifes and employments of the mind of man! and when it is once polifhed and cultivated, how agreeable are they all ! to invent and find out, to illuftrate and adorn, to prove and demonftrate, to weigh, difcriminate and diftinguifh, to deliberate calmly and impartially, to act with an abfolute liberty, to defpife little things, and look boldly on dangers; to do all
things

things dexterously, to converse with a
sweet and yet a *manly* air, in *honest* and *open*,
yet *taking, obliging* language! how delightful are these things in themselves! how
much do they conduce to the service, the
beauty, and dignity of human life! to these
accomplished minds we owe histories, sciences, arts, trades, laws. From all which,
if *others* reap an unspeakable *pleasure*, how
much more the *authors*, the *parents* of them?
And all this puts me in mind of *one* great
advantage which the *perfect* man enjoys
above the most *fortunate* sensualists; which
is, that he can never want an *opportunity* to
employ all the *vigour* of his mind, *usefully*
and *delightfully*. Whence it is, that *retirement*, which is the *prison* and the *punishment*
of the *fool*, is the *paradise* of the *wise* and
good.

But let us come at length to *that* pleasure
which depends upon *external* objects; where,
if any-where, the *fool* and *sinner* must dispute his title to *pleasure* with the *wise* and
good. How many things are there here
which force us to give the preference to
the *wise* man? I will not urge, that a *narrow*, a *private* fortune can furnish store
enough for all the *appetites* of *virtue*; that
a *wise* man need not at any time purchase his
pleasure at too *dear* a rate; he need not lie,
nor cheat, nor crouch, nor fawn: *this* is
the price of *sinful* pleasure. I will not, I

F 4　　　　　say,

fay, urge *thefe* and the *like* advantages, fince
the world thinks it want of *fpirit* to be *content* with a *little* ; and want of *wit* not to
practife thofe *arts*, let them be never fo
bafe, by which we may compafs *more*. I'll
only remark thefe few things. *Firft*, the
wife man's *profpect* is enlarged. He is like
an artift or philofopher, which difcovers a
thoufand pleafures and beauties in a *piece*,
wherein the *ideot* can fee *none*: he fees in all
the works, in all the providences of *God*,
thofe *depths*, thofe *contrivances*, which the
fool cannot *fathom*; that *order*, that *harmony*, which the *finner* is *infenfible* of. *Next*,
The pleafure of *fenfe*, that is not refined by
virtue, leaves a *ftain* upon the mind: 'tis
coarfe and *turbulent*, *empty* and *vexatious*.
The pleafure of *virtue* is like a *ftream*,
which runs indeed *within* its banks, but it
runs *fmooth* and *clear* ; and has a *fpring* that
always *feeds* the current: but the pleafure
of *fin* is like a *land-flood*, impetuous, mud-
dy, and irregular: and as foon as it *forfakes*
the ground it overflows, it leaves nothing
behind it, but *flime* and *filth*. Laftly, The
wife man forming a true *eftimate* of the objects of *fenfe*, and not looking upon them as
his *ultimate* end, *enjoys* all that is in them,
and is not fooled by an *expectation* of more.
Thus having confidered the *objects* of human *pleafure*, *two* things are plain: *Firft*,
That the *perfect* man has *many* fources or
fountains

fountains of *pleasure*, which the *sinner* never taftes of, which he cannot relifh, which he is a ftranger to; *Next*, As to *outward* things, that *he* has even here, many advantages above the *other*. But what is more *considerable* yet, is,

All the claim the *sinner* lays to *pleasure*, is confined to the *present* moment, which is extremely *short*, and extremely *uncertain*; the *time* that is *past* and to *come*, he *quits* all pretenfions to, or *ought* to do fo. As to the time *past*, the thing is *self-evident*: for the *sinner*, looking back, fees his *pleasures* and *satisfactions*; the *good man* his *trials* and *temptations* paft and gone: the *sinner* fees an *end* of his *beauty* and his *strength*; the *good man* of his *weaknesses* and *follies*: the *one* when he looks back is encountered with *sin* and *folly*, *wickedness* and *shame*; the *other* with *repentance* and *good works*: *guilt* and *fear* haunt the reflections of the *one*, *peace* and *hope* attend thofe of the *other*. As to the *time to come*, the *atheist* hath *no* profpect at all *beyond* the *grave*, the *wicked* Chriftian a very *dismal* one, the *weak* and *imperfect* a *doubtful* one; only the *wise* and *perfect* an *assured, joyful,* and *delightful* one. And this puts me in mind of *that* which is the proper *fruit* of *Perfection*, and the trueft and greateft *pleasure* of human *life*, that is, *assurance*, affurance of
the

the *pardon* of *fin*, affurance of the *divine favour*, affurance of *immortality* and *glory*.

Need I prove, that *affurance* is an unfpeakable *pleafure?* One would think, that to man, who is daily engaged in a *conflict* with fome *evil* or other, it were fuperfluous to prove that it is a mighty *pleafure* to be raifed, tho' *not* above the *affault*, tho' not above the *reach*, yet above the *venom* and *malignity* of *evils :* to be *filled* with joy, and ftrength, and confidence; to ride *triumphant* under the protection of the *divine favour*, and fee the fea of life, fwell and tofs itfelf in vain, *in vain threaten* the bark it *cannot fink, in vain invade* the cable it *cannot burft.* One would think, that to man, who lives all his life long in *bondage* for fear of *death*, it fhould be a furprizing *delight* to fee *death* lie *gafping* at his feet, naked and impotent, without *fting*, without *terror :* one would, finally, think, that to man, who lives rather by *hope* than *enjoyment*, it fhould not be neceffary to prove, that the *Chriftian's hope*, whofe confidence is greater, its objects more glorious, and its fuccefs more certain than *that* of any worldly fancy or project, is full of *pleafure;* and that it is a *delightful* profpect to fee the *heavens* opened, and *Jefus*, our *Jefus*, our *Prince* and *Saviour*, fitting at the *right* hand of *God.*

Thus

Thus I have, I think, sufficiently made out the subserviency of *Perfection* to the *happiness* of this *present* life; which was the thing proposed to be done in this *chapter*. Nor can I imagine what *objections* can be sprung to invalidate what I have said; unless there be any thing of colour in these two.

1. To reap the *pleasure*, will some one say, which you have described here, it requires something of an *exalted* genius, some *compass* of understanding, some *sagacity* and *penetration*. To this I *answer*, I grant indeed that some of those *pleasures* which I have reckoned up as belonging to the *perfect* man, demand a spirit *raised* a little above the *vulgar* : but the *richest* pleasures, not the most *polished* and *elevated* spirits, but the most *devout* and *charitable* souls are *best* capable of. *Such* are the *peace* and *tranquillity* which arises from the *conquest* and *reduction* of all inordinate affections : the *satisfaction* which accompanies a sincere and vigorous *discharge* of *duty*, and our *reflections* upon it; the *security* and *rest* which flows from *self-resignation*, and *confidence* in the *divine* protection : and lastly, the *joy* that springs from the *full* assurance of *hope*.

But 2*dly*, It may be objected, 'tis true all these things seem to hang together well enough in *speculation*; but when we come

to

to examine the matter of *fact*, we are almoft tempted to think, that all which you
have faid to prove *the ways of wifdom, ways
of pleafantnefs, and all her paths peace,* a-
mounts to no more than a pretty *amufement*
of the mind, and a *vifionary* fcheme of happinefs. For how *few* are there, if any,
who *feel* all this to be truth, and *experiment*
the *pleafure* you talk of? How *few* are
they in whom we can difcover any figns of
this fpiritual *joy,* or *fruits* of a divine *tranquillity* or *fecurity?* I *anfwer,* in a word,
the examples of a *perfect* and *mature* virtue are very *few*; *religion* runs very *low,*
and the *love* of *God* and *goodnefs* in the bo-
foms of *moft Chriftians* fuffers fuch an *allay*
and *mixture,* that it is *no* wonder at all, if
fo *imperfect* a *ftate* breed but very *weak*
and *imperfect hopes,* very *faint* and *doubtful joys.* But I fhall have occafion to *examine* the force of this *objection* more *fully,*
when I come to the *obftacles* of *Perfection.*

CHAP.

CHAP. V.

Of the attainment of Perfection: with a particular account of the manner, or the several steps, by which man advances or grows up to it: with three remarks to make this discourse more useful, and to free it from some scruples.

I Have in the *first, second,* and *third* chapters explained the *notion* of *Religious Perfection.* In the *fourth* chapter I have insisted on *two effects* of it, *assurance* and *pleasure:* my method therefore now leads me to the *attainment* of *Perfection.* Here I will do *two* things. *1st,* I will trace out the several *steps* and *advances* of the Christian towards it, and draw up, as it were, a short history of his spiritual *progress,* from the very infancy of virtue to its maturity and manhood. *2dly,* I will discourse briefly of the *motives* and *means* of *Perfection.*

Of the Christian's progress *towards* Perfection.

Many are the figures and metaphors by which the scripture describes this; alluding *one* while to the formation, nourishment, and growth of the natural man; *another* while to that of plants and vegetables: *one*
while

while to the dawning and increaſing light, that ſhines more and more to the perfect day. *Another* while to that ſucceſſion of labours and expectations which the husbandman runs thro' from ploughing to the harveſt. But of all the ſimilies which the ſpirit makes uſe of to this end, there is *one* eſpecially that ſeems to me to give us the trueſt, and the livelieſt image of the change of a ſinner into a ſaint. The ſcripture repreſents *ſin* as a ſtate of *bondage,* and *righteouſneſs* as a ſtate of *liberty*; and teaches us, that by the ſame ſteps by which an enſlaved and oppreſſed people arrive at their ſecular, by the very ſame does the Chriſtian at his ſpiritual liberty and happineſs.

Firſt then, as ſoon as any judgment or mercy, or any other ſort of call, awakens and penetrates the ſinner; as ſoon as a clear light breaks in upon him, and makes him ſee and conſider his own ſtate, he is preſently agitated by various paſſions, according to his different guilt and temper, or the different calls and motives by which he is wrought upon: one while fear, another while ſhame; one while indignation, another while hope, fills his ſoul: he reſents the tyranny, and complains of the perſecution of his luſts; he upbraids himſelf with his folly, and diſcovers a meanneſs and ſhamefulneſs in his vices, which he did

not

not reflect on fufficiently before; he is
vexed and troubled at the plagues and
mifchiefs his fin and folly have already
procured him, and thinks he has reafon to
fear, if he perfift, others far more intolerable. *Then* he calls to mind the goodnefs,
the long-fuffering of *God*, the love of
Jefus, the *demonftration of the Spirit and of
Power* ; and how diftant foever he be from
virtue, he difcerns there is a beauty and
pleafure in it; and cannot but judge the
righteous happy. *Thefe* thoughts, thefe
travels of the mind, if they be not
ftrangled in the birth by a man's own
wilfulnefs or pufillanimity, or unhappily
diverted upon fome temptations, do kindle
in the bofom of the finner, the defires
of righteoufnefs and *liberty*; they fill
him with regret and fhame, caft him
down, and humble him before God,
and make him finally refolve on fhaking
off the yoke. This may be called a
ftate of *illumination* ; and is a ftate of
preparation for, or *difpofition* to *repentance :* or, if it be *repentance* itfelf, 'tis
yet but an *embryo :* to *perfect* it, 'tis neceffary,

Secondly, that the finner make good his
refolutions, and actually break with his
lufts, he muft reject their follicitations,
and boldly oppofe their commands ; he
muft take part with reafon and religion,

keep

keep a watch and guard over his foul, and muft earneftly labour by mortification and difcipline, by meditation and prayer to root out vice, and plant virtue in his foul. This in the language of the prophet is *ceafing to do evil, and learning to do well,* Ifa. i. 16, 17. He that has proceeded thus far, though he feel a great conflict within; though the oppofition of luft be very ftrong, and confequently the difcharge of his duty very difficult, he is neverthelefs in a ftate of *grace,* but in a ftate of *childhood* too; he is *fincere,* but far from being *perfect.* And yet *this* is the ftate which many continue in to the end of their lives, being partly abufed by falfe notions, and taught to believe, from *Rom.* vii, that there is no higher or perfecter ftate; partly intangled and incumbered by fome unhappy circumftances of life : or, it may be, the force or *impetus* of the foul towards *Perfection,* is much abated by the fatisfaction of profperity, and the many diverfions and engagements of a fortunate life : but he that will be *perfect,* muft look upon this ftate as the beginning of virtue. For it muft be remember'd, that a ftubborn and powerful enemy will not be fubdued and totally brought under in a moment. The Chriftian therefore muft profecute this war till he has finifhed it; I will not fay by

extir-

extirpating, but difabling the enemy. But here I would have it well obferved, that the reducing the enemy to a low condition, is not always effected by an uninterrupted feries of *victories*; for feldom is any fo fortunate, or fo brave, fo wife, or fo watchful, as to meet with no check in the long courfe of a difficult war; 'tis enough if he be not difcouraged, but inftructed and awakened by it. And to prevent any fatal difafter, two errors muft carefully be avoided. *Firft*, A hafty and fond confidence in our felves, with an over-weening contempt and neglect of the enemy: and *next*, all falfe and cowardly projects of truces and accommodations: nor is the fitting down content with poor and low attainments very far removed from this latter. *This* is the *fecond* ftage of the Chriftian's advance toward *Perfection*; and may be called the ftate of *liberty*. The *third* and laft, which now follows, is the ftate of *zeal*, or *love*, or, as *miftick* writers delight to call it, the ftate of *union*.

The yoke of fin being once fhaken off, the love of righteoufnefs, and a delight in it, is more and more increafed: and *now* the man proceeds to the *laft* round in the fcale of *Perfection*. The wifdom, courage, and vigour of a convert, is generally at firft employed in fubduing his corruptions, in conquering his ill habits,

G and

and defeating his enemies; in watching
over his own heart, and guarding himself
against temptations. But this being once
done, he is in full *liberty* to pursue the
works of peace and love. Now he may
advance from *necessary* to *voluntary* acts of
self-denial, which before would have been
putting new wine into old bottles, contrary to
the advice of our *Master,* Mat. ix. 17. Now
he may enlarge his knowledge, and exchange
the *milk of the word* for *strong meat,* for the
wisdom and the mysteries of it : now
he may extend his watchfulness, his care ;
and whereas they were before wisely, for
the most part, confined to his own safety,
he may now, like our Saviour, *go about
doing good,* Acts. x. 38. protecting, strength-
ning, and rescuing his weak brethren ; propagating the faith, and inflaming the bo-
soms of men with the love of *Jesus* and his
truth. Now, in a word, he may give
himself up to a life of more exalted contemplation purity and charity, which will
be natural and easy now, though it were
not so in the beginning. And this life is
accompanied *with peace and joy in the Holy
Ghost*; with confidence and pleasure: now
the *yoke of Christ is easy, and his burden
light* ; now *he rejoices with joy unspeakable,
and hopes full of glory.* Now 'tis not so
much *he that lives, as Christ that lives in
him :* For the *life which he now leads,* is intirely

tirely the product of faith and love; and his greateſt buſineſs is to maintain the ground which he has got, and to hold faſt the ſtedfaſtneſs of his hope unto the end.

To render this ſhort account of the growth of virtue, from its very ſeed to maturity, the more *uſeful*, and to free it from ſome *ſcruples*, which it may otherwiſe give occaſion to; I will here add *two* or *three* remarks. *1*. That the ſtate and habit of *perfection*, is a different thing from ſome ſudden flights, or efforts of an extraordinary *paſſion*; and ſo is the fixt and eſtabliſhed tranquillity of the mind, from ſome ſudden guſts, and ſhort-liv'd fits of ſpiritual joy. No man attains to the habits of virtue and pleaſure but by degrees; and the natural method and order by which he advances to *either*, is that which I have ſet down. But as to ſome ſallies of the moſt pure and exalted paſſions, as to ſhort-liv'd fits of *perfection*, as to tranſient taſtes, ſhort and ſudden tranſports of ſpiritual pleaſure, it is very often otherwiſe. God ſometimes, either to allure the frailty of a new convert, or to fortify his reſolution againſt ſome hazardous trial, does raiſe him to an extraordinary height, by more than uſual communications of his bleſſed Spirit; and raviſhes him by ſome glances, as it were, of the beatifick viſion.

Raptures

Raptures. of love, the melting tenderness of a pious forrow, the ftrength of refolution and faith, the confidence and exultancy of affurance, do fometimes accompany fome fort' of Chriftians in the beginnings of righteoufnefs, or in the ftate of *illumination.* Where the conviction is full, the imagination lively, and the paffions tender, it is more eafy to *gain perfection,* than to *preferve* it. When a profligate finner in the *day of God's power* is fnatched like a firebrand out of the fire, refcued by fome amazing and furprizing call, like *Ifrael* by miracles out of *Egypt* ; I wonder not, if fuch a one *loves much,* becaufe *much has been forgiven him* ; I wonder not, if he be fwallowed up by the deepeft and the livelieft fenfe of guilt and mercy ; I wonder not, if fuch a one endeavour to repair his paft crimes by *heroick* acts, if he make hafte to redeem his loft time by a zeal and vigilance hard to be imitated, never to be parallel'd by others. Hence we read of *Judah's love in the day of her efpoufals,* Jer. ii. 2. And of the *firft love of the church of Ephefus,* Rev. ii. 4. as the moft perfect. And in the firft times of the gofpel, when men were converted by aftonifhing miracles ; when the prefence and example of *Jefus* and his *followers* ; when the perfpicuity and authority, the fpirit and power, the luftre and furprize
of

of the *word* of life and falvation dazzled, over-powered and tranfported the minds of men, and made a thorough change in a moment; and when again no man profeffed Chriftianity, but he expe&ted by his fufferings and martyrdom tò feal the truth of his profeffion; I wonder not, if virtue ripened faft under fuch miraculous influences of heaven ; or if *affurance* fprung up in a moment from thefe bright proofs of an unfhaken integrity. But we, who live in colder climates; who behold nothing in fo clear and bright a light as thofe happy fouls did, muft be content to make fhorter and flower fteps towards *perfettion*, and fatisfy our felves with a natural not miraculous progrefs. And we, whofe virtues are fo generally under-grown, and our tryals no other than common ones, have no reafon to expe&t the joys of a *perfe&t affurance*, till we go on to *Perfettion*.

2*dly*, As *Perfettion* is a work of time, fo is it of great expence and coft too; I mean, 'tis the effe&t of much labour and travel, felf-denial and watchfulnefs, refolution and conftancy. Many are the dangers which we are to encounter thro' our whole progrefs towards it; why elfe are we exhorted, to *learn to do good?* *To perfe&t holinefs in the fear of God*, 2 Cor. vii. 1, 2. *To be renewed in the fpirit of our minds from day to day*, Eph. iv. 23. *To*

watch,

watch, stand fast, to quit us like men, to be strong, 1 Cor xvi. 13. *To take to us the whole armour of God, that we may be able to stand against the wiles of the devil; and when we have done all, to stand,* Eph. vi. 11, 13. *To use all diligence to make our calling and election sure,* 2 Pet. i. 10. and such like? Nay, which is very remarkable, these and the like exhortations were addressed to *Christians* in *those* times, which had manifold advantages above these of *ours.* If I should say, that the Spirit of God, the sanctifying grace of God, was then poured forth in more plentiful measure than ever after, not only *scripture,* as I think, but *reason* too, would be on my side. The interest of the church of Christ required it; sanctity being as necessary as miracles to convert the Jew and the Gentile. But besides this, the then wonderful and surprizing light of the gospel, the presence of *Jesus* in the flesh, or of those who had been eye-witnesses of his glory; a croud of wondrous works and miracles, the expectation of terrible things, temporal and eternal judgments at the door, and an equal expectation of glorious ones too. All these things breaking in, beyond expectation, upon a *Jewish* and *Pagan* world, overwhelmed before by thick darkness, and whose abominations were too notorious to be concealed, and too detestable

testable to be excused or defended, could not but produce a very great and sudden change. Now therefore, if in these times many did start forth in a moment fit for *baptism* and *martyrdom;* if many amongst these were suddenly changed, justified and crowned, I wonder not. *This* was a *day of power,* a *day of glory* wherein God asserted Himself, exalted his Son, and rescued the world by *a stretched-out hand.* I should not therefore from hence be induced to expect any thing like at *this day.* But yet if, notwithstanding all this, Christians in those happy times, amidst so many advantages, stood in *need* of such exhortations, what do not we in these times? if so much watchfulness, prayer, patience, fear, abstinence, and earnest contention became them, when God as it were *bowed the heavens, and came down and dwelt amongst men ;* what becomes us in these days, in the dregs of time, when God stands as it were aloof off, to see what will be our latter end, retired behind a cloud, which our heresies and infidelities, schisms and divisions, sins and provocations have raised? To conclude, he that will be *perfect* must not sit like the lame man by *Bethesda's* pool, expecting till some *angel* come to cure him ; but, like our *Lord,* he must climb the mount, and pray, and then he may be transformed ; he may be raised as

G 4   much

much above the moral corruption of his nature by *Perfection*, as our Saviour was above the meanness and humility of his body, by his glorious *Transfiguration.* Thefe *two* obfervations are of manifold ufe. For *many* expect pleafure when they have no right to it; they would reap, before virtue be grown up and ripened; and being more intent upon the fruit of duty, than the difcharge of it, they are frequently difappointed and difcouraged. *Others* there are, who miftaking fome fits and flafhes of fpiritual joy for the habitual peace and pleafure of *Perfection*, do entertain too early confidences, and inftead of *perfecting holinefs in the fear of God*, they decline, or it may be, fall away through negligence and fecurity; or, which is as bad, the duties of religion grow taftelefs and infipid to them for want of that pleafure which they ignorantly or prefumptuoufly expect fhould conftantly attend them: and fo they are difheartened or difgufted, and give back; which they would never do, if they did rightly underftand, that *Perfection* is a work of time; that a fettled tranquillity, an habitual joy of fpirit, is the fruit only of *Perfection*; and that thofe fhort gleams of joy, which break in upon new converts, and fometimes on other imperfect Chriftians, do depend upon extraordinary circumftances, or are peculiar favours of heaven.

heaven. *Laftly*, there are *many*, who have entertained very odd fancies about the *attainment* of *Perfection*; they talk and act as if *Perfection* were the product, not of time and experience, but of an inftant; as if it were to be infufed in a moment, not acquired; as if it were a mere arbitrary favour, not the fruit of meditation and difcipline. 'Tis true, it cannot be doubted by a Chriftian, but that *Perfection* derives itfelf from heaven; and that the feed of it is the grace of God: yet it is true too, and can as little be doubted by any one who confults the gofpel, and the experience of the beft men, that we muft watch, and pray, and contend, labour, and perfevere, and that long too, ere we can attain it. And whoever fancies himfelf rapt up into the *third heaven* on a fudden, will find himfelf as fuddenly let down to the *earth* again; if he do not ufe his utmoft diligence to fortify his refolutions, to cherifh the new-born flame, and to guard and improve his virtues.

3*dly*, It may be *objected* againft the account I have given of the *growth* of virtue, that when I come to the maturity of it, my colours are *too* bright, my ftrokes *too* bold, and the form I have given it *too* divine. For you defcribe it, will one fay, as if man, now grown *perfect*, had nothing to do, but to enjoy God, and himfelf;

felf; as if he were already *entered into rest*, and did actually *fit down with Chrift in heavenly places* ; as if, in a word, *virtue* were no longer his task, but *pleafure* ; as if he had nothing to do but to rejoice continually, nothing further to prefs after, nothing to combat, nothing to contend with : whereas the *fathers* generally, and all judicious *modern* writers, feem to place *Perfection* in nothing higher, than in a perpetual progrefs towards it ; they look upon life as a perpetual warfare, and utterly deny any fuch height or eminence as is raifed above clouds and ftorms, above troubles and temptations. But to *this* I have *feveral* things to fay, which will *clear my* fenfe about this matter, and difpel all *objections.* *Firft,* I have defcribed the laft ftage of the Chriftian's fpiritual progrefs, which I call a ftate of zeal, and in which I fuppofe the Chriftian to commence perfect; this, I fay, I have defcribed in the fame manner, and, as near as I could, in the fame words which the fcripture does. *Secondly,* I do not pretend any where to affert, that there is any ftate in this life raifed above trials and temptations. Alas! the moft *perfect* man will find it work enough to make good the ground he has gained, and maintain the conqueft he has won ; much watchfulnefs and labour, much humility and fear, and many other virtues are

are neceſſary to perſeverance in a ſtate of
Perfection. Thirdly, As the world now
goes, and indeed ever did, *Perfection* is a
ſtate we arrive at very *late*; and all the
way to it full of labour and travel, full of
dangers and difficulties; ſo that upon this
account, the life of man may well enough
be ſaid to be a perpetual warfare. But,
Fourthly, I do by no means affirm, that
the *perfect* man is incapable of growth and
improvement. Of this I ſhall have occaſion to unfold my ſenſe more fully afterwards. In the mean time I cannot forbear
obſerving here, that there is a great difference between the growth of an *imperfect*
and a *perfect* Chriſtian; for ſuppoſing grace
to be always increaſing, and the very maturity of virtue to admit of degrees; yet
the marks and diſtinctions of ſuch different
degrees are ſo nice and delicate, that the
advances of the *perfect* man are ſcarcely
perceptible to himſelf, without the cloſeſt
and ſtricteſt enquiry, much leſs can they
fall under the obſervation of others. The
firſt change of a ſinner from darkneſs to
light, from vice to virtue, from an averſion for God and goodneſs, to a *ſincere,* tho'
not a *perfect* love of both, is very palpable: ſo *again,* the change from a ſtate of
weakneſs and inconſtancy, to one of
ſtrength; of conflict and difficulty, to
one of eaſe and liberty; of fear and
doubt,

doubt, to one of confidence and pleasure, is little less evident than sensible. *But* the several degrees of growth *afterwards*, the improvements, whatever they be, of a mature state, are of *another* nature, not confisting in a *change*, but *addition ;* and that made *insensibly.* Here therefore, the *perfect* man, in order to maintain the peace and pleasure of his mind, need not enter into a nice and scrupulous examination of the degrees and measures of his virtues ; 'tis sufficient that he make good his post; 'tis enough if he follow the advice of St. *Paul,* 1 Cor. xv. 58. *If he be stedfast and unmoveable, and always abounding in the work of the Lord,*

CHAP. VI.

Of the means *of Perfection. Five general observations, serving for directions in the use of gospel-means, and* instrumental-du-ties. 1. *The practice of* wisdom *and* vir-tue, *is the best way to improve and strength-en both.* 2. *The two general and imme-diate instruments, as of* conversion, *so of* Perfection *too, are the* gospel *and the* spirit. 3 *The natural and immediate fruit of* meditation, prayer, eucharist, psalmody, *and good* conversation *or* friendship, *is, the quickening and enli-vening*

vening the conscience, *the fortifying and confirming our* resolutions, *and the raising and keeping up an* heavenly frame of spirit. 4. *The immediate ends of* discipline, *are the subduing the* pride *of the heart, and the reducing the* appetites *of the body.* 5. *Some kinds of life are better suited to the great ends of religion and virtue, than others.*

SHould I insist particularly on every one of the *means* or *instruments* of *Perfection*, it would lead me through the whole system of religion ; it would oblige me to treat of all the articles of our faith, and all the parts of moral righteousness. For the virtues of the gospel do all afford mutual support and nourishment to one another ; and mutually minister to their own growth and strength. And *prayer* and the *Lord's supper*, not to mention *meditation, psalmody, conversation, discipline*, are founded upon the belief of all the mysteries of our religion ; and consist in the exercise of almost all Christian graces, as repentance, faith, hope, charity : but this would be an endless task. I purpose therefore here only to lay down some few *general observations*, which may serve for directions in the use of *gospel-means*, point out the *end* we are to aim at, and enable us to reap the utmost *benefit* from them.

§. 1.

§. 1. The *practice* of wisdom and virtue, is the best way to improve and
strengthen both. This is a proposition almost self-evident: for besides that it is
acknowledged on all hands, that the frequent repetition of single *acts* of virtue,
is the natural way to arrive at an *habit* of
it; the *practice* of virtue gives a man
great boldness towards God, mingles joy
and pleasure in all his addresses to him,
purifies and enlightens the mind, and en-
titles him to more plentiful measures of
grace, and higher degrees of favour. *If*
ye continue in my word, then are ye my dif-
ciples indeed; and ye shall know the truth,
and the truth shall make you free, John viii.
31, 32. *To him that hath, shall be given,*
and he shall have more abundance, Matth.
xiii. 12. If this be so, as undoubtedly it
is, it is plain, that we ought not to be
fond of such a solitude or retirement, as
cuts off the opportunity of many virtues,
which may be daily practised in a more
publick and active life. The true *Ancho-*
rite, or *hermite,* was at *first* little *better*
than a *pious extravagant* : I will not say
how much *worse* he is now. Meditation
and prayer are excellent duties; but meekness and charity, mercy and zeal, are
not one jot inferior to them. The *world*
is an excellent *school* to a good Christian ;

an ; the follies and the miseries, the trials and temptations of it, do not only exercise and employ our virtue, but cultivate and improve it: they afford us both *instruction* and *discipline*, and naturally advance us on towards solid wisdom, and a well-settled power over our selves. 'Tis our own fault if every accident that befals us, and every one whom we converse with, do not teach us somewhat ; occasion some wise *Reflection*, or inkindle some pious *affection* in us. We do not reflect on our words and actions, we do not observe the motions of our own hearts as diligently as we ought ; we make little or no application of what we see or hear, nor learn any thing from the wisdom and the virtue, the folly and the madness of *man*, and the consequences of both: and so we neither improve our *knowledge*, nor our *virtue*, but are the same to *day* we were *yesterday*, and life *wastes* away in common accidents, and customary actions, with as little alteration in us, as in our affairs : whereas, were we mindful, as we ought, of our true interest, and desirous to reap some spiritual benefit from every thing, the virtues of *good* men would inkindle our emulation, and the folly and madness of *sinners*, would confirm our abhorrence for sin ; from *one* we should learn content, from *another* industry ; here we
should

ſhould ſee a charm in meekneſs and charity, *there* in humility; in *this* man we
ſhould ſee reaſon to admire diſcretion and
command of himſelf; in *that* courage
and conſtancy, aſſiduity, and perſeverance: nor would it be leſs uſeful to us,
to obſerve, how vanity expoſes *one*, and
peeviſhneſs torments *another*; how pride
and ambition embroil a *third*; and how
hateful and contemptible avarice renders a *fourth*; and to trace all that variety of ruin, which luſt and prodigality, diſorder and ſloth, leave behind
them

And as this kind of obſervations will fill
us with ſolid and uſeful *knowledge*, ſo will
a diligent attention to the rules of righteouſneſs, and diſcretion in all the common
and daily actions of life, enrich us with
true *virtue*. *Religion* is not to be confined
to the *Church*, and to the *cloſet*, nor to be
exerciſed only in *prayers* and *ſacraments*,
meditations and *alms*; but every-where,
we are in the preſence of God, and every
word, every action, is capable of *morality*. Our defects and infirmities betray
themſelves in the daily accidents and the
common converſation of life; and *here*
they draw after the very important conſequences; and therefore *here* they are to
be watched over, regulated and governed,
as well as in our more *ſolemn* actions. 'Tis
to

to the virtues or the errors of our *common* converſation and *ordinary* deportment, that we owe both our friends and ene-mies, our good or bad character abroad, our domeſtick peace or troubles; and in a high degree, the improvement or depravation of our minds. Let no man then, that will be *perfect* or *happy*, aban-don himſelf to his humours or incli-nations in his carriage towards his acquain-tance, his children, his ſervants: let no man, that will be *perfect* or *happy*, follow *prejudice* or *faſhion* in the common and cuſtomary actions of life: but let him aſ-ſure himſelf, that by a daily endeavour to conform theſe more and more to the excel-lent rules of the goſpel, he is to train up himſelf by degrees to the moſt abſolute *wiſdom*, and the moſt *perfect* virtue, he is capable of And to this end he muſt firſt know himſelf, and thoſe he has to do with; he muſt diſcern the proper ſeaſon and the juſt occaſion of every virtue; and then he muſt apply himſelf to the acquiring the perfection of it by the daily exerciſe of it, even in thoſe things, which, for want of due reflection, do not commonly ſeem of any great importance. To one that is *thus* diſpoſed, the dulneſs or the careleſneſs of a ſervant, the ſtubbornneſs of a child, the ſourneſs of a parent, the inconſtancy of friends, the coldneſs of relations, the

H neglect

neglect or ingratitude of the world, will all prove extremely useful and beneficial; every thing will instruct him, every thing will afford an opportunity of exercising some virtue or another; so that such a one shall be *daily* learning, *daily* growing better and wiser.

§. 2. The *two* great *instruments,* not of *regeneration* only, but also of *perseverance* and *Perfection,* are the *Word* and the *Spirit* of *God.* This no man *doubts* that is a Christian: and therefore I will not go about to *prove* it: nor will I at present discourse of the energy and operation of the *one,* and the *other;* or examine what each is in its self, or wherein the one differs from the other. 'Tis abundantly enough, if we be assured that the *gospel* and the *Spirit* are proper and sufficient *means* to attain the great *ends* I have mentioned, namely, our *conversion* and *Perfection.* And that they are so, is very plain from those *texts* which do expresly assert, that the *gospel* contains all those truths that are necessary to the clear exposition of our duty, or to the moving and obliging us to the practice of it. And that the *Spirit* implies a supply of all that supernatural strength, be it what it will, that is necessary to enable us, not only to will, but to do that which the gospel convinces us to be our duty. *Such* are,

are, *Rom.* i. 2. *For the law of the spirit of life in Christ Jesus, hath made me free from the law of sin and death.* 2 Tim. iii. 16, 17. *All scripture is given by inspiration of God, and is profitable for doctrine, for reproof, for correction, for instruction in righteousness. That the man of God may be perfect, thoroughly furnished unto all good works.* 2 Cor. xii. 9. *And he said unto me, my grace is sufficient for thee, for my strength is made perfect in weakness. Most gladly therefore will I rather glory in my infirmities, that the power of Christ may rest upon me.* 1 Pet. i. 5. *Who are kept by the power of God through faith unto salvation, ready to be revealed in the last time.* 'Tis needless to multiply *texts* on this occasion; otherwise it were very easy to shew, that all things necessary to *life and godliness*, are contained in the *Word* and *Spirit*; that whatever is necessarily to be wrought in us to prepare us for, or entitle us to eternal salvation, is ascribed to the *gospel* and the *Spirit*. This truth then being unquestionable, that the *gospel* and the *Spirit* are the *two* great *instruments* of *Perfection*; we may from hence infer *two rules*, which are of the most universal use, and of the most powerful efficacy in the pursuit of *Perfection*. 1. We cannot have too great a value, too great a passion for the *Book of God*; nor fix our thoughts and hearts too earnestly upon the truths of

it.

it. We muft imitate the *Theffalonians*, in behalf of whom St. *Paul* thanks God, *because when they received the word of God which they heard of him, they received it not as the word of men; but as it is in truth, the word of God,* 1 Theff. ii. 13. that is, we muft entertain the *gospel*, as *that* which has infallible truth in all its doctrines, uncontroulable authority in all its precepts, a divine certainty in all its promifes and threats, and a divine wifdom in all its counfels and directions: and *he* that thus believes will certainly find the gofpel to work effectually in *him*, as it did in the *Theffalonians.* What light and beauty will he difcern in all its defcriptions of our duty! what force in all its perfuafions! what majefty, what dignity, what life, what power, what confolation, what fupport! in one word, what heavenly virtue will he difcern in each part of it, and what vaft and unfathomable wifdom in the whole compofure and contrivance of it! how will he then admire it, how will he love it, how will he ftudy it, how will he delight in it! how will he be tranfported by the promifes, and awed by the threats of it! how will he be pierced and ftruck through by thofe exaggerations of fin, and captivated and enamoured by thofe lively and divine defcriptions of virtue he meets in it! how will he adore the goodnefs of *God,*

confpi-

conspicuous in our redemption! how will
he be inflamed with the love of *Jesus*, and
be amazed at his condescension and humility! *this* and much more is the natural
effect of our receiving the *gospel* as we
ought, and pondering the truths of it with
devout and inceffant meditation. This
the royal *Pfalmift* was abundantly fenfible of, *Thy word have I hid in my heart,
that I might not fin againft thee*, Pfal. cxix.
11. *Thou through thy commandments haft
made me wifer than mine enemies: for they
are ever with me. I have more underftanding than all my teachers: for thy teftimonies are my meditation*, ver. 98. To which
I might add many other *verfes* out of
that *Pfalm*, containing the various and
mighty *effects* of the *word* of God. Nor
will any one think that I attribute too
much to the ftudy of this *word of life*,
who fhall confider that it is one of the great
works of the *Holy Spirit*, to *incline our
hearts to the teftimonies of God, to write his
laws in our hearts*, to difpofe us to attend to
revealed truths; and, in one word, to fix
our minds and thoughts upon them. 2.
Since the *Spirit*, together with the *gospel*,
is a joint principle of *regeneration* and
Perfection, 'tis manifeft, that we ought to
live in a continual dependance upon God.
He muft be our hope and confidence in the
day of trial: He muft be our praife and

H 3 boaft

boaſt in the *day of victory*, and in the *day of peace*: when we *lie down*, and when we *riſe up*, we muſt ſay with the *Pſalmiſt*, *'Tis thou, Lord, that makeſt me dwell in ſafety*, Pſal. iv. 8. We muſt look upon our ſelves as ſurrounded by enemies, and beſieged by *ſpiritual* dangers, as *David* was by *temporal*: and as *he* in the one, ſo muſt we in the *other*, expect ſtrength and ſalvation from *him*. *Through God we ſhall do valiantly, for he it is that ſhall tread down our enemies*, Pſal. lx. 12. *Many nations compaſs me round about ; but in the name of the Lord I will deſtroy them.* And when we have conquered temptations, and routed the powers of darkneſs, we muſt aſcribe all, not to our own ſtrength, nor to our own watchfulneſs, but to the grace and the power of God. *If the Lord himſelf had not been on our ſide, now may Iſrael ſay ; if the Lord himſelf had not been on our ſide*, when the legions of hell combined with the world and fleſh againſt us, *they had ſwallowed us up alive*, Pſal. cxxiv. 1, 2, 3. Now, *many* will be the happy *effects* of this dependance upon God ; we ſhall be paſſionately deſirous of his preſence, of his grace and favour; we ſhall dreſs and prepare our ſouls, we ſhall awaken and diſpoſe all our faculties to receive him ; we ſhall ever do the things that may invite and prevail with him to abide with us; we ſhall be apprehenſive of

his

his forfaking *us*, as the greateft evil that can befal us. *Lift up your heads, O ye gates, and be ye lift up, ye everlafting doors : and the king of glory fhall come in :* awake, O my foul, raife thy felf above this world and flefh, that thou mayeft be fit for the *king of glory* to dwell in thee: *Who is the king of glory? the Lord ftrong and mighty, the Lord mighty in battel*; that Holy Spirit that fub- dues our enemies, that ftrengthens us with might, and fills us with courage and holy alacrity, *Pfal.* xxiv. 7, 8. Nor does the *Pfalmift* prepare his foul for God by medi- tation only, and fpiritual recollection and foliloquies ; but by a careful and circum- fpect regulation of all his actions, *Pfal.* ci. 2, 3. *I will behave my felf wifely in a per- fect way: O when wilt thou come unto me? I will walk within my houfe with a perfect heart. I will fet no wicked thing before mine eyes: I hate the work of them that turn afide, it fhall not cleave to me.* And how earneftly does he pray againft God's forfaking him? *Pfal.* li. 11. *Caft me not away from thy pre- fence, and take not thy Holy Spirit from me.* The *refult* of all this, muft needs be *fted- faftnefs* and *growth* in holinefs and goodnefs. For, *firft*, This is the natural influence of fuch a dependance upon God ; it places us always before him, and makes us walk humbly and circumfpectly, as becomes thofe that are awed by the prefence of

fo

holy a Majefty: I have *fet the Lord always before me* ; *becaufe he is at my right-hand, I fhall not be moved*, Pfal. xvi. 1.   *Secondly*, We cannot doubt but that God will plentifully beftow his grace on thofe, who thus rely upon him. For where can He beftow it with more advantage to his glory, or to the propagation of holinefs ; both of which are fo dear to him ? Who is a fubject more 'capable of it, or who can be better entitled to it, than he who thus depends upon God? As he begs it *humbly*, and receives it *thankfully* ; fo he will husband it *carefully*, and employ it *zealoufly*.

§. 3. In *prayer, meditation*, and other *inftrumental* duties of religion, we are to aim at *one* or *all* of thefe *three* things. 1. The quickening and enlivening the *Confcience*. 2. The confirming and ftrengthening our *refolutions* of obedience. 3. The raifing and keeping up *holy* and *devout affections*. Great is the benefit of *each* of thefe. *Tendernefs* of *confcience* will keep us not only from evil, but every appearance of it ; increafe of *fpiritual ftrength* will render us ftedfaft and unmoveable in all the works of God; and *holy paffion* will make us abound in them. To fpiritual *paffion* we owe the zeal and pleafure ; to fpiritual *ftrength* and *liberty*, the conftancy

ftancy and uniformity of an holy life;
and both *ftrength* and *paffion* are generally owing to a *tender* and *enlightened confcience.* For while the *confcience* preferves a
quick and *nice* fenfe of good and evil, all
the great truths of the gofpel will have
their proper force and natural efficacy upon us. Thefe then are the genuine *fruits*
of *meditation,* the *eucharift, pfalmody,* and
fuch like. If they do not add life and
light to the *confcience*; if they do not aug-
ment our *ftrength,* nor exalt our *paffions*;
if they do not increafe our deteftation of
fin, and our love to God and goodnefs;
if they do not quicken and excite devout purpofes; if they do not engage
and refrefh the foul by holy joy and heavenly pleafure; if, I fay, they do not in
fome degree or other promote *thefe* things,
we reap *no* benefit at all from them, or
we can never be *certain* that we do. But
tho' the ends I have mentioned, be of
this great ufe to *all,* and confequently *all*
are obliged to aim at them, yet may the
different defeas and imperfeaions of *different* Chriftians, render *one* of thefe ends
more neeeffary than *another*; and by
confequence, it will be *wifdom* more immediately and direaly to intend and purfue *that.* For *example*; if a man's *temper* be fuch, that his *paffions* do foon kindle, and foon die again; that he is apt to
form

form wife and great projects, and as unapt to accomplish any thing; in *this* cafe,
it will be his duty to aim efpecially at
the *increafe of ftrength.* But if on the
other hand, a man's *temper be* cold and
phlegmatick, flow and heavy; it is but
fit that he fhould particularly apply himfelf to the awakening and exciting *devout
affections* in his foul. For *as* excellent purpofes do often mifcarry for want of conftancy and firmnefs of mind; *fo* fteadinefs
and firmnefs of mind doth feldom effect
any great matter, when it wants life and
paffion to put it into motion. *Again,* if
one's *paft* life has been very *finful,* or the
prefent be not very *fruitful,* it will behove
fuch a one to increafe the *tendernefs of
confcience,* to add more light and life to its
convictions; that, by a daily repetition of
contrition and compunction, he may wafh
off the *ftain,* or, by the fruitfulnefs of his
following life, repair the *barrennefs* of that
paft. Having thus in few words, both
made out the ufefulnefs of thofe *three ends*
I propofed to a Chriftian in the performance of *inftrumental* duties of religion,
and fhewed in what cafes he may be obliged to aim more immediately at *one* than
another; I will *now* enquire, and that as
briefly as I can, *how* thefe *three ends* may
be *fecured* and *promoted.*

1ft, Of

1st, Of *tenderness of conscience,* or the full and lively convictions of it.

To promote this, the *first* thing necessary is *meditation.* No man, who diligently searches and studies the *Book of God,* can be a stranger to *himself,* or to his *duty. Not* to his *duty;* for this *book* reveals the whole *will of God* in clear and full terms; it gives us such infallible *characters* of good and evil, right and wrong, as render our ignorance or error inexcusable: it points out the great *ends* of *life* so plainly, and conducts to them by such general and unerring *rules,* that there is no variety of circumstances can so perplex and ravel our duty, but that an *honest* man by the help of this may easily discover it. For this reason 'tis, that the *Word of God* is called *light,* because it does distinguish between good and evil, right and wrong; and like a *lamp* does manifest the path which we are to chuse, and disperses that *mist* and *darkness,* with which the lust of man, and the subtilty of hell has covered it. And for this reason 'tis, that the good have such a *value,* and the wicked such an *aversion* for the *Book of God.* For *every one that doth evil, hateth the light, neither cometh to the light, lest his deeds should be reproved. But he that doth truth, cometh to the light, that his deeds may be made manifest, that they are wrought in God,*

God, John iii. 20, 21. Nor can he that studies the *Word of God,* be a stranger to *himself* any more than to his duty. For this light ransacks all the recesses of the soul; it traces all its affections back to their first springs and sources; it lays open all its desires and projects, and strips its most secret purposes of all their disguise : *For the word of God is quick and powerful, and sharper than any two-edged sword; piercing even to the dividing asunder of soul and spirit, and of the joints and marrow; and is a discerner of the thoughts and intents of the heart,* Heb. iv. 12. In a word, if we would preserve the *conscience quick* and *sensible,* we must be daily conversant in the *Book of God.* For this commands with that authority, instructs with that clearness, persuades with that force, reproves with that purity, prudence, and charity, that we shall not easily be able to resist it; it describes righteousness and sin in such true and lively colours, proclaims rewards and punishments in such powerful and moving language, that it rouzes even the dead in sin, penetrates and wounds the stupid and obdurate.

To *meditation* we must add *prayer.* For this is a very proper and essential *means* to refresh and renew in the soul, the hatred of sin, and love of goodness ; and to improve those impressions which *meditation*

has

has made upon it. We cannot eafily put
up petitions to *God* with confidence, unlefs we do the things that *pleafe* him; for
our hearts will mifgive us, and our very
petitions will reproach us: and the mere
thought of entring more immediately into the prefence of God does oblige us to
a more careful tryal and examination of
our actions. For God being not only omnifcient, but juft and holy too, we can no
more flatter our felves with the hope of
pardon for any fin into which we are betrayed by fondnefs or negligence, than we
can imagine him ignorant of it. But this
is not all; we are to pray, that God would
enable us to *fearch* out and *difcover* our own
hearts. *Pfal.* cxxxix. 23, 24. *Search me, O
God, and know my heart: Try me and know my
thoughts; and fee if there be any wicked way in
me, and lead me in the way everlafting.* And if
we do this fincerely, God will undoubtedly
grant our requefts; and will lay open to us
all our prefent defects and infirmities, and
fhew us how far fhort we come of the *glory
of God:* that *Perfection* of holinefs and
happinefs, which many eminent *faints*
actually arrived at upon earth. And we
may be fure, *that* light which breaks in
upon our mind with this brightnefs, will
not fuffer any latent *corruptions* to continue
undifcovered; nor permit us to forget the
ftains and ruins, which the *fins* of our paft
life

life have left behind them. *Conversation* is
another way, by which we learn to know
our selves, and by which *conscience* is kept
awake, and in its *vigour.* How convictive,
how *moving* is the discourse of a devout
and pious *friend?* when he complains,
or when he rejoyces ; when he relate the
history of his own experience ; when he
lets us see the designs he has formed, and
the excellent ends his soul thirsts after ;
how does our heart burn within us? what
variety of *affections* does it *raise* in us, when
he makes his remarks on human nature
and the world; when he bewails the
dishonour of God and the decay of religion amongst us ; when he relates the misery and misfortune of sinners, and observes the particular sins and follies that
occasion it ? how often does he hereby
provoke us to wise *reflections* on our selves ?
how many new beauties does he *discover*
to us in virtue ? how many deformities
in sin, which had escaped *our* observations ? but 'tis not the *conversation* only of
my friend; but his *life* also, from which
I derive, or may do so, *instruction* and *ad-
monition.* The *Perfections* of my *friend,*
are the gentlest and the mildest, and yet
the most awakening *reproofs* too of my
own defects ; and by the freshness and lustre of the *virtue,* I discern best the weakness and the dimness of my *own.* How
often

often have I been moved to turn my thoughts with some *indignation* on my own heats and commotions, while I have admired and bless the sweetness and the gentleness, the softness and the calm, very conspicuous in an excellent friend? and when I have heard *another* mention his *nightly praises*, and those divine thoughts which filled the *intervals* of his *sleep*, and made those hours that are so burthensome to some, the most entertaining and delightful parts of his rest, how have I been inwardly filled with confusion and shame? how have I upbraided and reproached myself, condemned the sluggishness of my days, the dulness and the wanderings of my soul by night? and I believe every sincere man must find himself thus affected on the like occasions. For in *this* kind of *reproof*, which I talk of, there is something more of force and authority than is to be found in any *other*; for the example of friends, does not only teach us *what* we are to do, but demonstrates also that it *may* be done. Nor does virtue any-where appear with so lovely and charming an *air* as in a friend. But after all, amongst all the benefits we gain by excellent friendships, we ought not to reckon *this* as the *least*, that it is one, and that an indispensable *office* of *friendship*, to *admonish* and *reprove*: For *the reproofs of instruction are the paths of*
life,

life, Prov. vi. 23. But then, that we may be capable of this bleſſing, we muſt diſpoſe our minds to *expect* and *bear* reproof: we muſt ſtrive after an humble and teachable temper.; and we muſt invite and encourage our friends to this kindeſt office; not only by unaffected requeſts, but alſo by *obeying* their advice, *pardoning* whatever infirmity may be interſperſed with it, and *loving* them the better, as indeed they deſerve: for there is ſcarce any *better* proof of their affection, prudence and courage, which they are capable of giving us.

2dly, A *ſecond* end of *inſtrumental* duties is the *increaſe of ſpiritual ſtrength*. Now *ſpiritual ſtrength* conſiſts in the power and dominion we have over our affections and actions: and it ſtands upon *two baſes*; the *reduction of ſin*, and the *growth of virtue*; whatever does weaken and reduce our propenſions to ſin, whatever promotes the ſubjection of the body, adds power and authority to the mind, and renders virtue more eaſy and pleaſant. And becauſe virtues have a mutual connexion and dependance upon one another; therefore whatever promotes any one promotes all. But eſpecially, whatever ſtrengthens our hope, or quickens our fear, or enlarges our knowledge, and encreaſes our faith; this does confirm and

eſta-

eſtabliſh our reſolution more than any thing elſe. *Faith* is the *root, fear* the *guard,* and *hope* the *ſpur* of all our virtues. Faith convinces us what is our duty; fear makes us impartial, diligent, and watchful; hope, reſolved and active in the proſecution of it. It being thus clear *what* our *ſpiritual ſtrength* conſiſts in, it will be eaſy to diſ-cern by what *means* we are to gain it. But I can here only ſuggeſt thoſe hints and intimations which the *reader* muſt upon occaſion, as he needs, enlarge and improve.

1. *Meditation* is the *firſt* thing neceſſary. We muſt often ſurvey the grounds and foundations of our faith; we muſt conſi-der frequently and ſeriouſly the *ſcripture topicks* of hope and fear, ſuch are the death of *Jeſus,* a judgment to come, the holineſs and juſtice, and the omnipreſence of *God:* we muſt diligently obſerve the wiles and ſtratagems of *Satan,* the arts and inſinuations of the *world* and *fleſh,* and mark the progreſs of *ſin* from its very beginning to maturity ; and all this with a particular regard to the corruption of our own *nature,* and the deceitfulneſs of our own *hearts.* We muſt often ponder upon the beauty and peace of *holineſs,* the love of *God* and of *Jeſus,* the virtues, ſuf-ferings, and crowns of *martyrs.* And, *finally,* if we will increaſe in *ſtrength,*

I   we

we muſt practiſe this duty of *meditation* often, and we muſt not ſuffer our ſelves to be withdrawn from it, or be prevailed with to intermit it on any ſlight and trivial pretences. And becauſe we are not always *maſters* of our own *affairs,* nor conſequently of our *time*; therefore ought we to have ever ready at hand, a good collection of *texts,* which contain, in *few* words, the power and ſpirit of *goſpel motives,* the *perfection* and beauty of duties, and the ſubſtance of advice and counſel: and to fix theſe ſo in our *memory,* that they may ſerve as a *ſhield* for us to oppoſe, as our *Saviour* did, *againſt the darts of the devil,* and as a *ſupply* of excellent and uſeful thoughts upon a ſudden: ſo that in all the little interruptions of buſineſs, and the many little vacancies of the day, the mind, which is an active and buſy ſpirit, may never want a proper *ſubject* to work upon; much leſs loſe it ſelf in wild and lazy amuſements, or *defile* itſelf by vain or vicious thoughts. But we muſt not only take care that *meditation* be frequent, but alſo that it be not looſe and roving. To which end it will be neceſſary to ſtudy our *ſelves* as well as the *ſcriptures,* and to be intimately acquainted with the advantages and diſadvantages of our conſtitution, and our ſtate; ſo that in our *meditations* on the

ſcriptures,

fcriptures, we may more particularly have
an eye to thofe vices *we* are moft obnoxious to, and thofe virtues which are either
more neceffary, or more feeble and under-
grown.

Next after *meditation* muft follow *prayer.*
Great is the *power* of *prayer* in promoting
Chriftian ftrength and fortitude ; whether
we confider its *prevalence upon God,* or
its natural *influence upon our felves.* If
we confider the *latter,* what divine force
and energy is there in the confidences of
faith, the joys of hope, the earneft longings and defires of love, the tender forrows
of contrition, the delight of praifes and
thankfgivings, the adorations and felf-de-
preffions of a profound humility, and the
refolutions and vows of a perfect abhorrence of, and holy zeal and indignation
againft fin ! how do thefe things mellow
and enrich the foul ! how do they raife it
higher and higher above *the corruption
which is in the world through luft !* how do
they renew it daily, and make it a *partaker of the divine Nature !* the repetition
of the fame acts naturally begets an habit ; an habit is the ftrength and perfection of the foul ; for it is a difpofition ripened and confirmed by cuftom. How
naturally then muft *prayer* fortify the mind,
ripen good difpofitions, or add ftrength
and perfection to good habits ! fince it is

nothing

nothing elfe but a repeated *exercife* of almoft all the graces of the gofpel, repentance, faith, hope, charity, and the like:
and it ought to be obferved, that *prayer*
gives us a frequent opportunity of exercifing
thofe virtues, which we fhould not otherwife be fo often obliged to do. If, *fecondly*, we enquire into the *prevalence of prayer
with God*, we fhall have further reafons
yet to refolve, that it is a moft effectual
means of increafing our spiritual ftrength.
What will God deny to the prayer of a
righteous man? He may deny him temporal things, becaufe they are not good
for him. He may refufe to remove a
temptation, becaufe this is often an occafion of his own glory, and his fervant's
reward; but he will never refufe him
grace to conquer it. He will no more deny his Spirit to one that earneftly and fincerely begs it, than the natural parent will
bread to his hungry and craving child.
And no wonder, fince grace is as neceffary
to the fpiritual life as bread to the natural;
the goodnefs of God is more tender and
compaffionate than any inftinct in human
nature; and the purity and perfection of
God more zealoufly follicitous for the holinefs and immortality of *his* children, than
earthly parents can be for a fickly perifh-
ing life of theirs. Thus then 'tis plain,
that *prayer* contributes wonderfully to the
ftrengthening

ftrengthening and *eftablifhing* the mind of man in goodnefs. But then we muft remember, that it muft have thefe *two qualifications*; it muft be *frequent* and *inceffantly importunate.* 1. It muft be *frequent.* I would have this rule complied with as far as it may, even in our ftated, regular, and folemn addreffes to God. But becaufe bufinefs, and feveral obligations we lie under to the world, do often prefs hard upon us; therefore muft I give the fame counfel *here*, which I did before under the *head* of *meditation*; that is, to have always ready and imprinted in our *memory* feveral *texts of fcripture*, containing the moft weighty and important truths, in the moft piercing and moving language; that we may be able to form thefe on a fudden into *ejaculations*, in which our *fouls* may mount up into *heaven*, amidft the ardours and tranfports of defires and praife, as the angel did, in the flame of *Manoah's* facrifice. 2. *Prayer* muft be *inceffantly importunate. Importunate* it will be, if the foul be prepared and difpofed as it ought; that is, if it be difengaged from this world, and poffeffed entirely with the belief and earneft expeltation of a better; if it be humbled in itfelf, difclaim all ftrength and merit of its own, and reft wholly on the goodnefs and all-fufficiency of God. I add *inceffantly*, in conformity

to

to the *parables* of our *Lord*, Luke xi. 8.
and xviii. 5. and the ἀδιαλείπτως of the
apoſtle, 1 Theſſ. v. 17. And whoever
conſiders human nature well, and remem-
bers how ſoon pious motions vaniſh, and
how little they effect, will diſcern a plain
reaſon, both for *vehemence* and *perſeverance*
in *prayer* : for *vehemence*, that the ſoul
may be deeply impreſſed by pious paſſions;
for *perſeverance*, that ſuch impreſſions may
not be effaced and obliterated. Nor let
any one fancy, that *prayer* thus qualified
has not a better influence upon *God*, as
well as upon *our ſelves* : 'tis true, *God* is
void of the painfulneſs and defects of *human* paſſions, but not of the Perfection
of *divine* ones. Woe were to us, if God
were an inflexible, inexorable Deity, and
incapable of being wrought upon by the
inceſſant importunity of his poor creatures:
woe were to us, if the ſoftneſs and the
tenderneſs of the *divine Nature* did not
infinitely exceed the little reſemblances of
it in *man*. If, in a word, God did not
abound in goodneſs, mercy, and compaſſion,
more eaſily to be moved and excited than
thoſe human paſſions that bear ſome *ana-
logy* to them. Next to *converſation with God
by prayer*, the *converſation of good men* does
wonderfully contribute to the building us
up in faith and virtue. How does the
ſenſe and experience of ſuch as deſerve
our

our efteem and affection, fettle and eftablifh our judgment when they concur with
us! how does their knowledge enlighten
us, their reafon ftrengthen our faith, and
their example inflame us with emulation!
A pious friendfhip renders religion it felf
more engaging: it fanctifies our very diverfions and recreations, and makes them
minifter to virtue; it minds us when we
are forgetful, fupports and encourages us
when we faint and tire, reproves and cor-
rects us when we give back, and recalls us
into the right path when we go out of it.
This *is*, or this *fhould* be, the bufinefs of
converfation, the end and advantage of
friendfhip: we fhould be often *talking* together of the things of God, *communica-
ting* and laying open the ftate of our fouls,
our fears, our hopes, our improvements,
and defects; we fhould *watch* over one
another, *comfort* and *fupport* one another;
our *difcourfe* fhould always minifter new
warmth, or new ftrength to our holy faith
and love. But among *all* the *means of
grace*, there is *no one* does fo much *corroborate* and *nourifh* the foul of man as the
Holy Eucharift. How many wife and impartial reflections does the *preparation* for
it occafion? What unfeigned humility,
and what a profound awe of the divine
Majefty, does a previous *felf-examination*
beget in us? What a tender fenfe of the

I 4 divine

divine Love does the *contemplation* of the whole myftery inkindle? What firmnefs and refolution do we derive from frefh *vows* and repeated *engagements*; and thefe offered up with fo much *folemnity?* And how much, finally, is the habit of holinefs improved by that *fpiritual pleafure,* which the fenfible *affurances* of grace and falvation work in us, by that *awe* and holy *fear* which the whole action leaves behind on our minds, and the *zeal, vigilance,* and *circumfpection* it obliges us to for the time following? Not to mention here, how the participation of this *holy facrament* obliges us to a moft folemn *exercife* of repentance towards God, and faith in our Lord Jefus, of brotherly love and charity, and the hope of immortality and glory. *Here,* in a word, we prepare to meet *God,* as we would do in death and judgment; *here* we make an open profeffion of our holy faith, renounce the world and flefh, all our finful or vain defires; devote our felves to the fervice of *Jefus*; and learn to expect happinefs from nothing elfe, but the merits and the imitation of his Crofs. So profound is the *wifdom* of this inftitution, that it evidently fpeaks *God* the *author* of it, and proclaims the too common *neglect* of it in moft parts of *this nation,* an *inexcufable* fin and folly.

3. A

3. A *third end* of *instrumental* duties of religion, is the *raising* and *keeping up holy* and *devout affections.* I know not why *passion* is so commonly undervalued and disparaged in *religion*, unless they, who thus treat it, mean nothing by it, but a short-lived and superficial commotion of the mind, which leaves no print or relish behind it, and is presently succeeded by sin and folly. *Holy passion* is the vigour and strength of the soul; 'tis the state and frame of the mind when it is thoroughly moved and affected. And therefore to form to one's self *religion* destitute of *passion*, is little better than to content one's self with one that is lazy, lukewarm, and lifeless. And tho' there be some *tempers* very unapt to be *moved*, yet 'tis hard to imagine how even these can be wrought up to a resolution, or that resolution be supported and continued without their being affected so thoroughly, as to feel either a *real* passion, or something very nearly *approaching* one. 'Tis an excellent frame of spirit, when the soul is easily elevated and transported into *holy passion:* and I find that all those *virtues*, or rather *acts of virtue*, which are described to the life, and which are by all judged most perfect and lovely, have most of *passion* in them. How *warm* and *passionate* was the *love* of *David* for his *God!* what flame, what
vehemence

vehemence of desire was he moved by, when
he cries out, *Psal.* xlii. 1, 2. *As the hart
panteth after the water-brooks, so panteth my
soul after thee, O God : my soul thirsteth for
God, for the living God.* What awful con-
cussions and agitations of spirit did he
feel, when he thus describes his *fear!*
*My flesh trembleth for fear of thee, and I
am afraid of thy judgments,* Psal. cxix. 120.
What afflictions of soul. what tenderness of
heart do we meet with in the *repentance* of
St. *Peter,* when *he went forth and wept
bitterly!* of *Mary Magdalen,* or whoever
that *woman* in *Luke* vii. was, when *she
washed the feet of our Saviour with her tears,
and wiped them with the hairs of her head!*
and of the *royal Psalmist,* when he *watered
his couch with his tears,* Psal. vi. 6. Nor were
the pleasures of *assurance* less sensible and
vehement than the sorrows. of *repentance,*
when the *first Christians rejoiced with joy unspeakable, and hopes full of glory.* Shall I
here add *that* holy *indignation against sin,
that* vehement desire of making some *re-
paration* for it, which. is the effect of godly sorrow, that *zeal* and *fervency* of spirit
in the service of God, which is the *highest*
character of *Perfection* it self? Shall I call
these *passions?* I must not; for tho' they
have the heat and agitation of *passion,* they
have in them the firmness and steadiness
of an *habit.* And I wish with all my
heart,

heart, that all thofe other excellent *affecti-ons* of foul, which I before named, could be rendered *natural* and *habitual.* The *nearer* we come to *this*, undoubtedly the *perfecter.* I doubt mortality is incapable of any fuch height: but the more *frequent* as well as the more *vehement* and *fervent* fuch *affections* are, the *better* certainly; for great is the force and virtue of *holy paffi-on*; the flame of *love* refines our nature, and purifies it from all its drofs; the tears of a *godly forrow* extinguifh all our carnal and worldly lufts; and the agitations of *fear* preferve the chaftity and purity of the foul. 'Tis plain then, that our religi-on ought to be animated by *holy paffions*; that the more frequent and natural thefe grow, the more *perfect* we are; that be-ing the moft excellent frame of fpirit, when we are moft apt to be fenfibly and thoroughly *affected* by divine truths. By what *means* we may attain to this, is *now* briefly to be confidered. 'Tis certain, that great and important, wonderful and glo-rious *truths*, will not fail to affect us, and that throughly, unlefs luft or infidelity have rendered us ftupid and impenetrable. And that *gofpel-truths* are *fuch*, is no doubt at all; let the conviction be full, the re-prefentation lively, and the *truth* will do its work. 'Tis for want of fuch cir-cumftances and fuch fenfible notions of

an

an object as may strike the imagination; for want of close and particular applications, when *divine truths* do not move us. This now does not only call us to the frequent *meditation* of the most *affecting* subjects, the majesty and omnipresence of God; the suffering of Christ, death and judgment, heaven and hell; but it shews also, how to model and form our *meditations,* that they prove not cold and sluggish. Let the object of our thoughts be described by the most *sensible* images or resemblances; let it be clad with the most *natural* circumstances; let it be made as *particular* as it can, by fixing its eye *upon* us, and pointing its motion *towards* us: but above all, and in the first place, let the *proof* of it be clear and strong. *Prayer* is an exercise very apt to move the *passion:* the mind having disengaged it self from all earthly and bodily affections, is prepared for the impression of *truth* and the *Spirit of God* ; it draws nearer into the presence of God, and the sense of this sheds an awful reverence upon it; it has a clearer, calmer, and more serious *view* of divine things, than when it is obscured and disturbed by worldly objects. In a word, *meditation* is in *this* exercise rendered more *solemn* and more *particular*; and when the holy fire is kindled in the soul, it dilates and diffuses it self

more

more and more, till the ſtrength of deſire, the vehemence of holy love tranſcending the weakneſs of this mortal nature, we *faint* under the *paſſions* that we cannot *bear.* The *Lord's Supper* is an holy rite, wonderfully adapted to raiſe excellent *paſſions : Here* Chriſt is, as it were *ſet forth crucified amongſt us*; we ſee his *body* broken, and his *blood* poured forth ; *here* with a devout joy we receive and embrace him by faith and love in thoſe *ſymbols* of his body. and blood, and *pledges* of his love. The *ſoul* muſt be very *ill prepared*, it muſt have very imperfect notions of ſin and damnation, the croſs of Chriſt, grace and ſalvation, which is not ſenſible of a *croud* of holy *paſſions* ſpringing up in it at this ſacrament. Hymns and *Pſalms* have, by I know not what natural *magick*, a peculiar force and operation upon a pious mind. *Divine poetry* has a noble elevation of thoughts ; it does not deviſe and counterfeit *paſſions*, but only *vents* thoſe which it *feels* ; and theſe are pure and lovely, kindled from above. Therefore are all its characters natural, its deſcription lively, its language moving and powerful ; and all is ſo directly ſuited to a *devout* mind, that it preſently enters, moves, and actuates it, inſpires and informs it with the very *paſſions* it deſcribes. And though all good men are not *equally* moved in this duty,

duty, yet all, I believe, are *more* or *less*
moved. It was very much the bufinefs of
the *prophets*, and all of *prophetick education*; our *Lord* and his *difciples* practifed
it frequently; it was ever a great part of
religious joy, and one of the greateft pleafures of pious *retirement*: and I wifh
from my heart the efteem of it were re-
vived in *our* days; I perfwade myfelf it
would add much to the *warmth* and *pleafure* of devotion; it would contribute to
introduce *religion* into our *families*; and,
for ought I know, into our very *recreations*
and *friendſhips*. And this minds me, that
as I have under every *foregoing head* taken notice of the advantages of *converfation*, fo I fhould not forget it *here*. This
has a lively influence upon our minds, and
always kindles in the foul a gentle heat.
And did we but accuftom our felves to *entertain* one another with difcourfe about
another world; did we mingle the *praifes
of God* with the feafts and joys of life;
did we retire to our *country-houfes* to contemplate the variety and riches of divine
wifdom and bounty in thofe *natural* fcenes
of pleafure which the *country* affords, and
did we now and then invite our *friends* to
join with us in offering up *Hallelujahs* to
God on this account, with brightnefs and
ferenity, what calm and pleafure would
this diffufe through all our fouls, through
all

all our days! to this that I have said touching the exciting *holy paſſions*, I will only add one *obſervation*, formed upon thoſe words of the *apoſtle*, James v. 13. *Is any among you afflicted? let him pray. Is any merry? let him ſing Pſalms.* That *religion* muſt be accommodated to *nature*, and that devout *paſſions* will ſoon ſhoot up, when they are engrafted upon a *natural* ſtock. With which I will join this *other*, that ſince we are moſt affected by ſuch truths as are moſt particular, circumſtantiated, and ſenſible, and therefore imprint themſelves more eaſily and deeply on our imagination; for this reaſon I ſhould recommend the *reading* the *lives* of *ſaints* and *excellent perſons*, were they not generally writ ſo, that we have reaſon to deſire ſomewhat more of the ſpirit of *piety* in the *learned*, and more of *judgment* in the *pious*, who have employed their pens on this argument.

§. 4. The immediate *ends* of *diſcipline* are the *ſubduing the pride of the heart*, and the *reducing the appetites of the body:* By *diſcipline*, I here underſtand whatever *voluntary rigours* we impoſe upon our ſelves, or whatever *voluntary reſtraints* we lay upon our allowed *enjoyments*. And when I ſay, that the *humiliation* of the *heart*, and *ſubjection* of the *body* are the imme-

immediate ends of *both*, I do not exclude any *other* which may be *involved* in thefe, or *refult* from them. Nor, of what *importance* thefe two things are, I need not fhew. For fince all fin is diftinguifhed in fcripture into the filthinefs of the *fpirit* and the *flefh*, it is plain, that the *pride* of the *heart*, and the *luft* of the *body*, are the *two* great caufes of all immorality and uncleannefs. And therefore thefe are the *two* great *ends* which the wife and good have ever had in their *eye* in all their acts of *felf-denial* and *mortification.* This is fufficiently attefted by the example of *David*, Pfal. cxxxi. *Lord, I am not high-minded, I have no proud looks. I do not exercife myfelf in great matters, which are too high for me: But I refrain my foul, and keep it low, like as a child that is weaned from his mother; yea, my foul is even as a weaned child.* And from that other of St. *Paul*, 1 Cor. ix. 25. 26, 27. *And every one that ftriveth for the maftery, is temperate in all things: Now, they do it to obtain a corruptible crown; but we an incorruptible. I therefore fo run, not as uncertainly; fo fight I, not as one that beateth the air: but I keep under my body, and bring it into fubjection; left that by any means when I have preached to others, I myfelf fhould be a caft-away.* Whoever thus mortifies the *pride* of the *heart*, whoever thus brings under the *body*, will foon find himfelf

felf truly fet *free*, and *mafter* of Kimfelf and
fortune : he will be able to *run the way of
God's commandments*, and to advance on
fwiftly towards *Perfection*, and the pleafure and happinefs that attends it.

And to *attain* thefe bleffed *ends*, I do not
think that we need enfnare our fouls in
the perpetual bonds of *monaftick vows*; I
do not think that we are to expofe our
felves by any *ridiculous* or *fantaftick* obfervances: there is, I fay, no *need* of this;
for we may, as oft as we fhall fee fit, retrench our pleafures, abate of the fhew
and figure of life ; we may renounce our
own wills to comply with theirs who cannot fo well pretend either to authority or
difcretion: and if thefe things cannot be
done in fome cirumftances, without be-
coming *fools for Chrift*; that is, without
that tamenefs, that condefcenfion, that diminution of our felves which will never
comport with the humours and the fafhions
of the world ; here is ftill the more room for
mortification, and for a nearer and more
eminent imitation of the bleffed *Jefus :*
provided ftill we decline all affectation of
fingularity; and when we practife any extraordinary inftance of *felf-denial*, we be
ever able to juftify it to religious and judicious perfons, by the propofal of fome excellent end. *Fafting* indeed is plainly defcribed in *fcripture* ; and tho' the *obligation*

K   to

to it, with refpect to its frequency and
meafure, be not the fame on *all*, yet *all*
fhould fome time or other practife it, as
far as the rules of *Chriftian prudence* will
permit. And I have often thought, that
fafting fhould generally confift, rather in
abftinence from *pleafing meats*, than from
all; not the food which *nourifhes* our
ftrength, but that which *gratifies* the palate, miniftring moft directly to wantonnefs and luxury.

For the better regulating of voluntary
difcipline, I propofe, by way of advice,
three things. 1. I do not think it beft
to bring our felves under any perpetual and
unalterable ties in any inftance of felf-denial: there is a virtue in *enjoying* the world,
as well as in *renouncing* it; and 'tis as
great an excellence of religion to know
how to *abound*, as how to *fuffer want*.
Nay, what is more, all voluntary aufterities are in order to give us a power and dominion over our felves in the general courfe
of a profperous life. And, laftly, I very
much doubt, when once a man has long
and conftantly *accuftomed* himfelf to any
rigour, whether it *continue* to have much
of *mortification* in it, or whether it fo effectually tend to promote our *fpiritual liberty*, as it would if we did *return* to it but
now and *then*, as we faw occafion. 2. We
muft not multiply *unneceffary* feverities;
and

and that no man may think more needful
than really are, I obferve here, that as
there are very *few* who have not in their
nature very confiderable *infirmities*, fo are
there *as few* who have not in their *fortune*
very confiderable *inconveniences :* and if
they would apply themfelves to the *mafter-
ing* of both thefe as they ought, they would
ftand in *lefs need* of the *difcipline* of arbitrary aufterities   There are many things
too *trifling* to be taken notice of, which yet
do prove fufficient to difturb the quiet of
moft, and betray them to many paffions
and indecencies : nay, the weakneffes of
good men are fometimes fed by temptations of very little moment   Now, to *furmount* thefe temptations, and to frame and
accommodate the mind to bear the little
fhocks and juftles which we daily meet
with, without any difcompofure or dif-
pleafure, is a matter of great *ufe* to the
tranquillity of life, and the maturity of
virtue.   To be able to *bear* the pride of
one, and the ftupidity of another; one
while to encounter rudenefs, another
while neglect, without being *moved* by
either; to *fubmit* to noife, diforder, and
the diftraction of many little affairs, when
one is naturally a lover of quietnefs and
order, or when the mind is intent upon
things of importance; in a word, to *di-
geft* the perpetual difappointments which

we

we meet with, both in bufinefs and pleafure, and in all the little projeċts, which
not the elegant and ingenious only, but
people of all ftations and all capacities purfue ; to *fuffer* all the humours and follies,
the errors, artifices, indecencies, and faults
of thofe we have to do with, with that
temper we ought, that is, with a *calm-
nefs* which proceeds, not from an unconcernment for the good of others, but a
juft dominion over our own fpirits : *this*
is a great *height* ; and to train our felves
up to it daily with much patience, vigilance, and application of mind, is the *beft
difcipline :* tho' I do not mean hereby to
exclude all *voluntary impofitions* ; for, in
order to *mafter* the evils which we cannot
avoid, it may be of good ufe now and
then to form the mind by *voluntary tryals*
and difficulties of our own chufing.   3.
Laftly, We muft ever have a care not to
lofe the *fubftance* for the *fhadow* ; not to
reft in the *means,* and negleċt the *end* ; being much taken up in *difcipline,* without
producing any *fruit* of it   For this is taking much pains to little purpofe ; travel-
ling much without making any progrefs.
But much more muft we take care in the
next place, that the *difcipline* we put our
felves upon, do not produce any *ill fruit.*
To which end, we muft carefully obferve
three things.   1. That we keep to that *mo-*
                              deration

deration which spiritual *prudence* requires; neither exposing nor entangling our selves, nor discouraging others by *excesses* and *extravagancies.* 2. That our *self-denial* never betrays us into *pride* or *uncharitableness*; for if it tempts us to over-rate our selves and to despise others, this is a flat *contradiction* to one of the main ends of Christian discipline, which is, the *humiliation* of the *heart.* 3. That we ever preserve, nay, increase the *sweetness* and *gentleness* of our minds; for whatever makes us sour and morose, or peevish and unsociable, makes us certainly so much worse; and, instead of begetting in us nearer resemblances of the *Divine* Nature, gives us a very strong tincture of a *devilish* one. *Athanasius* therefore, in the life of *Anthony the hermite,* observes, amongst other his great virtues, that after thirty years spent in a strange kind of retired and solitary life, κ̀ ͑γ̀ ͑οὐκ ὡς ὄρει τϱαφεὶς κἀκεῖ γηρων γενόμψῦΘ., ἄγϱιον εἶχε τὸ ἦθΘ., ἀλλὰ κ̀ χαϱίεις ἦν, κ̀ πολιτικός. He did not appear to his friends with a sullen or savage, but with an obliging sociable *air:* and there is indeed but little reason, why the *look* should be louring and contracted, when the *heart* is filled with joy and charity, goodness and pleasure. A serene open countenance, and a chearful grave *deport-*

ment,

ment, does beft fuit the tranquillity, purity, and dignity of a Chriftian mind.

§. 5. *Laftly,. Some* kinds of *life* are better fuited and accommodated to the great
ends of religion and virtue than *others.*
I fhall not here enter into an examination
of the advantages or difadvantages there
are in the *feveral kinds of life* with reference to religion. The fettling *this* and
feveral *other* things relating to it, was one
main defign of my *laft book.* All therefore
that I have *here* to do, is but to make one
plain *inference* from all that has been advanced in *this chapter.* If *Perfection* and
happinefs cannot be obtained without a frequent and ferious *application* of our felves
to the *means* here infifted on; then 'tis plain
that we ought to caft our *lives,* if we can,
into fuch a *method,* that we may be in a *capacity* to do this. To fpeak more particularly and clofely; fince *meditation, prayer,*
and *holy converfation* are fo neceffary to *quicken* the *confcience, excite* our *paffions,* and
fortify our *refolutions*; it is evident that it is
as neceffary fo to model and form our lives,
that we may have time enough to beftow
on thefe. For they, whofe minds and
time are taken up by the *world,* have very
little leifure for things of *this* nature, and
are very little difpofed to them, and as ill
qualified for them. As to *converfation,* as
the

the world goes now, 'tis not to be expected that it should have in it any relish of
piety, unless between such as have entered
into a close and strict *friendship.* But the
worldly man is a stranger to true *friendship*;
'tis too sacred, too delicate a thing, for a
mind devoted to the *world*, to be capable
of. A regard to interest, to some outward forms and decencies; the gratification of some natural inclination, the necessity of some kind of diversion and enjoyment, may invite him to more *familiarity* with some, than others. But 'tis hard
to believe, that there should be any thing in
such *combinations*, of *that* which is the very
life and soul of *friendship*, a sincere and un-
designing passion, increased by mutual
confidences and obligations, and supported
and strengthened by virtue and honour.
As to *prayer, men of business* do, I doubt,
oftener *read* or *say prayers,* than *pray*; for
'tis very hard to imagine, that a soul that
grovels perpetually here upon earth, that
is incessantly sollicitous about the things
of this world, and that enters abruptly
upon this duty without any *preparation,*
should immediately take fire, be filled
with heavenly vigour, and be transported
with earnest and impatient desire of grace
and glory. Ah! how hard is it for him,
who hungers and thirsts perpetually after
the profits of *this world,* to *hunger and*

K 4 *thirst*

thirst after righteousness too! if such minds
as *these* retain the belief of a providence,
some awe of God, and some degree of
gratitude towards him, 'tis as *much* as may
reasonably be expected from them : and
may *this* avail them as far as it *can !* Lastly,
as to *meditation,* how can it be imagined,
that such, whose minds and bodies are fatigued and harrassed by *worldly business,*
should be much inclined to it, or well prepared for it ? How should *these* men form
any notion of a perfect and exalted virtue,
of devout and heavenly passion? What
conceptions can they have of the power
and joy of the Holy Ghost, of poverty of
spirit, or purity of heart, or the diffusion
of the love of God in our souls? What
idea's can they entertain of an heaven, or
of angelical pleasure and beatitude ? In a
word, the *religion* of men intent upon *this
world,* when they pretend to any, which
too often they do not, consists especially in
two things, in *abstaining* from *wickedness,*
and *doing the works* of their *civil calling ;*
and how far they may be sensible of *higher*
obligations, I determine not. Good God !
what a *mercy* it is to these poor creatures,
that 'tis the fashion of their country, as
well as a precept of our religion, to dedi-
cate *one* day in *seven* to the service of God
and their souls! but have I not often *taught,*
that *purity of intention* converts the *works*
                                             of

of a secular calling into the *works of God?*
I *have* so; 'tis univerfally taught; 'tis the
doctrine of the gofpel; and therefore I
fhall never *retract* it: but ah! how hard
a thing is it for a *worldly* man to *maintain* this *purity of intention!* how hard a
thing is it for a mind, eaten up by the
love and cares of *this world*, to do all to
the honour of God! tho' therefore I cannot *retract* this doctrine, yet the *longer* I
live, the *more* reafon do I fee for *qualify-
ing* and *guarding* it with this *caution:*
let no man that defires to be *faved*, much
lefs that defires to be *perfect*, take fanctua-
ry in *purity of intention*, while he fuffers
the works of his *fecular calling* to ingrofs
his foul, and entirely ufurp his time. If
fecular works exclude and thruft out of
doors fuch as are properly *religious*, it
will not be eafy to conceive, how the
power of godlinefs fhould be maintain-
ed, how any wife thoughts, or heavenly
defires fhould be preferved in fuch men;
or fhow, finally, thofe who have utterly
given up themfelves to the *wifdom of this
world*, fhould retain any true value for
thofe maxims of the gofpel, wherein confifts the *true wifdom that is from above.*
All that I have faid againft a life of *bufinefs*, may, with equal or greater force, be
urged againft a life of *pleafure;* I mean
that which they call *innocent pleafure :* the

one

one and the *other* entangle and enfnare the mind; the *one* and the *other* leave in it a peculiar relifh, which continues long after the hurry both of pleafure and bufinefs is over. But all this while, I would not have what I have *faid* to be *extended* further than I defign it, to raife *fcruples* in *virtuous* and *good* men, inftead of *reforming* the too eager applications of the *earthly* to the things of this world.

C H A P. VIII.

Of the motives *to Perfection.* Several motives *fumm'd up in fhort ; and that* great *one, of having the other* life *in our* view, *infifted upon.*

INnumerable are the *motives* to *Perfection,* which offer themfelves to any one that reflects ferioufly on this argument. An hearty endeavour after *Perfection* is the beft proof of *fincerity*; the neareft approach to *Perfection,* is the neareft approach to the utmoft *fecurity* this life is capable of. Great is the beauty and lovelinefs of an *exalted* virtue, great the honour and authority of it ; and a very happy influence it has even upon our temporal affairs ; and to this may be added, the peace and tranquillity of a wife

mind,

mind, sanctified affections, and a regular
life. Besides, the love of *God* is boundless, and the love of *Jesus* is so too; and
therefore demand not a lazy, feeble, or un-
steddy virtue, but a strong and vigorous
one, a warm and active; such as a true
faith, great *hopes*, and a passionate love
do naturally excite us to. To all this I
might add, that the *Spirit* of God is always pressing on and advancing, desirous
to communicate *himself* to us more and
more plentifully, if we be not backward
or negligent our selves. But these, and many other *inforcements* to the duty of *Perfection*, should I enlarge on them, would
swell this *treatise* to an intolerable bulk.
Nor indeed is it necessary: for the 4th
chapter, where I treat of the *Fruit of Perfection*, does contain such *motives* to it, as
are sufficient to excite, in any one that reads
them, a most vehement desire and thirst
after it. Here therefore all that I think
fit to do, is, to put my *reader* in mind of
another life: in the glories and pleasures
of which, I need not prove that the *perfect*
man will have the greatest share. *This* is
a *motive* that must never be out of the
thoughts of the man that will be *perfect*;
and that for *three* reasons, which I will but
just mention.

1. Without *another life*, we can never
form any true notion of a *perfect virtue*.
So-

Sociable and *civil* virtues may be supported by *temporal motives*, and framed and modelled by *worldly conveniences* ; but a *divine* virtue muſt be built upon a *divine* life, upon a *heavenly* kingdom. The reaſon of this aſſertion is plain ; the *means* muſt always bear proportion to the *end* ; where therefore the end is an imperfeċt temporal good, there needs no more than imperfeċt *unfiniſhed* virtue to attain it ; but where the end is heavenly and immortal, the virtue ought to be *ſo* too. Were there no *other* life, the ſtandard and meaſure of the good or evil to be found in aċtions would be their ſubſerviency to the temporal good or evil of *this* world ; and by a neceſſary conſequence, it would be impoſſible to prove any higher degrees of poverty of ſpirit, purity of heart, charity, and the like, to be truly *virtue*, than what we could prove truly *neceſſary* to procure the good, or guard us againſt the evil of *this* life : and if ſo, 'tis eaſy to conclude what *mean* and *beggarly* kind of virtues would be produced from this ground.

2. Without *another life*, all other *motives* to *Perfeċtion* will be inſufficient. For though, generally ſpeaking, ſuch is the contrivance of human nature, that neither the common good of civil *ſociety*, nor the more particular good of *private* men, can

can be provided for, or fecured, without
the practice of fociable and political *virtues*; yet 'tis certain, that not only in many
extraordinary cafes there would be no *reward* at all for *virtue*, if there were not
one referved for it in *another world*; but
alfo in *moft* cafes, if there were not a *future* pleafure, that did infinitely outweigh
the enjoyments of *this* life, men would
fee no *obligation* to *Perfection*. For what
fhould raife them above the love of *this*
world, if there were no *other?* or above the
love of the body, if when they died they
fhould be no more for ever? and certainly
our minds would never be able to foar very
high, nor fhould we ever arrive at any excellence or Perfection in any action, if we were
always under the influence of the love of the
world, and the *body*.

3. A *life to come* is alone a fufficient
motive to *Perfection*. Who will refufe to
*endure hardfhip as a good foldier of Chrift Je-
fus*, who firmly believes that *he* is now a
fpectator, and will very fuddenly come to
be a judge and rewarder of his fufferings?
how natural is it to *run with patience the
race that is fet before us*, to him who has
an eternal joy, an eternal crown always
in his eye? and if a *life to come* can
make a man rejoyce even in *fuffering evil*,
how much more in *doing good?* If it enable him to *conquer* in the day of the
church's

church's tryal and affliction, how much more will it enable him to *abound* in all *virtues* in the day of its peace and prosperity? how freely will a man give to the distressed *members of Christ,* who believes that he sees *Christ* himself standing by, and receiving it as it were by their hands, and placing it to his own account, to be repaid a thousand-fold in *the great day of the Lord?* how easily will a man allay the storms of passion, and cast away the weapon of revenge and anger, with indignation against himself, if his faith do but present him often with a view of that *Canaan,* which the *meek in heart shall inherit* for ever? how importunately will a man pray for the pardon of sin, whose sense, whose soul, whose imagination is struck with a dread of being for ever divided from God, and excluded from the joys and virtues of the blessed? how fervently will a man pray for the Spirit of God, for the increase of grace, whose thoughts are daily swallowed up with the contemplation of an eternity; and whose mind is as fully possessed of the certainty and the glory of *another world,* as of the emptiness and vanity of *this?* how natural, finally, will it be to be poor in spirit, and to delight in all the offices of an unfeigned humility, to that man who has the image of *Jesus washing the feet of his disciples,* and a

little

little after *afcending* up into *heaven*, always before him?

But I know it will be here *objected*, we *difcern* not this efficacy you attribute to this *motive*. The doctrine of *another life* is the great *article* of the Chriftian *faith*, and it is every-where preached throughout *Chriftendom*; and yet men generally feem to have as much fondnefs for *this* world, as they could were there no *other*: they practife no virtues but fuch as are profitable and fafhionable, or none any further than they are fo. To this I *anfwer*; tho' *moft* act thus, there are *many*, I hope *very many*, who do otherwife; and, that *all* in general do *not*, proceeds from want, either of due *confideration* or firm *belief* of this doctrine of another life. *Firft*, From not *confidering* it as we fhould. 'Tis the greateft difadvantage of the objects of *faith*, compared with thofe of *fenfe*, that they are diftant and invifible. *He* therefore that will be *perfect*, that will derive any ftrength and virtue from this *motive*, muft fupply this diftance by devout and daily *contemplation*; he muft fetch the remote objects of *faith* home to him; he muft render them, as it were, prefent; he muft fee and feel them by the ftrength of *faith*, and the force of *meditation*; which if he do, then will his *faith* certainly prove a vital and victorious *principle*; then will

no

no pleafure in this world be able to combat the affured hopes of an *heaven*, nor
any worldly evil or difficulty fuftained
for virtue, be able to confront the terrors of an *hell.* A *fecond* reafon why
this *motive* doth not operate as it fhould,
is want of *faith.* We doubt, we waver,
we ftagger, we take things upon truft;
affenting very flightly and fuperficially to
the doctrine of *another life*, and looking
upon good works rather as not injurious
to *this* world, than ferviceable to a *better:*
and then 'tis no more wonder that the *unbelieving Chriftian* does not enter into Perfection and reft, than that the *unbelieving
Jew* did not: 'tis no more wonder, if the
word of life do not profit the *Chriftian*
when *not believed* by him, than if it do not
profit a *pagan* who has *never heard* of it.
And what is here faid of *infidelity*, is in its
meafure and proportion true when applied
to a *weak* and *imperfect faith.* He therefore that will be *perfect* muft daily pray,
Lord, I believe; help thou mine unbelief. He
muft daily *confider* the grounds on which
the faith and hope of a Chriftian ftand;
the exprefs declarations of the divine will
concerning the future immortality and
glory of the children of God; the demonftration of this contained in the refurrection of Jefus from the dead, and
his afcenfion, and feffion at the right
hand

hand of God : and to this he may add, the love of God, the merits of Jesus, and the state and fortune of virtue in this world. From all which one may be able to infer the undoubted *certainty* of *another world.* The *sum* of all amounts to *this :* whoever will be *perfect,* must daily, I should, I think, have said almost hourly, ponder the *blessedness* that attends *Perfection* in *another life* ; he must ponder it *seriously,* that he may be throughly persuaded of it ; he must ponder it *often,* that the notions of it may be fresh and lively in his soul.

S E C T. II.

Of the several parts of Perfection, illumi-nation, liberty, *and* zeal.

WHAT the several *parts* of religious Perfection are, will be easily dis-cerned by a very slight reflection, either on the *nature* of man, or the general *noti-on* of *Perfection* already laid down. If we consider *man,* whose *Perfection* I am treat-ing of, as it is plain ; that he is made up of *soul* and *body,* so 'tis as plain that moral *Perfection* relates to the *soul,* as the chief subject of it, and to the *body* no otherwise than as the *instrument* of that righteous-ness which is planted in the *soul.* Now in the *soul* of man we find these three things ;

L *understand-*

understanding, will, and *affections:* in the improvement and accomplishment of which, human *Perfection* must consequently consist. And if we enquire wherein this improvement or accomplishment lies, 'tis a truth so obvious, that it will not need any proof, that *illumination* is the *Perfection* of the *understanding, liberty* of the *will,* and *zeal* of the *affections.* If, in the next place, we reflect upon the description I have before given of Perfection, nothing is more evident, than that to constitute a firm *habit* of righteousness, three things are necessary: 1. The *knowledge* of our *duty,* and our obligations to it. 2. The *subduing* our *lusts* and *passions,* that we may be enabled to perform it. Lastly, Not only a free, but warm and vigorous *prosecution* of it. In the *first* of these consists *illumination*; in the *second, liberty*; and in the *third, zeal.* Upon the whole then 'tis evident, both from the *nature* of *Perfection* and of *man,* that I am now to treat in order of these three things, *illumination, liberty,* and *zeal,* as so many essential *parts* of religious *Perfection.* Nor must I stop here, but must to those three unavoidably add *humility:* for whether we consider the sins of the *perfect* man's past life, or the slips and defects of his best state; or whether we consider man's continual dependance upon God in all respects, but especially in reference to the

the beginning, progress, and confummation of his *Perfection*; or whether, laftly,
we confider the fcantinefs and deficiency,
not only of this or that man's *Perfection* in
particular, but of human *Perfection* in general, we cannot but conclude, that nothing can become mortal man (even tho'
all the excellence human nature is capable
of were united in one) better than *humility*. *Humility* therefore muft begin and
compleat religious *Perfection*; it muft accompany the Chriftian in every ftage of
his fpiritual progrefs; it muft crown all
his actions, and add that beauty and excellence, that grace and luftre to all his
other virtues, that is wholly neceffary to
render them acceptable to God.

The general *notion* of *Perfection* being
thus refolved into its *parts*, 'tis plain I am
now to difcourfe of *each* of thefe. And
what I have to fay on *each* ought, accord-
ding to the ftrict rules of *method*, to be
comprized within the *fame* chapter : but to
confult the *eafe* and *benefit* of my *reader*,
I fhall flight this nicety, and diftribute my
thoughts into as *many chapters* as I fhall
judge moft convenient for the eafe and
fupport of the *memory*.

CHAP.

CHAP. I.

Of illlumination. I. *The distinguishing cha-*
racters of illuminating truths. 1. *They*
purify us. 2. *They nourish and strengthen*
us. 3. *They delight us.* 4. *They procure*
us a glorious reward. II. *The nature of*
illuminating knowledge. 1. *It must be*
deeply rooted. 2. *It must be distinct and*
clear. 3. *It must be thoroughly concocted.*

§. 1. **W**HAT it is. It happens in the
point of *illumination*, as it does
in that of *happiness:* all men, at first hearing,
form in general an agreeable and pleasing
notion of it; all men admire and love it;
but few have any distinct and true understanding of those things which 'tis made
up of. All men conceive *illumination* to
be a state of *light* and *knowledge*, as they
do *happiness* to be a state of *pleasure :* but
are as little agreed in particular, wherein
consists the light or knowledge which makes
the *one*, as wherein consists the pleasure
that makes the *other*. The lust and passion
of some, the superstition and prejudice of
others; curiosity and confidence, weakness
and design, enthusiasm and fancy, embroil
and perplex all things. However, every
honest man hath a *clue*, by which he may
escape out of this *labyrinth*. The *scripture*
shines with bright and gracious beams
through-

throughout all this darkneſs: and, if we will attend to it, we cannot wander into any dangerous miſtake. This deſcribes the ſtate of *illumination* very plainly to us, calling it ſometimes *wiſdom,* ſometimes *knowledge* and *underſtanding* ; ſometimes *faith,* ſometimes the *ſpirit of wiſdom* and *revelation.* Next, it acquaints us with the *deſign* and *end* of it ; namely, to *convert us from the power of Satan to the ſervice of the living God,* to purify and ſanctify us, to enable us to *approve the holy, acceptable, and perfect will of God,* and, in one word, *to make us wiſe unto ſalvation.* Nay, it proceeds further, and points out to us particularly the *truths,* in the knowledge of which *illumination* conſiſts. Thus the *Old Teſtament* reckons *wiſdom* to be, ſometimes the *knowledge of God,* ſometimes the *knowledge of his law,* ſometimes the *underſtanding of proverbs and parables* ; theſe containing as it were the ſoul of moral inſtruction, and wrapping up in a few and lively words, whatever the experience of the aged, or the obſervation of men of the moſt piercing judgment, thought beſt deſerved to be tranſmitted to poſterity. But all this amounts to the ſame thing, and all the deſcriptions of *wiſdom* in the *Old Teſtament* may be ſummed up into that one, *Job* xxvi i. 28. *Behold, the fear of the Lord, that is wiſdom, and to depart*

from

from evil is understanding. The *New Testament* tells us, *this is life eternal, to know
thee the only true God, and Jesus Christ whom
thou hast sent :* that *Christ is the way, the
truth and the life :* that *in him are hid all the
treasures of wisdom and knowledge :* that true
understanding consists in *knowing the will of
God ; which will is our sanctification.* And
when St. *Paul* understands by *wisdom,* as
sometimes he does, the penetrating into the
spirit and mystery, the depths and recesses
of the *Old Testament,* and discovering the
great *design* of *man's redemption,* carried on
through all the ages of the world, and
through a wise variety of dispensations,
this alters not the *notion* of *illumination :*
for this does not point out to us any new
or different truths ; but only regards one
peculiar way of explaining, or establishing
and confirming the great Christian doctrines. To conclude ; we may easily learn
what sort of *knowledge* the *Spirit of God*
recommends to us above all other, from
those *petitions* which St. *Paul* puts up for
the *Ephesians* and *Colossians.* For the *former*
he prays thus ; *that the God of our Lord
Jesus Christ, the Father of glory, may give
unto you the spirit of wisdom and revelation
in the knowledge of him ; the eyes of your understanding being enlightened, that ye may know
what is the hope of his calling, and what the
riches of the glory of his inheritance in the
saints,*

faints, and what is the exceeding greatness of his power to us-ward, who believe, according to the working of his mighty power, which he wrought in Christ, when he raised him from the dead, and set him at his own right hand in the heavenly places, &c. Eph. i. 17, 18, 19, 20. For the *latter* thus : *that ye might be filled with the knowledge of his will, in all wisdom and spiritual understanding ; that ye might walk worthy of the Lord unto all pleasing, being fruitful in every good work, and increasing in the knowledge of God,* Col. 1. 9, 10. If from these and the like *texts* we form a general *idea of illumination,* it will be this : *illumination* is a *state* of *knowledge,* consisting in the abolishing or relinquishing those *errors,* which deprave and pervert our affections, and undermine and supplant the empire and authority of reason ; and in entertaining and embracing those *truths,* which purify the one, and restore and establish the other : and all this in order to entitle us to the favour of God, and a blessed eternity. I might content my self with this general delineation of *illumination :* but because this is a subject from which we cannot but reap so much pleasure and advantage, as will abundantly requite whatever labour can be bestowed upon it ; I will proceed to a *fuller* discovery of it, if I can.

Illumi-

Illumination then being a *state* of *know-ledge*, and the *object* of this *knowledge* being *truth*, 'tis plain, that in order to form a just and distinct *notion* of *illumination*, it will be neceſſary to enquire into *two* things: *Firſt*, What kind of *truths*; and *next*, what kind of *knowledge* of theſe *truths*, conſtitutes *illumination*.

1. Of the *truths* which *illuminate*: we have many noble characters in the *Old Teſtament* and the *New*, which diſtinguiſh *theſe* from *truths* of an *inferior* nature: all which are, I think, comprized by *Solomon* in very few words; *Prov* xxiv. 13, 14. *My ſon*, ſaith he, *eat thou honey, becauſe it is good; and the honey-comb, which is ſweet to thy taſte; ſo ſhall the knowledge of wiſdom be unto thy ſoul, when thou haſt found it; then there ſhall be a reward, and thy expectation ſhall not be cut off.* *Solomon* here, as is very uſual with *inſpired writers*, does compare ſpiritual with corporeal things, or illuſtrates the *one* by the *other*. He tells us, that what *honey* is to the *body*, that *wiſdom* is to the *ſoul*: and recommending the *former* from two incomparable properties, its miniſtring to *health* and *pleaſure*, he recommends the *latter* from advantages, which bear indeed ſome *reſemblance*; but are as much *ſuperior* to theſe, as the *ſoul* is to the *body*. *My ſon, eat thou honey, becauſe it is good;* i. e. be-

cauſe

cauſe it both *cleanſes* and *purges* all noxious
humours, and *nouriſhes* and *ſtrengthens* the
body : *and the honey-comb, becauſe it is ſweet
to the taſte* ; which is the *ſecond excellence* of
this ſort of *food,* namely, its *pleaſantneſs* ;
and properly urged to invite the eater :
then, proceeding to compleat the compari-
ſon, he adds, *ſo ſhall the knowledge of wiſdom
be to thy ſoul, when thou haſt found it* ; i. e.
it ſhall miniſter to the *purification, ſtrength,*
and *delight* of thy *ſoul.* But this is not all :
tho' the parallel can be extended no further between *honey* and *wiſdom* ; yet he
does not think fit for that reaſon to omit
one of the greateſt *excellencies* of *wiſdom* :
and therefore he adds, *then there ſhall be a
reward, and thy expectation ſhall not be cut
off.* *Wiſdom* does not only *perfect* and *entertain* our minds ; but alſo it gives us a
title to thoſe *rewards,* for the enjoyment
of which it prepares and fits us. Here
then we have from *Solomon* the true *properties* of true *wiſdom :* by theſe we may
pronounce ſafely of all the different kinds
of *knowledge* ; diſtinguiſhing the *precious*
from the *vile,* and fixing the true *eſtimate*
of *each.* If there be any ſort of *truths,*
whoſe *knowledge* does not promote, but *obſtruct* theſe great ends, *theſe* we are to
deſpiſe and ſlight, to *ſhun* and *hate.* But
if there be any *knowledge,* that does *neither* oppoſe or hinder, *nor* yet contribute
to

to these ends, unless accidentally, and
very remotely; for *this* we may have
some, but *no* very *great* regard or esteem.
But whatever *knowledge* that be which is
attended by these *fruits*, *this* is that which
we are *to search for as for hidden treasure*: this is that which, when we have
found it, we are to value above *the gold
of Ophir, the Topaz*, and *the carbuncle*,
and *all precious stones*. The distinguishing
characters then of *illuminating truths* are
four.

1. They *purify* us.
2. They *nourish* and *strengthen* us.
3. They *entertain* and *delight* us.
4. They procure us a glorious *reward*.

1. They *purify* us. This is a *property*
which the *royal Psalmist* frequently attributes to the *word of God*, that it is *pure*
and *clean*, Psal. cxix. and elsewhere. And
the *New Testament* frequently ascribes to
faith and *hope*, that they *purify* the *heart*,
1 *John* iii. 3. *Acts* xv. And this sure is the
first thing necessary to the *perfecting* the
soul of man. 'Tis with the *soul*, as with
the *body*; it must be first *cleansed* from
hurtful humours, before it can be *fed* and
nourished; *purged* of its errors and vices,
ere it can be *enriched* with divine virtues,
and *attain* that liberty and strength,
where-

wherein confifts the true greatnefs and
excellence of the mind of man. The *firft
ftep* towards the *Perfection* of *virtue*, is the
relinquifhing our *vice* ; for *we muft ceafe to
do evil, ere we can learn to do good :* and the
firft ftep towards the *Perfection* of *wifdom,* is the *difpelling* thofe *errors,* which deceive and miflead the mind, and pervert
life. *What* thefe were in the *Jew* and
Gentiles, and what they are at *this* day in
us, it is eafy enough to difcern. The *mind*
of man, as far as I can obferve, is naturally *prone* to *Religious* worfhip. Not only the confideration of the wonderful me-
chanifm and contrivance of the *world,* and
of *events,* ftrange, fudden, and unaccountable ; but alfo the confcience of his own
impotence and *obnoxioufnefs,* inclining him
to the belief, and prompting him to feek
the patronage of an *invifible all-fufficient*
power. In the next place, the mind of
man is ever prone to propofe to him fome
great, fome foveraign *good* ; in which he
may acquiefce, and by which he may fecure himfelf as well as he can, againft the
indigence and poverty of his *nature,* and
the changes and revolutions, the difafters
and the miferies, to which this *mortal
ftate* is expofed. Thefe are two things
of that importance, that no man can err
in them, but the error muft prove fatal
to his repofe. He that fets up to himfelf
for

for his ultimate end, an *empty* and *uncertain good*, inftead of a *folid* and *eternal* one, muft needs be as miferably deluded and difappointed, as *he* muft, who fets up to himfelf a *falfe God* inftead of the *true*; or goes about to endear and recommend himfelf to the *true*, by a *falfe* and *fuperftitious* worfhip. Now in thefe points the *Jew* and *Gentile* were *miferably*, though not *equally*, miftaken. The *Gentile* worfhipped *devils*, inftead of God : their *myfteries* were either fenfual or cruel ; their *religion* did oftner encourage fin than virtue. And as to their foveraign *good*, their hearts were fet upon *this world*, upon the pomp and pleafure, upon the eafe and honour of it ; and they had either none, or very dark and uncertain profpects beyond the *grave :* all beyond it was an unknown region, full of fables and idle phantoms. The *Jews*, though they enjoyed the *oracles of God*, and generally preferved the worfhip of one *true* and *living God*, yet were they not free from very deplorable errors relating to thefe points : they feemed to have turned the *true God* into an *idol*, and to have entertained fome *notions* of *him* very repugnant to *his nature :* they looked upon him as *the God of the Jews, not of the Gentiles*; as a *refpecter of perfons*, as fond and *partial* to the nation; and as delighted with a religion, made up of
nume-

numerous *rites* and *ceremonies*, and *external* obfervances. And this could not but have a very fad influence upon their *religion*, as it really had: the *holinefs* which is truly acceptable to God, being neglected and abolifhed; and *Sadducifm* or *Pharifaifm*, i. e. *fenfuality* or *hypocrify*, introduced in the room of it. And as to their ultimate *end* or fupreme *good*, the *Sadducees* denied the *refurrection*, *angels*, and *fpirits*; and therefore 'tis not to be expected they fhould entertain any defign above the pleafure of the *body*. And though the *Pharifees* acknowledged *angels* and a *refurrection*; yet can we not difcern that they had a real value for any thing befides the honour, power, and wealth of this *world*. And no wonder, fince they could, upon their *principles*, fatisfy themfelves in a *religion* which had nothing of internal *purity* or folid *righteoufnefs* in it. So that upon the whole, the *Jew* and *Gentile* were alike wicked: only the wickednefs of the *Jews* had this *aggravation* in it above that of the *Gentiles*, that they enjoyed the *oracles of God*, and the favour of a peculiar *covenant*. This being the ftate of *darknefs*, which lay upon the face of the *Jewifh* and *Gentile* world, our *Lord*, who was to be *a light to lighten the Gentiles, and the glory of his people Ifrael*, advanced and eftablifh-ed in the world that doctrine, which
directly

directly tends to difpel thefe errors, and refcue mankind from the mifery that attends them. For all that the *gofpel* contains may be reduced to thefe *three* heads : *firft*, the affertion of *one* only true *God*, with a bright and full *revelation* of his divine *Attributes* and *Perfection*. *Secondly*, an account of the *will of God*, or the *worfhip* he delights in, which is a *fpiritual* one, together with fuitable *means* and *motives*; in which laft is contained a full *declaration* of *man's* fupreme *happinefs*. *Thirdly*, the *revelation* of *one Mediator between God and man, the man Chrift Jefus*; *through whom we have accefs with boldnefs to the throne of grace*; *through whom we have obtained from the Father, grace, and pardon, and adoption*; and through whom, *laftly*, all our oblations and performances are *acceptable* to him. The *defign* of this glorious manifeftation was to *open* mens *eyes, to turn them from darknefs to light, and from the power of Satan to the living God: that they might obtain remiffion of fins*, and an *inheritance of glory*. Thefe then are the *truths* which *illuminated* the *Gentile* and *Jewifh* world: and thefe are the *truths* which muft *illuminate us* at *this* day. Thefe difpel all deftructive *errors* that lead us to vice or mifery : Thefe point out our fupreme *felicity*, and the direct *way* to it: thefe open and enlarge the

eye

eye of the *soul,* enable it to diftinguifh and judge with an unerring *exactnefs* between *good* and *evil,* between *fubftantial* and *fuperficial, temporal* and *eternal* good. And I wifh from my foul, whatever *light* we pretend to at *this day,* we were well grounded and eftablifhed in *thefe truths.* I doubt notwithftanding our *belief* of *one God,* and *one Mediator ;* and notwithftanding we are well enough affured, that *God,* who is a *fpirit, muft be worfhipped in fpirit and in truth ;* and notwithftanding our pretending to believe a *life to come ;* I fay, I am afraid, that notwithftanding thefe things, we do generally err in *two* main points; namely, in the *notion* we ought to have of *religion,* and the *value* we are to fet upon the *world* and the *body.* For who, that reflects upon the pomp and *pride* of *life,* upon the eafe, the foftnefs and the luxury of it, upon the frothinefs and the freedom, the vanity and impertinence, to fay no worfe, of *converfation,* will not conclude, that either we have renounced our *religion,* or form to our felves too complaifant and indulgent a *notion* of it? for is *this* the imitation of *Jefus ?* is this to walk as *he* walked in the world ? can this be the deportment of men to whom the world and the body is crucified ? can fuch a life as this is flow from thofe divine fountains, *faith, love,* and *hope ? who*

again

again can reflect upon the paffion we difcover for *fuperiority* and *precedence,* our
thirft of *power,* or ravenous defire of
wealth, and not conclude, that we have
miftaken our main *end,* that we fet a wrong
value upon *things*; and that whatever we
talk of an *eternity,* we look upon this *prefent* world as our *portion,* and moft valua-
ble *good?* for can fuch a tender concern
for, fuch an eager purfuit after, *temporal*
things, flow from, nay confift with, *purity
of heart,* and *poverty of fpirit,* the *love of*
God, and a *defire of heaven?* Whoever then
will be *perfect* or *happy,* muft carefully
avoid both thefe *errors:* he muft never
think that *religion* can fubfift, without the
ftrength and vigour of our *affections:* or,
that the bent and vigour of our *fouls* can
be pointed towards *God,* and yet the *air* of
our *deportment* and *converfation* be earthly,
fenfual, and vain, conformed even to a
pagan pride, and *fhew of life.* *Next,* he
muft never cherifh in himfelf the love of
this world: he muft never look upon himfelf other than a *ftranger and pilgrim* in it:
he muft never be fond of the *pleafure* of
it: he muft never form vain *defigns* and
projects about it; nor look upon the beft
things in it, as *ingredients* of our *happinefs,*
but only as *inftruments* of *virtue,* or fhort
repafts and *refrefhments* in our journey.
And becaufe all our *miftakes* about the *nature*

ture and *Perfection* of *religion,* and the
value of *temporal* things do generally arife
from εὐπερισαίᾳ ἁμαρπα. that *peculiar* fin
to which our *conftitution* betrays us; therefore the *knowledge* of *our felves,* an intimate *acquaintance* with all our natural *propenfions* and *infirmities,* is no inconfiderable
part of *illumination.* For we fhall never
addrefs our felves heartily to the *cure* of
a *difeafe* which we know *nothing* of, or
to the *rectifying* any *inclination,* till we are
thoroughly convinced that 'tis *irregular* and
dangerous.

2. The *fecond* character of *illuminating
truths* is, that they are fuch as *feed* and
nourifh, corroborate and *improve* the mind
of man. Now the properties of *bodily*
ftrength are fuch as thefe: it enables us to
baffle and repel injuries, to bear toil and
travel, to perform difficult works with
fpeed and eafe; and finally, it prolongs
life to a much further date, than weak
and crazy conftitutions can arrive at. And
of all thefe we find fome *refemblances* in
fpiritual ftrength; but as much more *perfect* and *excellent,* as the *fpirit* is above
the *body. Thefe truths* then are indeed *illuminating,* which enable us to vanquifh
temptations, to *endure* with conftancy and
patience the toils and hardfhips of our
Chriftian *warfare,* to difcharge the *duties*
of our ftation with zeal and vigour; and

M   which,

which, laftly, render us firm, fteddy, and immortal. And thefe are the glorious ef-fects which are attributed to the *truths of God.* Hence is the *gofpel* called the *power of God unto falvation,* Rom. i. 16. And hence it is, that we read of the *armour of God,* Ephef. vi. 11. *The fword of the fpirit, the fhield of faith, the breaft-plate of righte-oufnefs,* &c. to intimate to us the *ftrength* and virtue of the *word of God,* and that it brings with it fafety and fuccefs. And hence it is, that the *word of God* is faid to *quicken* and *ftrengthen*; that *man* is faid *to live, not by bread only, but by every word that proceedeth out of the mouth of God*; that *righteoufnefs* is called *everlafting*; and that he that *doth the will of God* is affirmed to *abide for ever:* to teach us plainly, that there is nothing fteddy and unalterable, nothing durable, nothing eternal, but *God, divine truths,* and *thofe* that are *formed* and *moulded* by them.

There are *truths* indeed which are mere-ly *barren* and *unactive,* which amufe and fuf-pend the mind, but never benefit it : but there are *others* which are, in the language of *Solomon,* like *health to the navel, and mar-row to the bones:* wifdom and virtue, life and honour, the favour of God and man, at-tend them where'er they dwell. And thefe are the *truths* which *illuminate :* truths that are active and fruitful ; that make us
wife

wise and good, perfect and happy : such as
we have a mighty interest in, such as have
a strong influence upon us, such as give a
new *day* to the understanding, and new
strength and liberty to the will ; such as
raise and exalt our affections, and render
the whole man more rational, more steddy,
more constant, more uniform. *These* are the
truths which make men great and modest in
prosperity, erect and couragious in adversi-
ty ; always content with *this* world, yet
always full of the hopes of a *better* : serene,
calm, and well assured in the *present* state
of their souls, and yet thirsting after *Perfection, maturity,* and the absolute *consum-
mation* of righteousness in the *world to come.*
Now the *truths* that effect all this, are all
reducible to those which I have mentioned
under the former head: for in those we
find all that is *necessary to life an godliness,*
to *virtue* and *glory* ; in those we find all
that is necessary to raise and support true
magnanimity, to enlarge and free the mind,
and to add strength and courage to it. For
what can more certainly promote all this,
than *immortality* and *glory* ? what can be
a surer foundation for the hope of both to
rest on, than the favour of *God* himself ?
and what can more effectually reconcile
and ingratiate us with *God,* than sincere universal *righteousness,* and the *mediation* of his
dearly beloved *Son* ?

3. The *third* character of *illuminating truths*, is, that they are *pleasant* and *agreeable* to the soul. Hence it is, that the *royal Pfalmist* pronounces the *word of God fweeter than the honey and the honey-comb :* that he afcribes to it *delight* and *joy* ; for he tells us, that *it rejoices the heart*, that *it enlightens the eyes.* And accordingly we find the true fervants of God, not only continually blefling and praying God in the *temple*; but magnifying him by *Pfalms* and *Hymns* in their *prifons*, and *rejoicing* in the midft of *tirbulation.* But when I reckon *pleafure* and *delight* amongft the *fruits* of *Illumination*, I muft add, that there is a vaft difference between the *fits* and *flafhes* of *mirth*, and the ferenity of a *fixed* and *habitual delight* ; between the *titillations* of *fenfe*, and the folid *joys* of the *mind* ; and laftly, between the *pleafures* of *fancy*, and of *reafon.* And when I fay, *Illumination* confifts in the *knowledge* of *pleafant* and *agreeable truths*, I mean it of *rational* pleafure, an *habitual* tranquillity of the mind; and then the matter is beyond queftion. Whatever *truths* do contribute to promote *this*, the ftudy and contemplation of *them* muft be our true *wifdom.* Joy, when 'tis folid and rational, does enlarge and exalt the mind of man: 'tis as it were, *health to the navel, and marrow to the bones*; it renders us more thankful

- to

to God, more kind and courteous to man.
'Tis an excellent *preparation* to invite more
plentiful influxes of the *Spirit of God.* Hence
did *Elijah* call for a *musical instrument* when
he desired to *prophesy* : and we find the
company of *prophets* rejoycing with *hymns,
musick,* and *dances* ; all *outward* testimonies
of the *inward* transports and ravishments
of their *minds.* And as I am perswaded
that that which distinguishes a *godly* sorrow, from a *worldly* or *impious* one, *repentance* and *contrition,* from the agonies
and perplexities of *despair,* is the *peace* and
tranquillity which attends it ; so am I perswaded, that *God* does press and invite us
to *mourning* and *sorrow* for *sin,* for *this*
reason, not excluding *others,* because it
naturally leads on to *peace* and *joy* : a soft
and tender *sorrow* dissipating the fears and
distresses of *guilt,* like mild and fruitful
showers that do lay *storms.* In a word,
there is no such powerful antidote against
sin, nor spur to holy *industry,* as holy
pleasure, pious *joy,* or spiritual *peace* and
tranquillity. This is a partaking or anti-
cipating the *powers of the world to come* ;
and the mightiest corroboration of every
thing that is good in us. The study then
of *such truths,* is true *wisdom.* And *Illumination* thus far will consist in quitting
those *errors* which beget melancholy, superstition, desperation ; and in such *truths,*

as

as enlarge our view of the divine Perfections, and exhibit to us a nearer presence of his goodness and glory: *such,* again, as unfold the dignity of human nature, and the wise and gracious ends of our creation : *such,* lastly, as extend our prospect, and enlarge our hopes ; support our frailties, and excite our vigour.

4. The *last property* of those *truths* in the knowledge of which *Illumination* consists, is, that they are such as procure us a *reward.* If we reflect upon those *three* heads, under which I ranged those *truths,* which *illuminated* the *Gentiles* and *Jewish* world, we shall easily discern how well they fit this character: they fill the mind with *joy* and *peace,* and make it abound in *hope* ; they purge the man from his natural corruption, and fortify the mind against such impressions, from outward good or evil in this world, as disquiet and torment the sinner ; they procure him the protection of God's providence, and the assistance of his spirit in *this* life, and they invite him to hope for glories and pleasures in *another,* far above any thing that *the heart of man can conceive.* God is the God of hope; he has all *fulness* and *sufficiency in himself :* and therefore *blessed* must all *they be, who have the Lord for their* God. *Jesus* is the fountain of all *consolation : He is made unto us of God, wisdom* and

and *righteousness*, and *sanctification*, and *redemption* : happy is he that does *rejoice* always, and *glory* in *him*. *Righteousness* is a ftate of *health* and *ftrength*, of *Perfection* and *beauty*, of *peace* and *tranquillity*, of *reft* and *hope* : *bleffed* are they who are poffeffed of it, who are made *free from fin*, and *become fervants of God* ; who *have their fruits unto holiness, and the end everlafting life*. Such are already *pafs'd from death to life* ; for *the fpirit of life and holinefs, of God and glory, refts upon them*. This is the character that diftinguifhes *gofpel* knowledge from all *other* forts of knowledge. No knowledge of *arts* or *fciences*, and much lefs the moft exquifite knowledge of all the *myfteries* of the *kingdom of darknefs*, can pretend to an eternal *reward*. A fhort and impure *pleafure*, and a tranfient *intereft*, is all that *this* fort of *knowledge* can beftow, and very often, inftead of *pleafure* and *profit*, it requites its difciples with *pain* and *trouble*. The *gofpel* only contains thofe *truths*, which confer *life and immortality* on thofe that believe and obey them. 'Tis the *gofpel* alone that teaches us how we are to gain the love and favour of *God*; and 'tis *God* alone who *rules* and *governs* the vifible and invifible *world*. He therefore alone is to be *feared* ; and *he* alone is to be *loved*. *Fear not them*, faith our Saviour, *Matth.*

x. 28. *which kill the body, but are not able
to kill the soul; but rather fear him who is
able to destroy both soul and body in hell.* And
St. *John* gives the *same precept* concerning
the *world: Love not the world, neither the
things of the world:* and backs it by the
same reason; *for the world passeth away,
and the lust thereof: but he that doth the
will of God abideth for ever.* That is, the
world can at best but gratify for a *moment*
the appetites of the *body,* or the desires of
a sensual *fancy;* therefore *love* it *not;* but
love the *Father,* who, after the dissolution
of the vital union betwixt *soul* and *body,* is
able to confer *life* and *happiness* on *both* to
all *eternity.*

Thus I have considered the *characters*
of *illuminating truths.* And the *whole* of
what I have said amounts to these *two*
things. 1. There are *truths* of very *different* kinds: *truths* that are of *no use;* such
are those which are either *trifling* or merely *notional,* and can have no influence on
human life: *truths* that are of *ill use;* such
are those of which consists the arts of
sensuality, avarice, vanity, and *ambition:*
these are to be *detested,* the *former* to be
contemned by all that seek after true *wisdom.*
Again, there are *truths* of an *inferior use;*
such as concern our *fortunes,* our *relations,*
our *bodies;* and these may be allowed
their *proper place,* and a *reasonable value.*

But

But the *truths* which concern the peace
and pleasure, strength and liberty of our
souls; which procure us the *favour* of *God,*
and the *grace* of his *spirit*; the *truths,*
in a word, which secure our *temporal* and
eternal happiness ; these are *illuminating*
truths, these have a *transcendent* worth,
and *inestimable* excellence, or usefulness,
and consequently can never be too *dear* to
us.   2. Since the great *characters* of *illu-*
minating truths do exactly *fit* the *gospel of*
Jesus, 'tis plain, that *this* is that *system of*
knowledge, which we are to *study day and*
night; *this* is that *divine philosophy,* whose
principles and *laws* we must incessantly revolve and ponder.   'Tis not without reason, that the *Psalmist* bestows such glorious *elogies* upon the *word of God,* Psal.
xix. and elsewhere : that he magnifies one
while the intrinsick excellence and beauty,
another while the force and efficacy of it ;
and ever and anon enlarges himself upon
the advantages, the unspeakable advantages which reward the meditation and
practice of it.   *Of all Perfections I have*
seen an end; *but thy commandments are*
exceeding broad. They are pure, they en-
dure for ever; *they enlighten the eyes, and*
rejoice the heart.   Moreover by them thy ser-
vant is warned; *and in keeping of them there*
is great reward.   That is, by them we
are preserved from all *real evil,* and put in
possession

poſſeſſion of, or entitled to all *real good.* How well did St. *Peter* anſwer, when our *Lord* asked his diſciples, *will ye alſo go from me? Lord, whither ſhall we go? Thou haſt the words of eternal life.* And how wiſely did St. *Paul* reſolve, *to know nothing but Chriſt Jeſus and him crucified?* For *he is the way, the truth, and the life*; and in *him are hid all the treaſures of wiſdom and knowledge.*

But after all, as there is a *form of godli-neſs,* ſo there is a *form of knowledge,* without the *power* of it. The knowledge of the *ſame truths,* as I obſerved in the beginning, in *different perſons,* may be very *different,* as meeting with a very *different reception.* Our *conceptions* may be more clear or con-fuſed, more lively or faint, more perfect or maimed: and our *aſſent* may be ſtronger or weaker. In ſome they may only float ſu-perficially, in *others* they may penetrate deeper: and the degrees of their *influence* and *operation* will be certainly proportioned to the different manner of their *reception.* For this reaſon it will be neceſſary to the right underſtanding of a *ſtate* of *illumina-tion,* to diſcourſe,

2. Of the *nature* of that *knowledge* we muſt have of the *former truths*; to ſhew, *what* ſort of *conception* we muſt form of them, and what kind of *aſſent* we muſt pay them, and what kind of *conſideration* we muſt employ about them. As I have there-fore

fore laid down the *properties* of those *truths,*
so will I now lay down the *properties* of
that *knowledge of them,* which is essential
to *illumination.*

1. *Illuminating knowledge* must be deeply
rooted. This our *Saviour* has taught us in
that *parable,* wherein he has observed to us,
that the *seed which had not depth of earth,* as
it *soon sprang up,* so it *soon withered* and *dried
away.* We often know (or pretend to do so)
the *rudiments* of our *religion,* without the
grounds and *foundation* of it. We embrace
conclusions, without examining the *principles*
from whence they flow; and contrary to
the advice of the *apostle,* we are *unable to
give a reason to any one that asketh us of
the faith, and the hope that is in us.* And
then *ours* is not properly *knowledge,* but
opinion; 'tis not *faith* but *credulity:* 'tis
not a firm *persuasion,* but an *easy customary*
assent. And this is overthrown by every
temptation; defaced or much blurred by
every *atheistical suggestion* or *prophane objection.* Does the *world* or our *lust* tempt us,
as the *devil* did our *first parents, ye shall not
surely die?* How easily is that *faith* shak-
en, which is *no better founded?* How easily is a man induced to hope, that *sin* is
not very *fatal* and *pernicious,* that *God* will
easily be prevailed with to *pardon* it, that
the *flames of hell* are *metaphorical,* and its
eternity a *mistaken* notion and *groundless*
fancy,

fancy, if he be ignorant of the true *rea-sons of God's wrath* and *indignation,* which are founded in the very *nature of God* and *fin?* Whereas on the *other* hand, he that well underſtands *both* theſe ; the de-formity and tendency of ſin, and the ho-lineſs and the purity of the divine Na-ture, cannot but *diſcern* an irreconcileable *oppoſition* between them ; and be convin-ced, that were there *no tribunal* erected for the *finner,* yet would *fin* be its *own puniſhment* ; and that an intolerable *hell,* conſiſting in the *diſorder of nature,* an *ex-cluſion from God,* &c. would be the natu-ral and neceſſary *iſſue* of it. The *ſum* of this argument *is, that knowledge,* which has no deep *root,* is ſubject to be over-thrown by every *blaſt: that faith* which is little more than *credulity,* does very ſel-dom ſtand againſt any very rude *ſhock.* Now the *grounds* of our *faith* and *duty* are fully and clearly expounded in the *goſpel:* and *here* eſpecially we muſt *ſeek* them. When I ſay *this,* I reject no *col-lateral* arguments, I refuſe no *foreign* aids, which contribute any thing to *confirm* and *fortify* our belief of *goſpel truths.* The *faith* of St. *Thomas* did, in part at leaſt, depend upon the evidence of *ſenſe, Tho-mas, becauſe thou haſt ſeen thou haſt believ-ed,* John xx. 29. And ſo did that of the *reſt* of them, who were *eye-witneſſes* of
the

the *refurrection* and *afcenfion* of the *bleffed Jefus.* The *doctrine* of *one God*, and a *judgment to come*, may receive much *light* and *ftrength* from *natural reafon:* and whatever *eftablifhes* a *revealed truth*, will be fo far from diminifhing, that it will increafe the *virtue* and *efficacy* of it. All the *caution* I think fit to give here is, that we be fure that the ground be plain and firm, on which we build the belief of an *illuminating truth. Philofophy*, in many cafes is clear and convictive : St. *Paul* himfelf amongft the *Gentiles* frequently appeals to *reafon.* But too often we call our *fancy philofophy* ; and obtrude upon the world, the wild and undigefted *theories* of a warm and confident *imagination*, for new *difcoveries.* What ftrange *ftuff* was *Gnoftick philofophy* once ? What did it produce but the *corruption* of the *Chriftian faith?* And what can be expected from *myftick, euthnfiaftick philofophy* or *divinity* in *any* age, any man may guefs, without any deep penetration. Nor do I doubt but that all judicious and experienced men, do as much defpife and naufeate the blendures and mixtures of pretended *philofophy* with our *faith* and *morals*, as the world generally does the *fubtilties* and *perplexities* of the *fchools.* For my part, I can't endure to have my *religion* lean upon the rotten *props* of *precarious* notions. I admire, I love the *elevations*

vations and *enlargements* of soul: but I can have no value for unaccountable *amusements or rambles of fancy.* An itch of *novelty or curiosity* has a tincture in it of our *original corruption.* I ever suspect an *opinion* that carries an *air* of *novelty* in it; and does always prefer a *vulgar truth* before *refined error.* They are *vulgar truths,* which like *vulgar blessings,* are of *most use,* and *truest worth:* and surely our *Saviour* thought so, when he *thanked his Father, that he had hid these things from the wise and prudent, and revealed them unto babes.* And when he himself taught the people *with power and authority, and not as the scribes,* he did advance no subtil *theories,* but bright and dazling, useful and convictive *truths.* This minds me of another *property* of *illuminating knowledge.*

2. This *knowledge* must not be obscure and confused, but *distinct* and *clear.* Where the images of things are slight, faint, and vanishing, they move men but very weakly, and affect them but very coldly; especially in such matters as are not subject to our senses. And this I persuade my self is one chief *reason why* those glorious and wonderful *objects, God,* a *judgment to come, heaven,* and *hell,* do strike us so *feebly,* and operate so little. We have generally no lively, *distinct,* and clear *conception* of them: It being otherwise impossible, that things

in

in their own *nature dreadful* and *amazing*, should excite in us *no fear*; or that things in their own *nature* infinitely *amiable*, should inkindle in us *no passion, no desire*. The *notions* we have of *spiritual* and *invisible* things are *dim, dusky*, and *imperfect*: our *thoughts* pass over them so *slightly*, that they scarce retain any *print* or *traces* of them. Now this sort of *knowledge* will never do the work. These drowsy notices of things will never ferment and raise our *passions* for *heaven* high enough to confront and combat those we have for the *world*. From hence we may give a fair account, what the use is of *prophetick retirement*, and *prophetick eloquence*: what is the purpose of all those *schemes* and *tropes* which occur in *inspired writings*: and why the best of men have ever so much affected *solitude* and *retreats*, from the noise and the hurry of the world. Serious, frequent, and devout *contemplation* is necessary to form in our minds, clear, distinct, and sprightly *notions*: and to *communicate* these well to the world, they must be expressed in *moving* language, in *living* tropes and figures. Ah! did we but consider this, we should sure allot more time to the *study* of *divine truths*; and we should not think, that to discover them *throughly*, it were enough to let our thoughts *glance* upon them. But we should survey and

and ponder them with all the *exactnefs* and
diligence that were neceffary to make lafting and diftinct *impreffions* upon us. Could
we know by *intuition,* doubtlefs wonderful
objects would raife very extraordinary *paffions* in us. But this we cannot, let us
come as near it as we can : only let us
avoid forming *abfurd* and *falfe* notions of
things, whilft we endeavour after *diftinct*
and *clear* ones. *Spiritual* things do not
anfwer *corporeal,* like *face* to *face* in a
glafs : and therefore, tho' to give fome
light to things that are *above* us, we may
find out all the *refemblances* of them we
can in *thofe* things we are acquainted with
here below ; yet we muft ftill remember,
that the *one* do vaftly exceed the *other,* and
that we cannot thus get a juft adequate
notion of them.

3. This *knowledge* muft not lie in the
underftanding, *crude* and *undigefted*; but
it muft be throughly *concocted* and turned
into *nourifhment, blood,* and *fpirits.* We
muft know the true *value* and *ufe* of every
principle, of every *truth* ; and be able readily to *apply* them. For what does it fignify,
how important *truths* are in themfelves, if
they are not fo to me? What does it avail
that they are impregnated with *life* and
power, if I *feel* not any fuch influence? Of
what ufe is the knowledge of *gofpel-pro-
mifes* to *me,* if I reap no *comfort* from them?

Or

Or the knowledge of *gospel-threats,* if they are unable to *curb* and *restrain* my paffions? And fo is it with other *truths:* what will it avail me that I *know,* the *life of man confifts not in the multitude of the things which he poffeffes,* if notwithftanding I *cannot content* my felf with a *competency?* That *righteoufnefs* is the chief *good,* and the richeft *treafure* of the foul of man; if notwithftanding I feek *this world,* and the *things* of it, with a more *early* and *paffionate* concern? That *fin* and *pain* are the moft *confiderable,* if not *only, evils* of man; if notwithftanding I be *caft down* and *broken* under every *adverfity?* And thus I might go on, and fhew you, that the *knowledge* which is not digefted into *nourifhment* is, if not a burden, of no benefit to us. 'Tis plain, *that is to me* nothing worth, which I make *no ufe* of. We muft then follow the advice of *Solomon,* and never quit the fearch and meditation of *truth,* till we grow *intimate* and *familiar* with it; and fo have it always ready for a *guide* and *guard* for our *fupport* and *ftrength,* and for our *delight* and *pleafure.* We muft *bind it about our heart,* as he fpeaks, *and tie it as an ornament about our neck. Then, when we go forth it fhall lead us, when we fleep it fhall keep us, and when we awake it fhall talk with us: for the commandment is a lamp, and the law is light, and reproofs of inftruction are the way of life,* Prov.

N vi.

vi. In a word, nothing can render the moſt important *truths* powerful and operative in us, but ſuch a *digeſtion* of them by ſerious and devout *meditation,* as may in a manner incorporate them with us. And this the *ſcripture* plainly teaches, when to ſignify the force and virtue of the *goſpel* above that of the *law,* it uſes theſe words : *For this is the covenant that I will make with the houſe of Iſrael after thoſe days, ſaith the Lord,* I *will put my laws into their minds, and write them in their hearts,* Heb. viii. 10. intimating, that no *laws,* no *principles* can ever influence us, till they be deeply *imprinted* in our hearts.

To *wind up* all. There are *ſeveral* kinds of *knowledge* of the *ſame truths :* there is a *knowledge,* which ſerves us only as *Piſga's* top did *Moſes;* to ſhew us *Canaan,* but not to, *bring us* into it. There is again a *knowledge,* which ſerves us only as the *talent* did the *wicked ſervants;* not to procure *rewards,* but *puniſhments.* And finally, there is a *knowledge,* which like the *talents* in the hand of the *faithful* and *good ſteward, inriches us firſt,* and *recommends us afterwards* to *higher* truſts and dignities ; which *improves* and *perfects* our *nature* firſt, and then puts us into *poſſeſſion* of ſuch *bleſſings,* as only *nature* thus *improved* and *perfected* is capable of. And this *knowledge* muſt not be a ſlight, ſuperficial, and undigeſted one;

it

it muſt not be a confuſed and obſcure, a weak and imperfect one: *this is not the knowledge* which will bring forth thoſe excellent *fruits,* which we have reaſon to expect from true *illumination.* But it muſt be a *knowledge* that has all the quite *contrary* characters: even ſuch as I have *before* deſcribed at large. That *this* is an *obſervation* of the greateſt weight and moment, is *evident* to any one who will give himſelf leave to make any *reflection* on the *preſent* ſtate of *Chriſtianity.* For how does the power of *darkneſs* prevail amidſt the *light* of the goſpel? How has the *devil* erected *his throne* in the midſt of that *Church,* which ſhould be the *kingdom of God?* and ſin and death *reign* where life and immortality are *preached? Whence* is this? Are men *ignorant* of thoſe *truths* which make up the ſyſtem of true *wiſdom? This* is *not* eaſy to be *imagined*; ſcarcely of the darkeſt corners of the *popiſh* churches, much leſs of *ours.* And therefore we muſt conclude, that this is becauſe our *knowledge* is not *ſuch* as it *ought* to be, with reſpect to its *clearneſs, certainty,* and *digeſtion.*

CHAP.

C H A P. II.

Of the fruits *and* attainment *of illumination. That illumination does not depend so
much upon a man's* outward fortune, extraordinary *parts,* acquired learning, *&c.
as upon his moral* qualifications, *such as*
humility, impartiality, *and love* of the
truth. 4. *Directions for the attainment
of illumination.* 1. *That we do not suffer
our minds to be engaged in quest of know-*
ledge foreign *to our purpose.* 2. *That we
apply our selves with a very tender and sensible concern to the study of illuminating
truths.* 3. *That we act conformable to
those* measures *of light which we have attained.* 4. *That we frequently address our
selves to God by* prayer *for the illumination of his grace. The chapter concluded
with a prayer of* Fulgentius.

HAving difpatched the *notion* of *illumination* in the foregoing *chapter,*
and fhewed both what *truths,* and what
fort of *knowledge* of them is requifite to it;
I am next to treat,

    1. Of the *fruits :* and,
    2. Of the *attainment* of it.

    §. 1. As to the *fruits* of *illumination* I
have the lefs need to infift upon *them* becaufe whatever can be faid on *this* head, has
been

been in a manner *anticipated :* all the
characters of *illuminating truths* and *illuminating knowledge* being such as sufficiently
declare the blessed *effects* of *true illumination.*
I will therefore be very *short* on *this head ;*
and only just *mention two advantages* of *illumination.* As the use of *light* is especially *twofold,* to *delight* and *guide* us ; so do
we reap *two benefits* from *illumination.*

1. The *first* and most immediate one is,
that it *sets* the whole man, and the whole
life *right ;* that it fixes our *affections* on
their proper and natural *object,* and directs
all our *actions* to their true *end.* I do not
mean, that the *understanding* constantly and
necessarily *influences* and *determines* the *will.*
Experience tells us, that we have a *fatal liberty :* that our *affections* are too often *in-
dependant* of our *reason ;* that we *sin* against
the dictates of *conscience ;* that we pursue
false-pleasure, and a *false interest,* in opposition to the *true,* and in plain *opposition* to
our *judgment* too ; at least to a *sedate* and
calm one. And the *reason* of all this is, because we consist of *two* different and repugnant *principles,* a *body* and a *soul :* and are
follicited by *two* different-*worlds,* a *temporal* and an *eternal* one. But all this notwithstanding, 'tis certain that *illumination*
in the mind has a mighty influence upon
us : for it is continually exciting in us wise
desires and excellent *purposes :* 'Tis always

N 3   alluring

alluring and inviting us towards our foveraign *good,* and reftraining and deterring us
from *fin* and *death:* it alarms, difquiets,
difturbs, and perfecutes us as often as we
err and wander from the path of life. In
one word, the great *work* of *illumination*
is, to be always reprefenting the beauties
and pleafures, and the beatitude and glory
of *virtue*; and remonftrating the evils and
difhonours, the deformities and dangers of
vice : fo that a man will never be at *reft,*
who has this *light* within him, till it be
either *extinguifhed* or *obeyed,*

   2. This *light* within us, if it be followed and complied with, not muddied
and difturbed ; if it be not quenched and
extinguifhed by wilful fin, or unpardonable
ofcitancy and remifnefs ; if, in a word, its
influence be not interrupted, difperfes all
our *fears* as well as *errors,* creates an unfpeakable *tranquillity* in the foul, fpreads
over us a calm and glorious *sky,* and makes
every thing in us and about us look *gay,* and
verdant, and *beautiful.* The *diffipation* of
Pagan darknefs, and all participation or refemblances of it; *deliverance* from a ftate
of *bondage* and *wrath,* the *peace of God,* the
love of Jefus, the *fellowfhip of the Holy
Ghoft,* the *immortality of the foul,* the *refurrection of the body,* the *perfection* and *bleffednefs* of eternity. *Good God! what* furprizing, what ravifhing *themes* are thefe for the
thoughts

thoughts of an *enlightened* foul to dwell upon! bleffed and happy is he who enjoys this
pleasure upon earth. And that *we may,* I
am now to difcourfe,

§. 2. Of the *attainment* of *illumination.*
Now whatever advice can relate to *this,*
may be reduced under *two* heads :

1. *What qualifications* do render man *capable* of *illumination.*

2. *What* it is that one duly qualified is
to *do* in *purfuit* of it.

§. 1. To begin with the *qualifications* requifite to *illumination.* One man is diftinguifhed from *another* feveral ways: by his
eftate or *fortune* ; by *natural* or *acquired endowments,* and by *moral difpofitions* : and
each of thefe may have fome, tho' a very
different influence upon human *Perfection.*
For if we inquire after only the *effence* and
integrity of Perfection ; then are there *two*
or *three moral qualifications,* which are all
that is required in order to this : but if we
inquire after the *largenefs* of its ftature, the
fymmetry of its features, the *luftre* of its
complexion, and the *elegance* of its drefs ;
then may we allow fomething to be afcribed to *fortune,* to *nature,* and a liberal *education.* This is an *obfervation* very *neceffary* to be made. For tho' *every man may be*

N 4 *capable*

capable of *Perfection,* that is, *habitual holiness,* if it be not his own fault ; yet is not *every* man capable of being *equally perfect,* because of that accidental *variety* which I have suggested, and which flows from *different gifts of God,* which depend *not* on our *selves.* This being premised ; in order to prevent my being mistaken, I proceed and determine,

1. That *illumination* depends not upon a man's *outward fortune.* There are indeed *several* sorts of *knowledge,* which we can never arrive at without much *leisure* and much *expence:* and in order to support the one, and enjoy the other, it is requisite that we be masters of a *good fortune.* Hence is that *observation* of the *author of the Ecclesiasticus,* chap. xxxviii. 24. *The wisdom of a learned man cometh by opportunity of leisure ; and he that has little business shall become wise.* And therefore in the following verses, he excludes the *husbandman,* the *statuary,* the *engraver,* the *smith,* the *potter*; and all consequently whose time and mind is taken up in the *labours* of their *profession,* and in making the necessary *provision* for *life*; these, I say, he excludes from all pretensions to *wisdom. How can he get wisdom that holdeth the plough, and that glorieth in the goad, whose talk is of bullocks,* &c. But *this* is not the *wisdom* that I am inquiring after, and which constitutes *illumination. That* consists

not

not in the laws of our *earthly* but *heavenly*
country : not in *arts* and *sciences* which relate to the *body*, and minister to a *temporal*
life ; but in those *divine truths*, which purify
the *soul*, and minister to an *eternal one* : no,
not in *notional improvements* of the *mind*,
but in *spiritual* and *vital ones*. And therefore the *husbandman* and the *artist*, the *me-
chanick* and the *trader*, are as capable of
this sort of *wisdom*, as the man of *office*,
money, or *quality*. There needs no *wealth*
to render one *the child of light and of the
day*. There is the *book of nature* ; the *book
of revelation* ; *both* the *books of God*, *both
writ* throughout with glorious *illuminating*
truths : *these* lie wide *open* to every honest
Christian. The being and nature of God ;
the mediation of Jesus, and a judgment to
come ; the nature and necessity of holiness, are fully *revealed*, and unanswerably
proved. And tho' *every* honest man be not
able to discover *all* the *arguments* on which
they stand, yet may he discover *enough* :
and what is more, he may have an *inward,
vital, sensible* proof of them ; he may *feel*
the *power*, the *charms* of *holiness* ; *experiment* its *congruity* and *loveliness* to the *human* soul ; and observe a thousand demon-
strations of its *serviceableness* to the *honour*
of God, and the *good* of *mankind* : he may
have a full and convictive sense of the
manifestation of the *divine Perfections* in
the

the great work of our *redemption*; and the
excellent *tendency* of it may be so palpable
and conspicuous to him, as to leave no
room for *doubts* or *scruples.* But besides
all this, there is a *voice within*, there is a
divine teacher and *instructor*, which will
ever *abide with him*, and *lead him into all
necessary truths* : all which is implied in
those words of our Lord, *If any man will do
his will, he shall know of the doctrine, whether
it be of God, or whether I speak of my self*,
John vii. 17.

2. Extraordinary *natural parts*, such as
sagacity or acuteness of judgment, strength
of memory, the liveliness of imagination,
are not necessary to *illumination.* The
gospel, as I remember, takes *no notice* of
these. Such is the *beauty* of *holiness*, that
it requires rather *purity* of *heart*, than
quickness of *apprehension*, to render us *enamoured* of it. And the very same thing
may be said of the *power* and *energy* of all
gospel motives, and of the *proofs* and *evi-
diences* too of *divine truths.* To *convince*
and *affect* us, there is no need of sagacity
and penetration, but *probity* and *sincerity.*
However, I have *two* or *three reflections* to
make here, which may not be unuseful:
for though *acuteness* and *retention*, by
which I mean quickness in *discerning*, and
firmness in *preserving* truth, be commonly
accounted *natural parts*, and generally
are

are so; yet, I think, where the *one* or the *other* are most *defective*, they may be much *helped* and wonderfully *improved*. To which end I remark, *first*, That those *defects* of *understanding* or *memory*, which *some* are wont to accuse themselves of in *spiritual* things, are with more *justice* to be imputed to *want* of *concern* and *affection* for *such* things, than to any incapacity of *nature*. 'Tis plain, we easily *understand*, and easily *remember*, what we *desire* and *love*: and where-ever we follow the impulse or conduct of *strong inclinations*, we seldom fail of *excelling*. Let us therefore take care, that our *hearts* be *set* upon the *things* of *God*; and we shall soon see that our *judgment* and *memory* will no more fail us *here*, than in those *worldly interests* and *pleasures*, which we are most intent upon. *Secondly*, As to *memory*; it depends very much upon the *perspicuity, regularity*, and *order* of our notions. Many complain of want of *memory*, when the defect is in their *judgment*. And *others*, while they grasp at *all*, retain *nothing*. In order then to relieve this *infirmity* of *memory*, it were an excellent way to *confine* our search and *meditation* to a *few objects*, and to have these *clearly* and *methodically* handled. A *catechetical* way of expounding and asserting the *rudiments* of our faith, if done as it ought to be, is of great service to persons of *all capacities*; but

but efpecially to thofe of *meaner.* For *thus* they may not only be enriched with the *knowledge* of the moft *ufeful* things, and of the *grounds* on which our obligation either to *belief* or *practice* is bottom'd; but alfo may be furnifhed with general *principles* of *reafon,* by which that may. fteer their *judgment* in *all* cafes; and with certain *heads* of *faith* and *morals,* to which they may be able to reduce moft of what they *read* or *hear.* . *Thirdly,* 'Tis with the underftanding as with the eye of the body: *one* fees *further* off, and in a *fainter* light; but *another* fees as *well* with regard to all the *ufes* of life, who yet requires that the objects fhould be *nearer,* and the light *better.* Men of *flow* capacities muft not be *daring* or *precipitate* in paffing their *fentence* and forming their *notions.* They muft *examine,* whether the matters they *enquire* after be not too *remote* and *obfcure:* whether the object may be brought *nearer,* and placed in a *better light*; or whether they may be furnifhed with *telefcopes* or *microfcopes* fit for them. If *not,* they muft quit the fearch of *fuch* truths as *improper* and *unneceffary* for *them:* by which means they will, at leaft, avoid being *de-ceived* or *perplexed*; which is no fmall *advantage.* To be enriched with a kind of *univerfal knowledge* is a *great* thing; but I doubt *too great* for *man.* Next to this is, to be endowed with a knowledge of *neceffary*

and

and *important truths* ; and to be *freed* from *errors* and *perplexity* in matters of any *moment* : and methinks it were no great excefs of *modefty* or *humility*, for *man* to be *content* with *this*.

3. There is no great need of *acquired learning* in order to true *Illumination.* Our *Saviour* did not exact of his *difciples*, as a neceffary preparation for his doctrine, the *knowledge* of *tongues* ; the *hiftory* of *times*, or *nature* ; *logick, metaphyficks, mathematicks*, or the like *Thefe* indeed may be *ferviceable* to *many* excellent *ends* : they may be great *accomplifhments* of the mind; great *ornaments* and very engaging *entertainments* of life : they may be, finally, very excellent and neceffary *inftruments* of, or *introductions* to *feveral profeffions* or *employments.* But as to *Perfection* and *happinefs*, to *thefe* they can never be *indifpenfably* neceffary. A man may be excellently, habitually *good*, without more *languages* than *one* : he may be fully perfwaded of thofe great *truths*, that will render him mafter of his paffions, and independent of the world ; that will render him eafy and ufeful in *this* life, and glorious in *another*, though he be no *logician* nor *metaphyfician.* Yet would I not all this while be fuppofed to exclude the ufe of true *reafon* and folid *judgment.* Tho' the *meaneft* capacity may attain to its proper *Perfection* ; that is, fuch a meafure of *knowledge*,

as

as may make the man truly *wife* and *happy*;
yet the more *capacious* any man's *foul* is, and
the more *enlarged* his *knowledge*, the more
perfect and *happy* he.

4. The *qualifications* previoufly neceffary
to *Illumination*, are *two* or *three moral* ones,
implied in that *infant temper* our *Saviour*
required in thofe who would be his *difciples*.
Thefe are *humility, impartiality*, and a *thirft*
or *love* of *truth. Firft, Humility.* He that
will be *taught of God* muft not be *proud* or
confident in *himfelf.* He muft not *over-rate*
his own *parts* and *capacity*; nor lean too
ftiffly to his *own underftanding.* He muft
firmly believe, that *Illumination* is the
work of God; and on *him* he muft depend.
He muft confefs the *weaknefs* of his own
faculties, the natural *poverty* and *indigence*
of his *underftanding*; and fo look up to *God*,
who is the fountain of *wifdom*, and giveth
grace to the humble, but refifteth the proud.
Secondly, *impartiality, fincerity*, or a certain
purity or *innocence of judgment*, if I may be
allowed to fpeak fo. That the *underftanding*
may be *capable* of *divine light*, it muft not
be blurred and ftained by *falfe principles:*
it muft not be byafs'd nor influenced by any
corrupt inclinations. Some, to prove their
impartiality or *freedom* of judgment, aban-
don themfelves to the fcrupuloufnefs of
fcepticifm and a wanton itch of endlefs *dif-*
putation and *contradiction.* But I cannot
think

think it neceſſary to our *freedom* and *impartiality*, to deny the *evidence* of our *ſenſe*; to oppoſe the *univerſal reaſon* of *mankind*; and to ſhake off all *reverence* for the *integrity* of *man*, and the *veracity of God*. No, this favours too much, either of *oſtentation*, or of a raw and unexperienced *affection* of new theories and ſpeculations. *He* ſecures his *freedom* ſufficiently, who guards his *reaſon* againſt the force of groundleſs *prepoſſeſſions*, and ſenſeleſs *modes* and *cuſtoms*; againſt the *luſts* of the *body*, and the *prejudices* of *parties*; who keeps a ſtrict eye upon the motions and tendencies of his *inferiour* nature; who admits not the dictates of a *ſingle perſon* or *party* for *Catholick reaſon*; who conſiders, that there are *revolutions* of *philoſophy* and *opinions*, as well as of *ſtates* and *kingdoms*; and *judges* well of *times* and *men*, ere he pay much deference to *authority*. But, *thirdly*, this is not all that is neceſſary to any *compleat* degree of *Illumination*. *Impartiality* is neceſſary to the firſt *dawnings* of it; but if we would have it increaſe, and diffuſe itſelf into a *perfect day* of ſpiritual *wiſdom* and *underſtanding*, we muſt *hunger and thirſt* after *truths*. An *unprejudiced* mind is neceſſary to qualify us for the firſt *rudiments* of *truth*; but we muſt be inflamed with *deſire* and *love* of it, ere we ſhall enter into the *ſanctuary* or *receſſes* of it: therefore our *Saviour* invites

to

to him *every one that thirfts,* John vii. 27.
And St. *Peter* exhorts us, *as new born babes,*
to defire the fincere milk of the word, that we
may grow thereby, 1 Epift. ii 2.   And St.
Paul imputes the damnation of *thofe that*
perifh, to *want of love of the truth,* 2 Theff.
ii. 10.   'Tis too *trifling* to *object* here, how
come we to *thirft* after what we do not
know? for it concerns *every* man to *enquire*
what will *become* of him *for ever* ; and if he
be already *affured* that there is *another world,*
and a glorious *falvation* to be attained, it
is *natural* to *thirft* after the *refolution* of
fuch queftions as *thefe,* *what* fhall I *do* to be
faved? *what* fhall I *do* to inherit an *eternal*
life? and fuch is the *beauty* of *illuminating*
truth, that every *glance* of it kindles in our
hearts the love of it ; and fuch its *boundlefs*
Perfection, that the more we *know,* the
more ftill fhall we *defire to know.* Having
thus confidered what *qualifies* man for *Illumi-*
nation, my *next* bufinefs is to enquire,

§. 2. *What* one thus qualified is to *do* for the actual *attainment* of it. All the advice that I can think fit here to be given, may be reduced to *four* heads:

1. That we do not suffer our minds to be *engaged* in queft of knowledge *foreign* to our purpofe.

2. That we apply our felves with a very tender and *fenfible concern* to the *ftudy* of *illuminating truths.*

3. That we act *conformable* to thofe *meafures* of *light* which we have *attained.*

4. That we frequently and conftantly addrefs our felves to *God* by *prayer,* for the *illumination* of his *grace.*

1. That we do not fuffer, *&c.* *This* is a natural and neceffary *confequence* of what has been already faid concerning *illumination.* For if *illumination* confift in the *knowledge,* not of *all* forts of *truths,* but the moft *neceffary* and *important,* fuch as *purify* and *perfect* our nature ; fuch as procure us *facred* and *ftable pleafure,* and all the *rewards* that flow from our *adoption* to *God;* it is then plain, he, who would be *perfect,* ought not to amufe and diftract his mind in purfuit of *trifling* or *divertive knowledge:* that he ought to fhun, and not to admit, whatever is apt to *entangle, perplex,* or *defile* him ; and to *fix* his thoughts, and *confine* his me-

O   ditations

ditations to the *great truths* of the *gospel.*
He, that *knows the only true God, and Jesus
Christ, whom he hath sent,* knows *enough* to
oblige him to *virtue,* and to open the way
to *glory* and *everlasting life.* He, that *knows
nothing but Jesus Christ, and him crucified,*
knows *enough* in order to *peace, grace,* and
joy; enough to promote *holiness* and *hope:
hope* that abounds in *joy unspeakable and full
of glory.*

    2. We muſt apply our ſelves with a very
tender and ſenſible *concern* to the ſtudy of *illuminating truths.* This *rule* muſt be underſtood to enjoin *three* things. 1. Great
care and *caution* in examining doctrines pro-
poſed ; and in *diſtinguiſhing* between *truth*
and *falſhood.* 2. Great *diligence* and *induſtry* to increaſe and enlarge our *knowledge.*
3. Frequent and ſerious *reflections* upon the
truths we *know.*

    1. There is need of great *caution* in the
trial and *examination* of *doctrines.* This
the *ſcripture* it ſelf frequently puts us in
mind of : and not without reaſon ; becauſe
the devil *ſows his tares amongſt the wheat* ;
errors, and theſe too fatal and deſtructive
ones, are frequently obtruded upon the
world for the *revelations* of *God* ; and every *party,* nay, every *ſingle author,* lays the
ſtreſs of *ſalvation* on their *peculiar* and *diſtinguiſhing* opinions. *Beloved, believe not
every*

*every spirit, but try the spirits whether they
are of God : because many false prophets are
gone out into the world,* 1 John iv. 1. 'Tis
needless to multiply *texts* or *words* on this
occasion. When the peace and purity of
our mind, the rectitude and happiness of
our lives, and the blessedness of eternity
has so close and necessary a dependance upon the *doctrines* we imbibe, that we hereby either *secure* or *forfeit* them; who sees
not, unless he be stupid and infatuated, that
greater *care* and *solicitude* is necessary *here,*
than in *any* matter whatever, because there
is *no* other of *equal* moment? Bad *money,*
or bad *wares,* instead of good; an ill *title,*
or *conveyance,* instead of a firm and clear
one, may *impoverish* us : bad *drugs,* instead
of good, may *infect* the *body,* and *destroy*
the *health:* but what is all *this* to the dismal consequences of *error* and *heresy,* which
impoverishes and *infects* the *mind, perverts*
the *life,* and *damns* the *man* to all *eternity?* The example of the *Bereans* is never *forgot* ; and indeed never *ought* to be
on *this* occasion. We must admit nothing *hastily* ; assent to nothing without
examining the *grounds* on which it stands.
Credulity, precipitation and *confidence* are
irreconcilable enemies to *knowledge* and
wisdom.

2. We

2. We are to use great *diligence* and *industry* to enlarge and increase our *knowledge.* The treasures of *divine wisdom* are almost infinite; and it fares with *those* that *study* them, as with a *traveller* when he ascends a *rising* ground : every *new* step almost *enlarges* his *horizon,* and presents *new* countries, *new* pleasures to his eye. 'Tis our own negligence, if we do not daily extend the *compass* of our *knowledge :* if our *view* of things grow not more distinct and clear, and our *belief* of them more firm and steddy. This is, to *grow in grace and in the knowledge of Christ Jesus our Lord,* 2 Pet. iii. 18. This is, to *have the eye of our understanding opened,* Eph. i. 17. This is, to *be filled with the knowledge of God, in all wisdom and understanding,* Col. i. 9. This is, finally, *for the word of God to dwell in us richly,* Col. iii. 16. And of what *importance* this is, is manifest from what I have before proved; namely, that *illumination* consists not in a credulous and ill-grounded, in a slight and superficial, or a confused and obscure, or imperfect sort of *knowledge ;* but in a clear, distinct, firm, and well established one. And the acquiring such a one demands a very *diligent* and an *indefatigable study* of the *word of life.* To fill the mind with numerous, great, and beautiful *ideas,* and *these* clear and distinct ; to have them engraven in the me-

mory in deep and lafting *characters*; to have them lodged and difpofed in that *order*, as to be able in an inftant to have refcourfe to them, to difcern and demonftrate plainly the *connexion* and *dependance* of one upon another, and the unqueftionable *evidence* of each; this is a work of *time* and *labour*; the fruit of a regular and affiduous *fearch* after *truth*; and, if the capacities and fortunes of all men will not fuffer them to come up to *this*, they muft come as near as they can. But if fuch a *fearch* as this be *not* neceffary to *penetrate* the depths, and to *difcover* the beauties of *divine truths*, or to *convince* the world and our felves of the certainty of them; yet certainly *without* it we fhall never be able to *extract* their *force* and *virtue*, and to *derive purity* and *nourifhment* from them; which is the *next* thing implied in the rule laid down.

3. We muft make frequent and ferious *reflections* on the *truths* we *do know*. This again naturally follows from the *notion* of *illumination* as it is before fettled. For if it is not *every knowledge* of the *beft* things that fuffices for *illumination*, but a *vital* and *operative* one, that is, a well-grounded, clear, diftinct, and well-digefted one; it is plain, that conftant, daily, and devout meditation is neceffary to *illumination*; becaufe 'tis not a tranfient and perfuncto-

ry

ry reflection upon the moſt *important* truths; 'tis not a fleeting, rambling, irregular, and defultory meditation of them that will poſſeſs us with *ſuch* a kind of *knowledge.* To imprint a *truth* in *lively* notions upon our minds, to digeſt it into *nouriſhment* and *ſtrength,* and make it *mix* it ſelf with all our *affections* and all our *actions,* it is neceſſary that we *dwell* upon it with conſtancy and delight. And accordingly we find, that excellent and elevated ſouls, both under the *Old Teſtament* and the *New,* have been daily, nay, almoſt hourly converſant in the *Book of God:* they have been paſſionately *devoted* to the *ſtudy* of it, and *delighted* more in *it,* than in *treaſures* or *honours,* than in the moſt profitable *employments* or engaging *diverſions* of life. 'Tis *this* kind of *meditation* on *God,* on *Jeſus,* the *world,* and our *ſelves,* that can alone acquaint us thoroughly with *each;* 'tis *this* kind of *meditation* on *death* and *judgment, heaven* and *hell,* that can *make us wiſe unto ſalvation.*

The *ſum* of all that I have ſaid on this rule amounts to *this:* that *illumination* is not to be attained without *labour* and *travel.* It is indeed the *gift of God:* but ſuch a one as he will *never* beſtow, but upon thoſe who *ask,* and *ſeek,* and *knock.* *Divine bounty* and *human induſtry* do here very well *accord:* the *Spirit of God* ge-

nerally *joins* them together ; and 'tis *boldness* and *impiety* in *man* to go about to *divide them,* Prov. ii. 4, 5, 6. *If thou seekest
her as silver, and searchest for her as hid
treasures*; *then shalt thou understand the fear
of the Lord, and find the knowledge of God.
For the Lord giveth wisdom*; *out of his mouth
cometh knowledge and understanding.* Nor
will any one surely think it much to devote
his *time* and *labour* to the *attainment* of *illumination.* For what is there that can more
justly *challenge,* or better *deserve both?* Can
pleasure? There is none but what flows
from *wisdom,* that is either *pure, great,* or
lasting. Can *business?* What business can
be of *greater* importance, than what secures
our *salvation,* our *eternity? Wisdom then is
the principal thing, therefore get wisdom : and
with all thy getting, get understanding,* Prov.
iv. 7. for without *this,* the most desirable
possessions and *pleasures* of life are but *cheats*
and *illusions, mischiefs* and *snares. For the
turning away of the simple shall slay them,
and the prosperity of fools shall destroy them,*
Prov. i. 32.

3. That we act *conformable* to those *measures* of *light* which we have *attained.* The
more *spiritual* we grow, the *fitter* we are
for the residence of *God's Spirit,* and the
more *capable* of his *influences.* The more
we subdue all *inordinate affections,* the *clearer* does the *understanding* grow, and the

O 4 more

more *absolute* its *authority.* The *grace* of *God,* if it be complied with and obeyed, while it renders us more *like* God, renders us more *dear* to him too: and *one favour,* if it be not our own fault, qualifies us for *another.* Whoever shall observe the *scriptures,* will find that *holiness* and *illumination* advance with *equal* steps, and grow up by the *same* degrees of maturity: that as we pass on from the *infancy* to the *manhood* of *virtue,* so do we from the first *rudiments* of *wisdom* to the *heights* and *mysteries* of it. But on the other hand, *lust* obscures and eclipses the *light* within : *sin* depraves and corrupts our *principles :* and while we renounce our *virtue,* we *quench* or *chase away* the *Spirit: Into a malicious soul wisdom shall not enter ; nor dwell in the body that is subject unto sin : for the holy spirit of discipline will flee deceit, and remove from thoughts that are without understanding; and will not abide when unrighteousness cometh in,* Wisd. i. 4, 5.

4. We must frequently and constantly address our selves to God by *prayer,* for the *illumination* of his *grace.* There is *nothing* that we do not receive from *above :* and if the most *inconsiderable* things be the *gift* of *God,* from *what* fountain but from *him* can we expect *illumination ?* The raptures of *poets,* the wisdom of *law-givers,* the noblest pieces of *philosophy,* and indeed all

all *heroic* and *extraordinary* performances
were by the *Pagans* themselves generally
attributed to a *divine inspiration.* And
the *Old Testament* ascribes a transcendent
skill even in *arts* and *trades* to the *Spirit
of God.* It is not therefore to be wondered at, if *illumination* be attributed to *Him*
in the *New. Wisdom* and *understanding*
are essential *parts* of *sanctity* ; and therefore must proceed from the *sanctifying Spirit.* We must therefore constantly look up
to *God,* and depend upon *Him* for *illumination*; we must earnestly *pray* in the words
of St. *Paul, That the God of our Lord Jesus Christ, the Father of glory, would give
unto us the spirit of wisdom and revelation,* Eph. i. 17. This dependance upon
God, in expectation of his *blessing* on our
search after *knowledge,* puts the mind into
the best *disposition* and *frame* to attain it ;
because it naturally frees and disengages it
from those *passions, prejudices,* and *distrac-
tions,* which otherwise entangle and difturb it, and render it incapable of raised,
fedate, and coherent thoughts. But what
is *more* than this; there are repeated and
express *promises* made it ; so that it can never fail of success : *Ask, and it shall be
given you, seek, and ye shall find, knock, and it
shall be opened to you.* The reason of which
is added; *If ye then, being evil, know how to
give good gifts unto your children; how much*
more

more shall your Father which is in heaven give good things (or as it is *Luke* xi. *the Holy Spirit*) *to them that ask him?* Mat. vii. 7, 11. *If any of you lack wisdom, let him ask of God, that giveth to all men liberally, and upbraideth not; and it shall be given him,* Jam. i. 5. nor do I doubt but *every* good man has these *promises* verified to him. There are *sudden* suggestions, *unexpected* manifestations, *extraordinary* elevations of mind, which are never to be accounted for, but by a *divine principle.* Nor does this doctrine of *spiritual illumination* or *irradiation* in the least diminish the power and excellence of the *gospel of Christ*, no more than the *instruction* of the *gospel* does supersede that of the *Spirit.* For we must not think that the *Spirit* does now reveal any *new* truth of *general* use or importance; since the *canon* of *scripture* would on this supposal be but a defective *rule* of *faith* and *manners.* But, *first*, The *Spirit* may *assist* us in making a fuller *discovery* of the *sense* of *scripture. Secondly*, The *Spirit* may help us to form *clearer* and *distincter notions* of those things we have yet but an *imperfect* and *general* knowledge of; and to fix and imprint them in more *lasting*, as well as more *legible* characters in our minds: or it may recall to our *remembrance* such things as are obliterated and forgotten:

ten : or, finally, it may produce in us a more earneft and fteddy application to the truth of God, *Thirdly,* I fee no rea- fon why the *Spirit* may not vouchfafe us particular *impulfes, directions,* and *intima- tions* upon *extraordinary* occafions and *fud- den* emergencies ; where *holy writ* affords us no *light,* and *human prudence* is at a lofs. Nor does any thing, that I attribute to the *Spirit* in all this, detract or dero- gate from the dignity or the efficacy of the *fcripture.* This then, I conceive, is *what* the *Spirit* does in the work of *Illumination.* But *how* it does it, is not *neceffary,* nor, I doubt, *poffible* to be determined. Nor ought our *ignorance* of this to be objected againft the *truth* of *divine Illumination.* We are fure we *underftand* and *remember,* and exer- cife a *freedom* or *liberty* of will, in our choices, refolutions and actions : but the *manner* how we do this, is an enquiry that does hitherto, for ought I can fee, wholly furpafs and tranfcend our *philo- fophy.*

I will here clofe this *chapter* with a *prayer* of *Fulgentius, lib.* 1. *cap.* 4. After he has in the beginning of the *chapter* dif- claimed all *pretences* to the fetting up him- felf a *mafter, doctor,* or *dictator* to his *brethren,* he breaks out into thefe devout and pious words —— ' I will not ceafe ' to pray, that our true *Mafter* and *Doctor* ' *Chrift*

' *Chrift Jefus,* either by the *oracles* of his
' *gofpel,* or by the *converfation* of my *bre-*
' *thren* or *joint-difciples*; or elfe by the fe-
' cret and delightful inftruction of *divine*
' *infpiration,* in which, without the ele-
' ments of letters, or the found of fpeech,
' *truth* fpeaks with fo much the *fweeter,* as
' the *ftiller* and *fofter* voice ; would vouch-
' fafe to *teach* me thofe things, which I may
' *fo* propofe, and *fo* affert, that in all my ex-
' pofitions and affertions, I may be ever
' found conformable, and obedient, and
' firm to *that truth,* which can neither
' *deceive,* nor be *deceived.* For it is *truth*
' itfelf that enlightens, confirms, and aids
' me, that I may always obey and affent
' to the *truth.* By *truth* I defire to be
' informed of thofe many *more* things
' which I am *ignorant* of, from *whom* I
' have received the *few* I know. Of *truth*
' I beg, through preventing and affifting
' grace, to be inftructed in whatever I
' *yet* know not, which conduces to the
' intereft of my virtue and happinefs ;
' to be preferved and kept ftedfaft in *thofe*
' truths which I *know* ; to be reformed
' and rectified in thofe points, in which,
' as is common to man, I am *miftaken* ;
' to be confirmed and eftablifhed in thofe
' truths wherein I *waver* ; and to be de-
' livered from thofe opinions that are *er-*
' *roneous* or *hurtful.* I beg, laftly, that
                                        ' *truth*

' *truth* may ever find, both in my thoughts
' and ſpeeches, all that ſound and whole-
' ſome doctrine I have received from *its*
' gift ; and that *it* would always cauſe me to
' utter thoſe things which are agreeable to
' *itſelf* in the *firſt* place; and conſequently
' acceptable to *all* faithful *Chriſtians* in the
' *next.*'

CHAP. III.

*Of liberty in general. The notion of it tru-
ly ſtated, and guarded. The fruits of this
liberty. 1. Sin being a great evil, deliverance from it is great happineſs. 2. A
freedom and pleaſure in the acts of righteouſneſs and good works. 3. The near relation it creates between God and us.. 4. The
great fruit of all, eternal life ; with a brief
exhortation to endeavour after deliverance
from ſin.*

AFTER *Illumination,* which is the
Perfection of the *underſtanding,* follows *liberty,* which is the *Perfection* of the
will. In treating of which, I ſhall, *firſt,*
give an account of *liberty* in *general* : and
then diſcourſe of the ſeveral *parts* of it ; as it
regards *wickedneſs, unfruitfulneſs, human
infirmities,* and *original corruption.*

§. 1. What

§. 1. What *liberty* is. There have been several *mistakes* about this matter : but these have been so absurd or extravagant, so designing or sensual, that they *need* not, I think, a serious *refutation.* However, 'tis necessary in a word or two to remove this *rubbish* and *lumber* out of my way, that I may build up and establish the *truth* more easily and regularly. *Some* then have placed Christian *liberty* in deliverance from the *Mosaic yoke.* But this is to make our *liberty* consist in freedom from a *yoke* to which we were *never* subject; and to make our glorious Redemption, from the tyranny of *sin* and the *misery* that attends it, dwindle into an immunity from *external* rites and observances. 'Tis true, the *Mosaic* institution, as far as it consisted in *outward* observances and *typical* rites, is now dissolved ; the *Messias* being come, who was the *substance* of those *shadows* ; and the *beauty of holiness* being unfolded and displayed, without any *veil* upon her face. But what is this to *ecclesiastical authority* ? or to those *ecclesiastical institutions,* which are no part of the *Mosaic* yoke ? from the abrogation indeed, or abolition of *ritual* and *typical* religion, one may infer, *first,* That *Christianity* must be a *rational* worship, a *moral spiritual* service. And therefore, *secondly,* That *human* institutions, when they enjoyn

joyn any thing as a *neceſſary* and *eſſential*
part of religion, which *God* has not made
ſo, or when they impoſe ſuch *rites*, as, thro'
the number or nature of them, cheriſh
ſuperſtition, *obſcure* the *goſpel*, weaken its
force, or prove *burthenſome* to us, are to be
rejeſted and not complied with. Thus
much is plain, and nothing farther. There
have been *others*, who have run into more
intolerable *errors*. For ſome have placed
Chriſtian liberty in exemption from the
laws of *man* : and *others*, advancing
higher, in exemption even from the *moral* and *immutable* laws of *God*. But the
folly and *wickedneſs* of theſe opinions ſufficiently *confute* them : ſince 'tis notorious to
every one, that *diſobedience* and *anarchy* is
as flat a contradiction to the *peaceableneſs*,
as *voluptuouſneſs* and *luxury* is to the *purity* of that *wiſdom which is from above*.
But how abſurd and wicked ſoever theſe
notions are, yet do we find them greedily
embraced and induſtriouſly propagated at
this day ; and behold, with amazement,
the baffled and deſpicable *Gnoſticks*, *Priſ-
cilianiſts*, *Libertines*, and I know not what
other ſpawn of *hell*, reviving in *deiſts* and
atheiſts. *Theſe* indeed do not advance
their errors under a pretence of *Chriſtian
liberty* ; but, which is more ingenuous, and
leſs ſcandalous of the two, in open *defiance*
and confeſſed *oppoſition* to *Chriſtianity*. They
tell

tell us, that we impoſe upon the world *falſe* and *fantaſticks* notions of *virtue* and *liberty:* that *religion* does *enſlave* man, not ſet him *free*; awing the mind by groundleſs and ſuperſtitious principles, and reſtraining and infringing our true and natural *liberty:* which, if we will believe *them,* conſiſts in giving *nature* its full ſwing; letting looſe the reins to the moſt headſtrong *luſts,* and the wildeſt and the moſt corrupt *imaginations.* But to this 'tis eaſy to anſwer, that while theſe men attempt to eſtabliſh their errors, and fortify their minds in them, by *arguments* of ſome ſort or other, as they do; 'tis plain, that *they* ſuppoſe and acknowledge with *us,* that they ought to be ruled and governed by *reaſon:* and if *this* be true, then, by undeniable conſequence, true *liberty* muſt conſiſt, not in doing what we *liſt,* but what we *ought*; not in following our *luſt* or *fancy,* but our *reaſon*; not in being *exempt* from *law,* but in *being a law to our ſelves.* And then I appeal to all the world, whether the diſcipline of *virtue,* or *libertiniſm*; whether the ſchools of *Epicurus,* or *Chriſt,* be the way to true *liberty.* I appeal to the *experience* of mankind, whether *ſpiritual* or *ſenſual* pleaſure; whether the *love* of God and *virtue,* or the *love* of the *world* and *body,* be the more like to qualify and diſpoſe us to obey
the

the dictates of ſober and ſolid *reaſon.* But the truth is, here is no need of *arguments*; the *lives* and *fortunes* of *atheiſts* and *deiſts* proclaim aloud what a glorious kind of *liberty* they are like to bleſs the world with, 2 *Pet.* ii. 19. *Whilſt they promiſe liberty, they themſelves are the ſervants of corruption.* And this *corruption* draws on their *ruin.* The diſhonourable and miſerable *courſes,* in which theſe poor wretches are plunged, and in which, generally, they periſh before their time, are ſuch an open *contradiction* to *reaſon,* that no man doubts but that they have abandoned *its* conduct, that they have given themſelves up to that of *luſt* and *humour* ; and that they earneſtly endeavour to force or betray their *reaſon* into a *compliance* to *ſcreen* themſelves from the reproach and diſturbance of their own *minds,* and from the ſhame and contempt of the *world.* I have dwelt long enough on *this* argument. 'Tis now time to paſs *on,* and reſolve what *Chriſtian liberty* really *is.*

This is in a manner evident from what has been ſuggeſted already. For if *reaſon* be the governing faculty in *man,* then the *liberty of man* muſt conſiſt in his *ſubjection* to *reaſon* : and ſo *Chriſtian liberty* will be nothing elſe but *ſubjection* to *reaſon* enlightened by *revelation.* *Two* things therefore are *eſſential* to true *liberty:* A

P

clear

clear and unbyassed *judgment* ; and a power
and capacity of acting *conformable* to it.
This is a very *short*, but *full* account of
liberty. *Darkness* and *impotence* constitute
our *slavery*: light and *strength* our *freedom*. Man is then *free*, when his *reason*
is not awed by vile *fears*, or bribed by
viler *hopes*: when it is not tumultuously
transported and hurried away by *lusts* and
passions; nor cheated and deluded by the
gilded appearances of *sophisticated* good ;
but it deliberates *impartially*, and commands
effectually. And because the great *obstacle*
of this *liberty* is *sin* ; because natural and
contracted *corruption* are the *fetters* in
which we are bound; because the *law in
the body wars against the law in the mind*, ob-
scuring the *light*, and enfeebling the *authority* of *reason*; hence it is, that *Christian
liberty* is as truly as commonly described
by a *dominion* over the *body*, by the subduing our corrupt *affections*, and by *deliverance* from *sin*. This notion of *liberty* may be sufficiently established upon
that account of *servitude* or *bondage* which
the *apostle* gives us, *Rom.* vii. where he represents it as consisting in *impotence* or *in-
ability* to do those things, which *God* commands, and *reason* approves : *For to will is
present with me; but how to perform that which
is good, I find not*, ver. 18. *Liberty* therefore must on the *contrary* consist in being
able,

able not only to *will,* but to *do* good ; in *obeying* thoſe *commandments,* which we cannot but acknowledge to be *holy,* and *juſt,* and *good.* And this is the very notion which our *Lord* and *Maſter* gives us of it, *Joh.* viii. For, when the *Jews* bragged of their *freedom,* he lets them·know, that *freedom* could not conſiſt with *ſubjection* to *ſin : He that committeth ſin is the ſervant of ſin,* ver. 34. That honourable *parentage,* and the *freedom* of the *body,* was but a falſe and ludicrous *appearance* of *liberty :* that if they would be *free indeed, the Son muſt make them ſo,* ver. 36. *i. e.* they muſt, by his *ſpirit* and *doctrine* be reſcued from the *ſervitude* of *luſt* and *error,* and be ſet at *liberty* to work *righteouſneſs. If ye continue in my word, then are ye my diſciples indeed ; and ye ſhall know the truth, and the truth ſhall make you free,* ver. 31, 32. Finally, not to multiply *proofs* of a truth that is ſcarce liable to be *controverted,* as the *apoſtle* deſcribes the *bondage* of a *ſinner* in *Rom.* vii; ſo does he the *liberty* of a *ſaint* in *Rom.* viii. For there, *ver.* 2. he tells us, that the *law of the ſpirit of life* has ſet the true Chriſtian *free from the law of ſin* and *death.* And then he lets us know *wherein* this *liberty* conſiſts ; *in walking, not after the fleſh, but after the ſpirit ;* in the *mortification* of the *body of ſin,* and *reſtitution* of the *mind* to its juſt *empire*

and

and *authority.* *If Chriſt be in you, the body is dead becauſe of ſin; but the ſpirit is life becauſe of righteouſneſs,* ver. 10. And all this is the ſame thing with his *deſcription* of *liberty,* chap. vi. where, 'tis nothing elſe, but for a man to be made *free from ſin, and become the ſervant of God.* Thus then we have a plain account of *bondage* and *liberty.* Yet for the clearer underſtanding of *both,* it will not be amiſs to obſerve, that they are *each* capable of different *degrees*; and both the *one* and the *other* may be *more* or *leſs* entire, compleat, and abſolute, according to the different *progreſs* of men in *vice* and *virtue.* Thus, in *ſome* men, not their *will* only, but their very *reaſon* is enſlaved. Their *underſtanding* is ſo far infatuated, their affections ſo *intirely* captivated, that there is no *conflict* at all between the *mind* and the *body:* they commit *ſin* without any *reluctancy* beforehand, or any *remorſe* afterwards: their *ſeared conſcience* making no *remonſtrance,* inflicting no *wounds,* nor denouncing any *threats.* This is the *laſt* degree of *vaſſalage.* Such are ſaid in *ſcripture* to be *dead in treſpaſſes and ſins. Others* there are, in whom their luſt and appetite *prevails* indeed, but not without *oppoſition.* They *reaſon* rightly; and, which is the natural reſult of this, have ſome *deſires* and *wiſhes* of *righteouſneſs.:* but through
the

the prevalency of the *body*, they are unable to act and live *conformable* to their
reason. Their *understanding* has indeed
light, but not *authority :* it *consents* to the
law of *God*, but it has no power, no force
to make it be *obeyed :* it produces indeed
some good *inclinations, purposes,* and *efforts ;*
but they prove *weak* and *ineffectual* ones,
and *unable* to grapple with the stronger
passion raised by the *body.* And as *bondage,* so *liberty* is of different *degrees,* and
different *strength.* For though *liberty* may
be able to *subsist,* where there is much *opposition* from the *body ;* yet 'tis plain *that
liberty* is most *absolute* and *compleat,* where
the *opposition* is *least,* where the *body* is reduced to an entire *submission* and *obsequi-
ousness,* and the *spirit* reigns with an un-
controuled and unlimited *authority.* And
this *latter* is *that liberty* which I would
have my *perfect* man possessed of. I know
very well 'tis *commonly* taught by *some,* that
there is *no* such state: But, I think, this
doctrine, if it be throughly considered, has
neither *scripture, reason,* nor *experience* to
support it. For as to those places, *Rom.* vii.
and *Gal.* v. urged in favour of an almost
incessant, strong, and too frequently prevalent *lusting of the flesh against the spirit ;*
it has been often answered, and proved
too, that they are so far from belonging
to the *perfect,* that they belong not to

the

the *regenerate*. But, on the contrary, thoſe *texts* that repreſent the *yoke of Chriſt eaſy, and his burthen light*; which affirm the *commandments of Chriſt not to be grievous to ſuch as are made perfect in love*; do all bear witneſs to *that liberty* which I contend for. *Nor* does *reaſon* favour my opinion leſs than *ſcripture*. For if the *perfect* man be a *new creature*; if he be *tranſformed* into a *new nature*; if his *body* be *dead to ſin, and his ſpirit live to righteouſneſs*; in one word, if the *world be as much crucified to him, as he to it*; I cannot ſee why it ſhould not be *eaſy* for him to act *conſonant* to his *nature*; why he ſhould not with pleaſure and readineſs *follow* that *ſpirit*, and *obey* thoſe *affections*, which *reign* and *rule* in him. Nor can I ſee why a *habit of righteouſneſs* ſhould not have the ſame *properties* with *other habits*; that is, be attended with *eaſe* and *pleaſure* in its operations and actions. 'Tis true, I can eaſily ſee why the *habits of righteouſneſs* are *acquired* with more *difficulty* than thoſe of any *other* kind : but, I ſay, I cannot ſee, when they *are* acquired, why they ſhould not be as *natural* and *delightful* to us as any *other*. *Laſtly*, How *degenerate* ſoever ages *paſt* have been, or the *preſent* is, I dare not ſo far diſtruſt the goodneſs of my cauſe, or the virtue of *mankind*, as not to refer myſelf willingly, in this point,

to

to the decifion of *experience.* I am very well affured, that truth and juftice, de-.votion and charity, honour and integrity, are to a great many fo dear and delightful, fo natural, fo eafy, that it is hard to determine, whether they are more ftrongly moved by a fenfe of *duty,* or the inftigations of *love* and *inclination ;* and that they cannot do a *bafe* thing without the utmoft *mortification* and *violence* to their *nature.* Nor is all this to be wondered at, if we again reflect on what I juft now intimated, that the *perfect* man is a *new creature, transformed daily from glory to. glory :* that he is moved by *new affections,* raifed and fortified by *new principles :* that he is animated by a *divine energy,* and *fees .* all things by a *truer* and *brighter light ;* through *which* the *things of God* appear *lovely* and *beautiful,* the things of the *world deformed* and *worthlefs ;* juft as to him who views them through a *microfcope,* the *works of God* appear *exact* and *elegant ;* but *thofe of man, coarfe,* and *bungling,* and *ugly.* My *opinion* then, which afferts the *abfolute liberty* of the *perfect* man, is fufficiently *proved here,* and in *chapter the firft.* And *if* I thought it were *not,* I could eafily *reinforce* it with frefh *recruits.* For the glorious *characters* that are given us in *fcripture,* of the *liberty* of the *children of God,* and the bleffed *fruit* of it, *peace*

and

and *joy in the Holy Ghost*, would easily furnish me with invincible *arguments* : nor
would the *contrary* opinion ever have been
able to have kept the *field* so *long* as it has
done, had it not been favoured by a
weak and *decayed piety* ; by the *fondnesses*
of men for *themselves*, in spight of their
sins and *frailties* ; and by many *mistaken*
texts.

But that this matter may, if possible,
be freed from *all objections*. 1. I here *di-*
stinguish between *inordinate* and *natural*
affections. By *inordinate affections*, I mean
the tendencies of the soul towards that
which is *unlawful:* by *natural*, its propension to the *body* with which it is invest-
ted ; the desire of its *health* and *ease*, and
the *conveniencies* and *necessaries of life* for
this end. Now when *religion* enjoyns
repugnances to the *former* appetites, the
obedience of the *perfect* man has *no reluc-*
tancy in it : but when it enjoyns things,
as sometimes occasionally it does, which
thwart and cross the *latter* ; here the
obedience even of *Christ* himself could not
be exempt from *conflict* ; for our *natural*
appetites, in *this* sense of them, will *never*
be put off till our *bodies* be. I think this
is so *clear*, it needs not be illustrated by
instances: or else 'twere easy to shew,
that tho' good men have practised *tem-*
perance, chastity, charity, and other virtues

tues of this kind with *eaſe* and *pleaſure* too; yet has nature *ſhrunk* and *ſtartled* at *perſecution* and *martyrdom:* tho' even *here* too the courage and reſolution of *ſome* hath appeared to be much *above* what *human nature* ever ſeemed *capable* of. 2. I do not in the leaſt ſuppoſe that *nature* is ſo *changed,* but that the *inclinations* to ſinful pleaſure, or profit, or any other forbidden objeƈt, will ſoon *revive* again, even in the *perfeƈt* man, unleſs he keep a *watch* and *guard* upon himſelf, and *paſs the time of his ſojourning here in fear.* Not to be ſubjeƈt to *diſorderly deſires,* not to be liable to *irregular motions,* is the privilege of *ſouls* when ſtripped of a *mortal* body, or cloathed with an *immortal* one. Till *then,* the conjunƈtion of *fleſh* and *blood* will ever render the poor *ſoul* obnoxious to *carnal* and *worldly* appetites: and the *natural* appetites of the body do ſo eaſily paſs thoſe bounds that divide them from *ſinful* ones, that the *beſt* of men can never be *ſecure,* but when the mind is taken up in *contemplation, devotion, good works,* or engaged in the *proſecution* of ſome juſt and honeſt *deſign,* or amuſed by ſome innocent *recreation:* for in *theſe* caſes the *body* is either made the *inſtrument of righteouſneſs;* or at leaſtwiſe, 'tis innocently *buſied* and *diverted* from thoſe *objeƈts,* to which it has too impetuous a *tendency.* I have now,

now, I think, sufficiently *stated* the *notion*
of *true liberty* ; and, I hope, sufficiently
guarded it: and have nothing to do but to
proceed to the *fruits* of it; which will serve
for so many *motives* or *inducements* to its
attainment.

§. 2. Of the *fruits* of *liberty.*

These may · be reduced under four
beads.

1. *Sin* being a great *evil, deliverance*
from it is great *happiness.*
2. A second fruit of this *liberty* is *good
works.*
3. It gives us a near *relation* to God.
4. The great and last *fruit* of it is *eternal life.*

These are *all* comprised by the *apostle* in
Rom. vi. 21, 22, 23. *What fruit had ye then
in those things, whereof ye are now ashamed?
For the end of those things is death. But
now being made free from sin, and become servants to God, ye have your fruit unto holiness, and the end everlasting life. For the
wages of sin is death ; but the gift of God is
eternal life, through Jesus Christ our Lord.*
And these are the great *ends* which the
gospel, that *perfect law of liberty,* aims at,
and for which it was *preached* to the
world ;

world; as appears from those *words* of our *Lord* to St. *Paul*, Acts xxvi. 17, 18. *Unto whom now I send thee; to open their eyes, and to turn them from darkness to light, and from the power of Satan unto God; that they may receive forgiveness of sins, and inheritance among them which are sanctified by faith that is in me.* I will *here* insist on these blessed *effects* of *Christian liberty*; not only because the *design* of the *chapter* demands it, but also to prevent the being obliged to any tedious *repetition* of them hereafter, under every distinct *branch* of *Christian liberty*.

§. 1. *Sin* is a great *evil*; and therefore *deliverance* from the *dominion* of it is a great *good*. To make this evident, we need but reflect a little on the *nature* and *effects* of *sin*. If we inquire into the *nature* of *sin*, we shall find that it is *founded* in the *subversion* of the dignity, and *defacing* the beauty of *human nature:* and that it *consists* in the *darkness* of our understanding, the *depravity* of our affections, and the *feebleness* and *impotence* of the will. The *understanding* of a *sinner* is incapable of *discerning* the certainty and force of divine truths, the loveliness of virtue, the unspeakable pleasure which now flows from the great and precious *promises* of the gospel, and the incomparably
bly

bly greater which will one day flow from the accompliſhment and fruition of them. His *affections*, which is fixed and bent on *virtue*, had been *incentives*, as they were deſigned by God, to *noble* and *worthy* actions, being *byaſſed* and *perverted*, do now hurry him on to *lewd* and *wicked* ones. And by *theſe* the *mind*, if at any time it chance to be awakened and rendered ſenſible of its happineſs and duty, is *overpowered* and *oppreſſed*. If *this* were not the true *ſtate* of a *ſinner* ; if the *ſtrength* of *ſin* did not thus conſiſt in the *diſorder* and *impotence* of all the *faculties* of the *ſoul*, whence is it that the *ſinner* acts as he *does?* Is it not evident that his *underſtanding* is *infatuated*, when he lives as if he were merely, wholly, *body?* As if he had *no ſoul*, or none but one *reſulting from*, and *diſſolved with*, its *temperament* and *contexture?* One deſigned to no higher purpoſe, than to contrive, miniſter to, and partake in its *ſenſualities?* Is it not evident that *he* has little expectation of *another world*, who *lays up his treaſures* only in *this* ; and lives as if he were born only *to make proviſion for the fleſh to fulfil the luſts thereof?* 'Tis true, *all ſinners* are not *equally* ſtupid or obdurate : but even in thoſe in whom ſome *ſparks of underſtanding* and *conſcience* remain *unextinguiſhed*, how are the *weak* deſires of *virtue* baffled and

over-

over-powered by the much *stronger* paffions which they have for the *body* and
the *world?* Do they not find themfelves
reduced to that wretched *state of bondage*,
wherein the *good* that *they would do, that
they do not*; *but the evil that they would not
do, that is prefent with them?* 'Tis plain
then that *fin* is a *difeafe* in our nature:
that it not only *extinguifhes* the *grace* of
the *Spirit*, and *obliterates* the *image of
God* ftamped on the foul in its creation;
but alfo fcatters and diffufes I know not
what *venom* and *infection* thorough it, that
makes it eagerly *purfue* its *own mifery*.
'Tis a *difeafe* that produces more *intolerable* effects in the *foul*, than *any* whatever
can in the *body*. The predominancy of
any noxious *humour* can breed no *pain*,
no *difturbance*, equal to that of a predominant *paffion:* no *fcars* or *ruins* which
the worft *difeafe* leaves behind it, are half
fo *deformed* and *loathfome* as thofe of *vice:*
nay, that laft *change*, which *death* it felf
produces, when it converts a *beautiful*
body into *duft* and *rottennefs*, is not half
fo *contemptible* or *hateful* as that of *fin*;
when it transforms *man* into a *beaft* or
devil. If we do not yet fufficiently comprehend the *nature* of *fin*, by viewing
it as it exifts in our *minds* and *hearts*, we
may contemplate it in our *actions*. And
here, 'tis blindnefs and folly, rafhnefs and
madnefs,

madness, incogitance, levity, falshood, and cowardise; 'tis *every thing* that is *mean* and *base*: and all this *aggravated* by the most accursed *ingratitude* that human nature is capable of. These and the like *reflections* on the *nature* of *sin*, cannot chuse but render it *hateful*. And if,

Secondly, We make any serious ones on the *effects* of it, they cannot fail of rendering it *frightful* and *dreadful* to *us*. These *effects* may be especially reduced to *three*: 1. The ill influence *sin* has upon our *temporal* concerns. 2. *Guilt*. And, 3. *Fear*. As to the *first* of these, I shall only say, that we suffer very few *evils* but what are owing to our own *sins*: that it is very rarely any *calamity* befals us, but we may put our finger on the *fountain*, the *sin*, I mean, from whence the mischief flows. *Whence comes wars and fightings amongst you,* faith St. *James, come they not from your lusts, which war in your members?* This is every jot as applicable to *private* as *publick* contentions: and *where envy, strife, and contention is,* no *evil work,* no *disaster* will be long *absent*. I might run through all the different *kinds* of *evils* that infest the *body*, or embroil the *fortune*; that blast our *hopes*, or stain our *desires*: and easily shew, that they all generally spring from our

our *vices.* Nay, what is worfe yet, I could
fhew that *fin* converts our *good things* into
evil, and our *enjoyments* into *punifhments:*
that it renders the *flighteft* evils *intolerable;*
turns *fcratches* into *wounds,* and *wounds* into *gangrenes.* But this is too *copious* a
fubjeƈt ; and would infenfibly render me
voluminous, when I would be as *fhort* as
poffibly I can. A *fecond effeƈt* of *fin* is
guilt; which is nothing elfe, but a *confcioufnefs* of having *done ill,* and an *obligation* to *punifhment* refulting from it. And
tho' men often *fin* with *hopes* of *impunity;*
yet it is hard to imagine, even on *this*
fuppofal, that they fhould *fin* without fuffering the *reproaches* of their *own minds;*
which furely muft be very *uneafy* to them :
to be perpetually *vexed* at one's *own folly;*
to *commit* thofe things which we inwardly
condemn, and be in continual *pain* left they
fhould *come to light;* to be always *difpleafed*
at *one's felf,* and *afraid,* not only of the
refleƈtions of *others,* but our *own :* this is,
methinks, a *great* evil, did no *other* attend
our *fin.* But, *thirdly, fear* is almoft infe-
parably joined with *guilt:* for *guilt* does
not only damp the *chearfulnefs,* and en-
feeble the *vigour* of the *mind;* it does not
only deftroy that *confidence* man would
otherwife *naturally* have in *God,* and render him *cowardly* and *pufillanimous;* but it
terrifies his foul with *melancholy* apprehen-
fions,

fions, and makes him live continually in *fear* of *death* and *punishment*. And thus *scripture* represents the *state* of a *sinner :* *The wicked flee when none pursue* ; *but the righteous are as bold as a lion,* Prov. xxviii. 1. *If our heart condemn us, God is greater than our heart, and knoweth all things,* 1 John iii. 2. *There is no peace to the wicked, saith the Lord,* Isa. xlviii. 22. *To deliver them, who through fear of death, were all their life time. subject to bondage,* Heb. ii. 15. *The sinners in Zion are afraid, fearfulness has surprised the hypocrites* ; *who among us shall dwell with the devouring fire? who amongst us shall dwell with everlasting burnings?* Isa. xxxiii. 14. Nor let any one wonder, that notwithstanding the *outward gaiety* of the *sinner,* the *Spirit* thus *describes* the *inward condition* of his *soul.* As long as men retain the *belief* of a *God,* it is impossible they should wholly free themselves from the *fear* of him. They may indeed *forget* him in the *fits* of *lust* or *passion :* but in their *intermissions* his *terrors* will *return* upon them with *more violence. Again,* as long as men retain the common principles of *truth* and *justice* ; if they acknowledge but the obligation of that *universal law, Thou shalt do to others, as thou wouldest they should do unto thee,* 'tis impossible they should *reflect* on their *fins* without *regret* and *uneafiness* ; for there is no *fin* but has more or lefs,

Re-

repugnancy in it to *truth, juſtice,* and *good-neſs.* *Finally,* As long as men are per-ſuaded that there is ſuch a faculty as *con-ſcience,* that *God* has preſcribed them a *law,* and that they are *accountable* to *him*; the *natural conſcience* cannot chuſe, but by *fits,* and upon *occaſions,* ſcourge and torture, lance and gaſh them. And 'tis a hard matter to *wear* out *theſe notions:* they are ſo *natural* and *obvious*; the *proofs* of them are ſo *clear*; their *reputation* and *autho-rity* in the world is ſo well *eſtabliſhed*; and the *providence* of *God* ſo frequently *incul-cates* them. Men may eaſily wear out all ſenſe of the *beauty,* and of their *obliga-tions* to their *heights* and *perfections* of *vir-tue:* but they cannot ſo eaſily do this in reference to *virtue* in *general*; becauſe 'tis tempered and accommodated to *human na-ture* and *ſociety*; and neceſſary to the tole-rable *well-doing* of the *world.* Men may ſoon, I confeſs, extinguiſh their *Chriſtia-nity,* but not *humanity:* and while *this* re-mains, *ſin* will leave a *ſtain* and *guilt* be-hind it; and *guilt* will be attended by *un-eaſineſs* and *fear.* The very *pagans,* who had advanced *ſo far* in wickedneſs, as to be *given up* to all *diſhonourable* paſſions, and to *commit all uncleanneſs with greedineſs,* had not yet ſo *mortified* and *ſtupified* their *conſcience,* but that *it* gave much *diſtur-bance,* Rom. i. *ver.* 32. 'tis ſaid of them,

Q   that

that *they knew the judgment of God, that they which committed ſuch things, were worthy of death.* And Rom. ii. 15. *Their conſciences* are ſaid *to accuſe and condemn them.* And 'tis of *very wicked* men, that the *author* to the *Hebrews* affirms, that *through fear of death they were all their life-time ſubjeҍ to bondage.*

But are there not, will ſome ſay, many *ingenuous* and *brave* ſpirits, who have *diſperſed* thoſe vain *ſpeҍres,* and burſt thoſe ſuperſtitious *fetters,* by which you labour to *ſcare* and *enſlave* the world? I do not doubt, indeed, but that there are *too many* who have vigorouſly endeavoured to caſhier all *principles* of natural and revealed *religion,* and utterly to extinguiſh all *conſcience* of *good* and *evil.* But *this* is ſuch an *attempt,* in which, I confeſs, I could never have *believed,* that the moſt *daring ſinner* could have proved *ſucceſsful,* had not the *ſcriptures* told me, that there are ſome *who are paſt feeling,* Eph. iv. 19. *of a ſeared conſcience,* 2 Tim. iv. 2. *who are not aſhamed when they have committed iniquity neither can they bluſh,* Jer. vi. 15. *who call good evil, and evil good; that put darkneſs for light, and light for darkneſs; that put bitter for ſweet, and ſweet for bitter,* Iſai. v. 20. *Such ſinners* there *are* then: but *what* does this amount to? *what* can *their* ſenſe or example *weigh?* I am ſure theſe

poor

poor wretches are as far diftant from any *true happiness*, as from *fenfe*; and de- ferve our *pity*, not *imitation*. As will ea- fily appear from thefe following *confide- rations.*

1. 'Tis true, *confcience* depends upon *opinion :* but what if this *opinion* depend upon *fenfe* and *truth?* what if it be built upon the *demonftration of the fpirit and of power?* in what a deplorable *condition* are thefe *men of wit?* the *fear* of an *angry God, a judgment* to come, and *an hell,* is no *common* or *ordinary fear.* 'Tis not the *fear* of a *fcratch* or *wound* in the *body ;* of a *baffle* in the purfuit of *preferment,* or a *difappointment* in that of *pleafure* ; 'tis not the *lofs* or the *forfeiture* of *eftate,* in part, or whole : 'tis not a *blot* upon our *repu- tation* ; 'tis not the *death* of a *child,* a bro- ther, or, what is *more,* if *he* be fuch, a *friend :* 'tis not any thing of *this* kind that is the *objeĉt* of *this fear* ; but *mifery* pure and unallayed ; complicated, accumu- lated *mifery* ; *mifery* unalterable, incurable, and lafting as long as *eternity.* Methinks, before one fhould *venture* on a *fin,* which is *threatened* with fuch a *ftate* as this ; and much more, before one fhould refolve to *continue* in it, it were reafonable to be ve- ry *fure,* that the *notion* of a *hell* were *falfe,* and the doĉtrine of *eternal punifh- ment* a *mere bugbear.* Nay, I proteſt, in a

Q 2 mat-

matter of this *importance*, I think one should scarce trust to a *demonstration*, unless it had passed the *test* of the most *solid* and *impartial* part of mankind, and stood the *shock* and *tryal* of many *ages*. But, alas, after the utmost *efforts* of *wit* and *lust*, what has ever *yet* been produced, that has been able to undergo the *examination* even of an *honest man?* what *arguments* have yet been started against a *judgment to come*, that have been *able* to work upon *any* who were truly *serious* in the point? and if a *judgment to come*, why not an *hell?* *revelation* is plain; and *reason* can find no inconsistency in the doctrine. *Human laws* punish a *single* offence sometimes with *death* or *banishment*; with *loss* of *estate* : and by *this*, and divers *other* ways, extend the punishment of the criminal to his *posterity* : that is, make it as *eternal* as they *can*. And shall it be thought *unjust* in *God* to punish the *repeated* provocations of an *impenitent life*; the *neglect* of that *great salvation* wrought by the *blood*, and *published* by the *mouth* of *his dearly beloved son*; and all this *wilfully* in *defiance* of the *light* of the *gospel*, and *solicitations* of the *spirit*; in defiance of *mercies* and *chastisements*; shall it, I say, be thought *unjust* in *God* to punish *this* by a *miserable eternity?* when *infinite goodness* has in vain *tried* all imaginable *means* to

reclaim

reclaim a *sinner*, what has *he* to complain of, if *God* leave him to the *effects* of his own *choice*? *sin*, as it alienates our *affections* from *God here*, so must it certainly exclude *us* from *his presence* and his *favour hereafter*. And what can be the case of that *wretched creature*, who is banished *for ever* to those *black* and *dismal* regions, which no *ray*, no *influence* of divine *goodness* can ever reach? where shall those *unhappy creatures* dwell, which shall be chased by the *presence* and *glory of God* out of the *new heaven* and the *new earth*, (or which rather can never approach either) *but* in that *outward darkness*, which is parted from the world of the *blessed* by an *unpassable gulph*? Ah then! if this be *so, what* do wretched men *gain* by growing *impudent* in *wickedness?* Alas! the more *insensible* men are of the deformity and danger of *sin*, the more *desperate* their *state*, the more *incurable* their *disease*; and the nearer *they* to *death* and *destruction: My spirit shall not always strive with man. This is* indeed a *blessed advantage*, to stand upon the brink of *damnation!* 'tis a *glorious victory*, to have *defeated* all the means of *grace* and *happiness!* 'tis an *heroick atchievement* to be able to *extinguish* all true *sense* and *reason*, as well as *religion*, and become impregnable, impenetrable to all *arguments*, to all *motives*, which either the tenderest *love*

or the profoundest *wisdom* of *God* and *man*
can attack us by !

2. I cannot but think that those *very*
men, who for the *most part* are *obdurate*
and *insensible*, do suffer *some*, though *rare*
returns of *anxiety* and *fear*. *Why* else are
they such avowed *enemies* to *solitude* and
retirement? to all serious and calm *reflections*; that they are ready to take up with
a most trifling and contemptible *business* or
diversion? nay, *tired* with a dull and taste-
less *repetition* of a *folly* ; they chuse to *repeat* it to their *lives end*, rather than be
alone, and *thoughtful?* what is this, but to
confess that there is something *within*, which
they are afraid to *awaken?* that there is
such a *brightness* in divine *truth*, that they
dare not open their *eyes* upon it, left it
should fill their souls with the *terrors* of
God? this *height* of *wickedness* then at
best is a state fit only for *fortunate sinners*,
who can rowl and tumble from *folly* to
folly, from *one* impertinence or extravagance to *another*, *endlesly :* and yet what
becomes of those poor things, when a *difafter*, when a *disease*, nay, but a *wakeful*
hour by night forces them to *retire* into
themselves?

3. A *sinner* does not *soon* arrive at this
state of *insensibility*. It costs him very
dear to grow *impudent* in his lust. Many
a *pang*, many a *torment* has he suffered
firft ;

firſt ; often has he felt the *wounds* of *con-ſcience* ; often has he trembled and ſhrunk at the *menaces* of *God.* The *ſoul* can no more be reconciled to *ſin*, than the *body* to *exceſs*, but by *paſſing* through many *painful* and *ſickly* fits, many *uneaſie* pangs and qualms. And is it not worth the *while* to *endure* ſo *much* in order to be *damned* ? is it not an infallible *mark* of more than vulgar *wiſdom*, to purchaſe *miſery* at ſo *dear* a rate ? to *endure hardſhip as good ſoldiers of Chriſt Jeſus,* for a *crown*, a *never-fading crown* ; *this* with them is an undertaking that deſerves to be *expoſed*, and *laſhed* with the utmoſt *ſeverity* of ſpight and confidence : but to *ſuffer*, as it were, *repeated martyrdoms* to gain an *hell*, this is what they think *becomes* men of *their parts* and *gallantry.* Bleſſed God ! to what degree of *madneſs* and *ſtupidity* may men of the *fineſt* natural parts ſink, when *abandoned* by thee ? or rather, when *they* themſelves *abandon thee*, and that *light* which thou haſt ſet up in the *world* ? our *Lord* and *Maſter* thought the *profits* and *pleaſures* of the *whole* world a *poor* compenſation for the *loſs* of the *ſoul* : *What is a man profited, if he gain the whole world,* &c. Matt. xvi. But *theſe* men, rather than it ſhould *not* periſh for ever, will charge through *ſhame* and *pain, remorſe* and *ſickneſs*, and *all* the *obſtacles* that

God

God has set between *us* and a desperate height of *wickedness.*

4. Though a *sinner* may come to that pass, as to *suppress* his *conscience,* and *master* his *fears*; yet he must ever be *conscious* to himself of the *fruitlesness* and the *meanness* of a course of *sin.* He must needs be inwardly sensible, that he has *wearied* himself to commit iniquity to. *no purpose*; that his *mind* has been *restless* and *tempestuous*, *like a troubled sea, casting up its own mire and dirt :* he must be conscious to himself, that *he* is *false* and *unjust*, *unconstant* and *ingrateful*, and in *bondage* to *such* lusts as are *mean* and *poor*, and injurious to his *repose*, and which he has often *wished* himself *free* from. And *this*, no doubt, must be a *blessed* condition, when a man's *own mind* does to his face assure him, that *he* is *that* very thing which *all the world condemns and scorns*, and which he cannot *endure* to be *charged* with, without *resenting* it as the highest *affront !* certainly it were better that *all the world* should *call me fool*, and *knave*, and *villain*, than that *I* should *call myself so*, and *know it* to be *true.* My *peace* and *happiness* depends upon my *own* opinion of *myself*, not *that* of *others:* 'tis the *inward* sentiments that *I have* of *myself*, that *raise* or *deject* me ; and my *mind* can no more be pleased with any *sensation* but its *own*, than the *body* can

can be gratified by the relishes of another's *palate.*

5. The more *insensible* a *sinner* grows, the more *intolerable* is the *disorder* and *distraction* which *sin* produces in his affairs. While men are under any little restraints of *conscience*; while they are held in by *scruples,* and *fears,* and *fits* of *regret*; while, in a word, they *sin* with any *modesty,* so long *sin* will tolerably comport with their *interest* and *reputation*; but as soon as they grow *insensible* and *impudent,* they pass all *bounds,* and there is nothing so *dear* and *considerable* to them, which they will not *sacrifice* to their *wickedness.* Now wife and children, friends, estate, laws, vows, compacts, oaths, are no *stronger ties* to them than *Sampson's withes,* or *cords.* Such a one as *this* is very well *described* in the *prophet*; *Thou art a swift dromedary, traversing her ways*; *a wild ass used to the wilderness, that snuffeth up the wind at her pleasure*; *in her occasion who can turn her away?* Jer. ii. 23 And again, he is fitly represented to an *horse rushing into the battel.* He has as much *contempt* for his *safety* and *happiness,* as for *reason* and *religion*; he defies *shame, ruin,* and *death,* as much as he does *God* and *providence* : in one word, with an impudent and *lewd stupidity* he makes all the *haste* he can to be *undone*; and since he *will* be so, it were well

if

if he could be undone *alone*. I am fure we
have too *many* inftances at *this day* of the
miferable and fatal *effects* of *atheifm* and
deifm, to leave any room to doubt whether
I have *ftrained* the point here or no.

Upon the whole it does appear, that *fin*
is a *great evil*; and that the *evil* of it is
not *leffened*, but *increafed* by *obduration*.
And from hence the *propofition* inferred does
naturally *follow*, that *deliverance* from it is
a *great good*; fo *great*, that if we eftimate
it by the *evil* there is in *fin*, *health* to the
fick, *liberty* to the *captive*, *day* to the be-
nighted, weary, and wandering *traveller*;
a *calm*, a *port* to *paffengers* in a *ftorm*;
pardon to men *adjudged to death*, are but
weak and imperfect *images* or *refemblances*
of it. A *difeafe* will at worft terminate
with the *body*, and *life* and *pain* will have
an end *together:* but the *pain* that *fin*
caufes will endure to all *eternity*; for the
worm dies not, and *the fire will not be
quenched*. The *error* of the *traveller* will
be corrected by the approaching *day*, and
his *wearinefs* refrefhed at the next *ftage*
he comes to ; but he that errs impeni-
tently from the *path of life*, is *loft* for
ever: when the *day of grace* is once *fet*
upon him, no *light* fhall e'er *recall* his wandering *feet* into the *path of righteoufnefs
and peace*; no *eafe*, no *refrefhment* fhall
                                        e'er

e'er relieve his *toil* and *misery*. Whilst the *feet* of the *captive* are loaded with *fetters*, his *soul* may enjoy its truest *liberty*; and in the midst of *dangers* and *dungeons*, like *Paul* and *Silas*, he may sing *songs of praise and triumph* : but the *captivity of sin* defiles, oppresses, and enslaves the *mind*, and delivers up the miserable man to those *intolerable* and *endless* evils, which inexorable *justice* and almighty *wrath* inflicts upon *ingratitude* and *obstinacy*. A *storm* can but wreck the *body*, a frail and worthless *bark* ; the *soul* will escape safe to *shore*, the *blessed* shore, where the happy *inhabitants* enjoy an undisturbed, an everlasting *calm* : but *sin* makes *shipwreck of faith and a good conscience*, and he that *perishes* in it does but pass into a *more miserable* state; *for on the wicked God will rain snares, fire and brimstone, storm and tempest* ; *this shall be their portion for ever*. Psal. xi. And, *lastly*, a *pardon* sends back a *condemned criminal* to *life*, that is, to sins and sufferings, to toils and troubles, which *death*, if death were the *utmost* he had to fear, would have *freed* him from : but *he*, that is once *delivered* from *sin*, is *pass'd from death to life*; and from *this life* of *faith*, of *love*, of *hope*, shall soon pass to another of *fruition* and *glory*.

§. 2. A

§. 2. A *second fruit* of *liberty* is *good works.* *Here* I will shew *two* things : *First,* and this but *briefly,* that the *works* of *righteousness* contribute mightily to our *happiness;* and that *immediately.* *Secondly,* That *deliverance* from *sin* removes the great *obstacles* and *impediments* of *righteousness,* and throws off that *weight* which would otherwise *encumber* and *tire* us in our *race.* 1. *Holiness* is no small *pleasure,* no small *advantage,* to him who is *exercised* therein. When *nature* is *renewed* and *restored,* the *works* of *righteousness* are properly and truly the *works of nature :* and to *do good* to *man,* and offer up our *praises* and *devotions* to *God,* is to gratify the *strongest* and most *delightful inclinations* we have. These indeed are at first *stifled* and *oppressed* by *original corruption, false principles,* and *vicious customs :* but when once *they* have broke through *these,* like *seeds* through the *earthy coats* they are enclosed and imprisoned in, and are impregnated, warmed, and cherished by an *heavenly influence,* they naturally shoot up into *good works.* *Virtue* has a celestial *original,* and a celestial *tendency :* from God it *comes,* and *towards* God it moves : and can it be *otherwise* than *amiable* and *pleasant? Virtue* is all *beauty,* all harmony and *order;* and therefore we may view and review, consider and reflect upon it with *delight.* It procures us the *favour*

vour of *God* and *man*; it makes our *affairs* naturally run *smoothly* and *calmly* on; and fills our minds with *courage, chearfulness,* and *good hopes.* In one word, *diversion* and *amusements* give us a *fanciful* pleasure; an *animal sensitive* life, a *short* and *mean* one: *sin,* a *deceitful, false,* and *fatal* one: only *virtue,* a *pure,* a *rational,* a *glorious,* and *lasting* one. And this is *enough* to be said *here :* the *loveliness* of *holiness* being a *subject* which ever and anon I have, *occasion* to engage in.

2. I am *next* to shew, that *deliverance* from *sin* removes the *impediments* of *virtue.* This will easily be made out, by examining what influence *selfishness, sensuality,* and the *love of this world,* which are the *three* great principles or sources of *wickedness,* have upon the *several parts* of evangelical *righteousness.* 1. The *first part* is that, which contains *those duties* that more immediately relate to *ourselves. These* are especially *two, sobriety* and *temperance.* By *sobriety,* I mean a serious and impartial examination of things; or such a state of mind as qualifies us for it. By *temperance,* I mean the moderation of our affections and enjoyments, even in lawful and allowed instances. From these proceed *vigilance, industry, prudence, fortitude ;* or *patience* and *steadiness* of mind in the prosecution of what is best. Without *these*

'tis

'tis in vain to expeƈt, either *devotion* towards *God,* or *juſtice* and *charity* towards *man.* Nay, nothing *good* or *great* can be accompliſhed without them: ſince without them we have no ground to hope for, either the aſſiſtance of divine *grace,* or the proteƈtion and concurrence of divine *providence.* Only the *pure* and *chaſte* ſoul is a fit *temple* for the reſidence of the *Spirit :* and the *providence* of *God* watches over none, or at leaſt none have reaſon to expeƈt it ſhould, but ſuch as are themſelves *vigilant* and *induſtrious.* But now, how repugnant to, how inconſiſtent with thoſe virtues, is that *infatuation* of *mind,* and that *debauchery* of *affeƈtions,* wherein *ſin* conſiſts? How incapable either of *ſobriety* or *temperance* do *ſelfiſhneſs, ſenſuality,* and the *love of this world,* render us ? What a *falſe eſtimate* of things do they cauſe us to form? How *inſatiable* do they render us in our *deſire* of *ſuch* things, as have but *falſe* and *empty* appearances of good? And how imperiouſly do they precipitate us into thoſe *ſins,* which are the *pollution* and *diſhonour* of our nature ? On the contrary, let man be but once *enlightened* by *faith* ; let him but once come to believe, that his *ſoul* is *himſelf,* that he is *a ſtranger and pilgrim upon earth,* that *heaven* is his *country,* and that to do *good works* is to *lay up his treaſure* in it ; let him,

him, I ſay, but once believe *this*, and then, how *ſober*, how *temperate*, how *wiſe*, how *vigilant*, and *induſtrious* will he grow? And this he will ſoon be induced to *believe*, if he be not actually under the influence of vicious *principles* and vicious *cuſtoms*. When the *mind* is undeceived and diſabuſed, and the *affections* diſengaged, 'tis *natural* to man to think *calmly*, and to deſire and enjoy with a *moderation*, ſuited to *juſt* and *ſober* notions of worldly things: for *this* is to think and act as a *man*. A ſecond part of *holineſs* regards *God* as its immediate *object*, and conſiſts in the *fear* and *love* of him, in *dependance* and *ſelf-reſignation*, in *contemplation* and *devotion*. As to this, 'tis plain, that whoever is under the *dominion* of any *ſin*, muſt be an *enemy*, or at leaſt a *ſtranger* to it. The *infidel* knows no *God*; and the *wicked* will not, or dares not, approach one. Their *guilt*, or their averſion keeps them from it. *Selfiſhneſs*, *ſenſuality*, and the *love of the world*, are inconſiſtent with the *love of the Father*, and all the ſeveral *duties* we owe him: they *alienate* the minds of men from *him*, and ſet up *other* gods in his room. Hence the *covetous* are pronounced guilty of *idolatry*, Col. iii. 5. and the *luxurious* and *unclean* are ſaid to make *their belly their god*, and to *glory in their ſhame*, Phil. iii. 19. But as ſoon as a poor man diſ-
cerns

cerns that he has set his heart upon *false*
goods ; as soon as he finds himself *cheated*
and *deceived* in all his expectations by the
world, and is convinced that *God* is his
proper and his foveraign *good* ; how natural is it to *turn* his defires and hopes
from the *creature* upon the *Creator*? How
natural is it to *contemplate* his *greatness* and
goodness, to *thirst* impatiently for his *favour,* and *dread* his *displeasure*? And *such*
a man will certainly make the *worship* of
God a great part, at least, of the *business*
and *employment* of *life.* With *this* he will
begin, and with *this* he will *end* the day :
nor will he rest *here* ; his foul will be
ever and anon *mounting* towards *heaven,*
in *ejaculations* ; and there will be fcarce
any *action,* any *event,* that will not *excite*
him to *praise* and *adore God,* or engage
him in fome wife *reflections* on his *attributes.*
But all *this,* will the *loose* and *atheistical*
fay, may be well *spared* ; 'tis only a vain
and idle *amusement. War* and *peace,* bu-
siness and *trade,* have no *dependance* upon
it ; *kingdoms* and *common-wealths* may *stand*
and *flourish,* and fensible *men* may be *rich*
and *happy without* it. But to this I *answer,*
religion towards God, is the *foundation* of all
true *virtue* towards our *neighbour. Laws*
would want the better part of their *authority,* if they were not enforced by an
awe of God : the wifest *counsels* would
have

have no *effect*, did not *virtue* and *religion*
help to execute them : *kingdoms* and *com-*
mon-wealths would be *dissolved*, and burst
to pieces, if they were not united and held
in by *these bonds :* and *wickedness* would reduce the *world* to one great *solitude* and *ruin*,
were it not *tempered* and *restrained*, not
only by the *virtues* and *examples*, but by
the *supplications* and *intercessions* too, of *de-*
vout men. Finally, This is an *objection* fit
for none to make, but the *sottish* and the
ignorant; men of *desperate confidence*, and
little knowledge. For whoever is *able* to
consider, by what *motives mankind* has ever
been wont to be most strongly *affected*; by
what *principles* the *world* has ever been *led*
and *governed*; how great an interest even
superstition has had, either in the *civilizing*
and *reforming* barbarous nations, or the
martial successes of the first *founders* of *mo-*
narchies, and the like; whoever, I say, is
able to *reflect*, tho' but slightly, on these
things, can never be so silly, as to demand
what the *use* of *religion* is ; or to imagine
it *possible* to *root up* its *authority* in the
world.

The *third part* of *holiness* regards our
neighbour ; and consists in the exercise of
truth, justice, and *charity.* And *no-where*
is the ill influence of *selfishness, sensuality,*
and the *love of the world*, more notorious
than *here :* for these rendring us *impatient*

R   and

and *inſatiable* in our *deſires*, *violent* in the *proſecution* of them, *extravagant* and *exceſſive* in our *enjoyments*; and the *things* of this *world* being *few* and *finite*, and unable to *ſatisfy* ſuch *inordinate* appetites; we ſtand in *one another's* light, in *one another's* way to *profit* and *pleaſures*, or, too often at leaſt, *ſeem* to do ſo: and this muſt unavoidably produce a thouſand *miſerable conſequences*. Accordingly, we daily ſee that theſe paſſions, *ſelfiſhneſs*, *ſenſuality*, and the *love of the world*, are the *parents* of *envy* and *emulation*, *avarice*, *ambition*, *ſtrife* and *contention*, *hypocriſy* and *corruption*, *lewdneſs*, *luxury* and *prodigality*; but are utter *enemies* to *honour*, *truth* and *integrity*; to *generoſity* and *charity*. To obviate therefore the miſchievous *effects* of theſe vicious *principles*, *religion* aims at implanting in the world *others* of a *benign* and *beneficent* nature; *oppoſing* againſt the *love of the world*, *hope*; againſt *ſelfiſhneſs*, *charity*; and againſt *ſenſuality*, *faith*: and to the end the *different tendency* of theſe *different principles* may be the more conſpicuous, I will briefly compare the *effects* they have in reference to our *neighbour*. *Selfiſhneſs* makes a man look upon the *world* as made for *him* alone; and upon *all* as his *enemies*, who do any way *interfere* with, or *obſtruct* his *deſigns*: it *ſeals* up all our *treaſures*; *confines* all our *care* and *thoughts*

. to

to our *private* interest, honour, or pleasure; *employs* all our *parts*, *power*, and *wealth*, and all our *time* too, in pursuit of our *particular* advantage. *Sensuality* tempts a man to *abandon* the care and concern for his *country*, his *friends* and *relations*, and *neglect* the *duties* of his *station*, that he may give himself to some sottish and dishonourable *vice:* it prevails with him to refuse *alms* to the poor, *assistance* to any publick or neighbourly good work, and even a *decent*, nay, sometimes a *necessary allowance* to his *family*, that he may waste and lavish out his fortune upon some vile and expensive *lust*. In a word, it makes him incapable of the fatigues of *civil business*; and much more of the hardships and hazards of *war:* so that instead of imitating the glorious example of *Uriah*, who would not suffer himself to be courted into the enjoyment even of *allowed* pleasures, nor indulge himself in the tendernesses and caresses of a *wife* and *children*, while *Joab* and the armies of *Israel* were in the *field*; he, on the contrary, *dissolves* and *melts down* his life and fortune in *uncleanness* and *luxury*, the shame and burden of his country and his family, at a time when not only the *honour*, but the *safety* of his *country* lies at stake, and *prince* and *people* defend it by their *toil* and *blood*. What should I mention the

R 2

love

love of the world? Are not the *effects* of
it as visible amongst us, as *deplorable?*
Does not this, where-ever it reigns, fill
all places with *bribery* and *corruption, falfhood, treachery,* and *cowardise?* Worse can-
not be said on't, and *more needs* not: for
what *societies* can *thrive,* or which way
can *credit* and *reputation* be *supported?*
What *treasures,* what *counsels,* what *armies,* what *conduct,* can fave a people,
where these *vices* prevail? Let us now,
on the other fide, suppose *selfishness, sensuality,* and the *love of the world,* cashiered;
and *faith, hope* and *charity* entertained
in their room; what a blessed *change* will
this effect in the world? How foon will
honour and *integrity, truth* and *justice,*
and a *publick spirit* revive? How serviceable and *eminent* will these render *every*
man in his *charge? These* are the true *principles* of great and brave *actions: these,*
these alone, can render our *duty* dearer to
us than any *temporal* consideration : these
will enable us to do *good works,* without
an eye to the *return* they will make us:
these will make it appear to us very reafonable, to *sacrifice* fortune, life, every
thing, when the *honour* of God and *publick good,* demand it of us. The *belief*
and *hope* of *heaven* is a sufficient *encouragement* to *virtue,* when all others fail:
the *love of God, as our supreme good,* will
make

make us eaſily *ſurmount* the conſideration
of *expence*, *difficulty* or *hazard*, in ſuch
attempts as we are ſure will *pleaſe* him;
and the *love of our neighbour as our ſelves*
will make us *compaſſionate* to his evils and
wants, *tender* to his *infirmities*, and *zealous*
of *his good* as of *our own*. How *happy* then
would *theſe* principles make the *world?*
And how much is it the *intereſt* of *every*
one to *encourage* and *propagate theſe*, and to
diſcountenance and *ſuppreſs* the *contrary*
ones? I have done with the *ſecond effect* of
Chriſtian Liberty; and will paſs on to the
third, as ſoon as I have made *two remarks*
on this laſt *paragraph*. *Firſt*, 'Tis very
evident from what has been ſaid in it, that
ſolid *virtue* can be *grafted* on no *ſtock*, but
that of *religion:* that *univerſal righteouſneſs* can be raiſed on none but *goſpel principles*; who is *he that overcometh the world,
but he that believeth that Jeſus is the Chriſt?*
1 John v. 5. I do not *oppoſe* this *propoſition*
againſt *Jew* or *Gentile*. *God* vouchſafed *in
ſundry times and in divers manners*, ſuch
revelations of his *truth*, and ſuch *communications* of his *grace*, as he ſaw fit: and
to *theſe* is their *righteouſneſs* therefore,
whatever it was, to be *attributed*; not to
the *law* of *nature* or *Moſes*. But I *oppoſe*
it againſt the *bold* pretenſions of *libertines*
and *atheiſts* at *this day*. *Honour* and *juſtice*
in *their* mouths is a vain *boaſt*; and the

natural

natural power they pretend to over their own actions, to *square* and *govern* them according to the rules of *right reason*, is only a *malicious* design to *supplant* the honour of divine *grace*; and is as *false* and *groundless* as *arrogant.* Alas! they talk of a *liberty* which they do not *understand*: for did they but once admit *purity* of heart into their *notion* of it, they would soon discern what *strangers* they are to it. How is it possible, but that *they* should be the servants of the *body*, who reject and disbelieve the *dignity* and *pre-eminence* of the *soul?* How is it possible, *they* should not be *lovers of pleasure more than lovers of God*, who either believe *no God*, or *none* that *concerns* himself much about us? And how can they chuse but be *selfish* and *sensual*, and doat upon this *world*, who expect *no better*, who believe *no other?* Take away *Providence* and a *life to come*, and what can *oblige* a man to any *action*, that shall *cross* his temporal *interest* or his *pleasure?* What shall *reward* his *espousing virtue*, when it has no *dowry*, but *losses*, *reproaches* and *persecutions?* What shall *curb* him in the career of a *lust*, when he may *commit* it, not only with *impunity*, but, as the world sometimes goes, with *honour* and *preferment* too? Though, therefore, such men as these may possibly restrain their *outward actions*, yet are they all the while

enslaved

enflaved and *defiled* in their *affections* ; and
the very *liberty* they boaſt of in their *conduct* and *management* of *themſelves* openly,
ſprings from their *ſecret ſervitude* to ſome
vile *paſſion*, or other. Nor yet can I be
ſo ſoft and eaſy as to grant, that *ſuch men*
as theſe either do or can *arrive* at the *liberty* they pretend to: I mean, that of
regulating and *governing* all their *outward
actions* by the rules of *virtue.* They too
often throw off the *diſguiſe*, which either
hypocriſy or *enmity to religion* makes them
put on; and *prove* too plainly to the
world, that when they lay *reſtraints* on
themſelves in *this* or *that ſin*, 'tis only to
indulge themſelves the more *freely* and *ſe-
curely* in *others.* Secondly, My *next* remark
is, that it is groſs ſtupidity, or impudence,
to *deny* a *providence* and *another world*,
when the *belief* of *both* is ſo indiſpenſably
neceſſary to the well-being of *this.* The
frame and nature of *man*, and the neceſſities of *this world* require *both.* Without
theſe, *ſelfiſhneſs* muſt undoubtedly be the
predominant principle. This would breed
unreaſonable deſires; and theſe would fill
us with *fears* and *jealouſies:* ſo that a
ſtate of nature would indeed be a *ſtate of
war*; and our *enmity* againſt one another
would *not* be *extinguiſhed* by *civil ſociety*;
but only *concealed* and *reſtrained*, till a fit
occaſion for its breaking out ſhould preſent

R 4   it

it felf: *laws* would want that *force*, *com-mon-wealths* that *bond* or *cement*, *converſati-on* that *confidence*, and our *poſſeſſions* that *ſe-curity* which is neceſſary to render them *bleſſings* to us.

§. 3. A *third fruit* of *Chriſtian Liberty* is that *relation* which it creates between *God* and *us*. We are no longer *of the world*, but are *ſeparated* and *ſanctified*, *devoted* and *dedicated* to God. Thus St. *Peter*, 1 Epiſt. ii. 9. *Ye are a choſen generation, a royal prieſthood, a holy nation, a peculiar people.* And thus St. *Paul*, Rom. viii. 15, 16. *Ye have not received the ſpirit of bondage again to fear ; but ye have received the ſpirit of adoption, whereby we cry, Abba, Father. The Spirit it ſelf beareth witneſs with our ſpi-rit, that we are the children of God : and if children, then heirs ; heirs of God, and joint-heirs with Chriſt.* God is *our God*; we are *his people.* He is *our Father*, and *we* are *his children*, we are *ingrafted* into *his fami-ly*. The *conſequence* of this is, his *dearly beloved* and *only begotten Son* is our *Advocate at his right-hand*, the *Propitiation for our ſins*, and *Interceſſor* for us. His *Spirit* re-ſides with us to *comfort* and *aſſiſt* us ; his *angels* guard us, and miniſter to us; for we are no longer the *object* of his *wrath*, but of his *love* and *care*. How does the *apoſtle* triumph on *this* argument, *Heb.* xii.

18,

18, 19, &c. *For ye are not come unto the mount that might be touched, and that burned with fire; nor unto blackneſs and darkneſs, and tempeſt, and the ſound of a trumpet, and the voice of words; which voice they who heard, intreated that the word ſhould not be ſpoken to them any more: (for they could not endure that which was commanded; and if ſo much as a beaſt touch the mountain it ſhall be ſtoned, or thruſt through with a dart: and ſo terrible was the ſight, that Moſes ſaid, I exceedingly fear and quake:) but ye are come unto mount Sion, and unto the city of the living God, the heavenly Jeruſalem; and to an innumerable company of angels; to the general aſſembly and church of the firſt-born, which are written in heaven; and to God, the judge of all, and to the ſpirits of juſt men made perfect: and to Jeſus, the Mediator of the new covenant; and to the blood of ſprinkling, that ſpeaketh better things than that of Abel.* And thus again, 1 Cor. iii 2. *Therefore let no man glory in men; for all things are yours; whether Paul, or Apollos, or Cephas, or the world, or life, or death, or things preſent, or things to come; all are yours, and ye are Chriſt's, and Chriſt is God's.* Theſe are *great* and *glorious* things. What *dignity* and *eminence* does this *adoption* raiſe us to? What *bleſſedneſs* flows from *communion* and *fellowſhip* with *God?* What can we

want,

want, or what can we *fear*, when we have
so mighty an *interest* in the *Soveraign of
heaven and earth*; when all his divine
Perfections, are employed to promote and
secure our *happiness*? Now sure we may *rejoice*, now we may *glory* and *triumph*; for
certainly *all things* must *work together for
our good.* But as *fallen angels* envied the
happiness of *new-created man*; so do *apostate
and debauched men* envy that of the *godly.*
And one of these will be apt to *say*, hold,
Sir, you run too *fast*; these glorious *pri-
vileges* are yet but in *embryo*, and all your
happiness is yet but in the *reverfion*: notwithstanding all these big *words*, you must
grant me that you are *yet* but in a *state of
probation*; that you are to undergo *hardships*
and *difficulties*, and to live upon the thin
diet of *hope* and *expectation*: and so I
think I might take you down from *heirs
of God*, to *servants* at the best. Well, I
will grant, that we *yet live by faith*, and
wait for the hope of glory: nor will I at
present contend about *those* pleasures that
are but in the *bud*: I will for once quit all
that *preference* both as to *nobility* and *pleasure*, which *adoption* and the full *assurance*
of *hope* gives a *godly man* above a *sinner*;
and I will take the *state* of *a child of God*,
to be as the *objector* would have it; I will
suppose him to be *under age* till he come to
another

another life; and to differ nothing from a servant whilst he is so, though he be heir of all. Yet after all, if I can prove that 'tis our *duty* to *serve God*, it will be no contemptible *fruit*, no *small commendation* of *liberty*, that it *enables* us to *do* our *duty*. And that it is our *duty to serve God*, is plain: for is it not fit that *he*, who *made* and still *upholds the world*, should *govern* it? ought we not to pay *obedience* to his laws, whose infinite *Perfections* and immense *beneficence* invest him with an *absolute* and uncontroulable *sovereignty* over us? *whom* should we *honour* with our *soul* and *body*, but *him* who is the *author* of *both*? to *whom* should we *devote* and *sacrifice* what we *have*, but to *him* from *whom* we received all? *whose praise* should we *shew forth*, but *his* who has *called us out of darkness into his marvellous light*? *whom* should we *obey* and *adore*, but *him* who has *translated us out of bondage* into *liberty*, out of the *servitude* of *satan* into the *kingdom of his dear Son*; having *redeemed us* by the *blood* of *his Son* from that *wrath* to which our *sins* had deservedly *subjected* us? But this is not all; I shall prove it not only to be our *duty*, but our *honour* and our *happiness*, to *serve God*; even on the *supposition* on which the *objection* proceeds, and which I at *present grant*.

1. 'Tis our *honour* to *serve him* whom an-

gels

gels ferve, to *whom all things in heaven and in
earth do bow and obey.* 'Tis the highest
prerogative we can derive from *grace* or
nature, to be *capable* of *ferving him.* His
divine *Perfections* tranfcend the *conceptions*
of *inferiour creatures,* and can be *known,*
contemplated, and *adored* by none, but fuch
as are *made but a little lower than the angels*;
fuch as are *endued,* not only with the *light*
of *reafon,* but with a far *brighter,* that of
the *Spirit of God. This* is indeed *our* utmoft
Perfection, and muft be our utmoft *ambition: this* alone makes us *confiderable,* who
are in all *other* refpects but *mean* and *contemptible*; for we draw but a *precarious* and
dependent breath; and the *world* we inhabit
is a *dark* and *tempeftuous* one, full of *folly*
and *mifery.* But even *this* will ferve for a
further *confirmation* of what I *further* contend for. For being *indigent* and *needy,*
ftanding at an *infinite* diftance from *felf-
fufficiency,* 'tis plain that what we cannot
find *within* us, we muft feek *without* us.
Some *all-fufficient* good we muft *find* out ;
fomething we muft *reft* in, and *repofe* our
felves upon ; and *this will* be our *God, this*
we fhall *ferve* and *adore.* And *what* fhall
this *be ?* fhall we ferve *evil fpirits ? thefe*
are our avowed and inveterate *enemies,* and
- *go about like a roaring lion feeking whom they
may devour.* Shall we ferve the *good ?*
                                                    this

this were to *dishonour* our *nature*, to serve
our *fellow-creatures* and *fellow-servants* : besides, that *such* will never *sacrilegiously* usurp
their *Maker's honour*, nor *admit* that *service* which is *due* to *him* alone. Shall we
then serve *man?* alas! the *breath* of *great
ones* is *in their nostrils*; their *life is but a
vapour*, tossed to and fro with restless noise
and motion; and then it *vanishes*; they
die, and *all their thoughts and projects perish.*
What then; shall we at length be reduced
to serve our *lusts?* this is worse than
pagan idolatry; *stocks and stones* indeed
could not *help* or *reward* their *votaries*; but
our *lusts*, like *wild* and *savage tyrants*, de-
stroy where *they rule*, and oppress and over-
whelm us with *ruins* and *mischiefs*, while
we *servilely* court and flatter them. I have
not done *yet:* I have proved it indeed to
be our *duty* and *honour* to *serve God*; but
these with *some* are *cold* and *lifeless topicks:*
I will now prove it to be our *interest* and
happiness; and this too, laying aside at
present, as I promised, the consideration
of a *future reward*, and the *joys* springing
from it. To make good this *assertion*, it
will be necessary briefly to examine *two*
things. *First*, The *design* or *end:* and,
secondly, The *nature* of *this service.* If
we enquire after the *end* of it, 'tis evident
ly our *own* advantage and happiness. The
lusts

lusts or the *humours*, the *wants* and *ne-
cessities* of man, may put *him* upon *invad-
ing* our *liberty*, or *purchasing* and *contract-
ing* with us for our *servitude*: but *God* is
all-sufficient to *himself*, and has no *need* of
our *service*: when he will be *glorified* by
us, 'tis that *we* may enjoy his *protection* and
bounty: when he obliges us to *obey* his
commands, 'tis in order to *perfect* our *natures*, and *purify* and *qualifie* us for the enjoyment of *spiritual* and *divine* *pleasure*:
when he enjoins us *prayer*, 'tis because it
does *exalt* and *enlarge* our minds, and *fit*
us for the *blessings* it obtains: when he
prescribes us *self-resignation*, 'tis because
he will *chuse for* us, and *manage* our affairs
better than *we* can our *selves*. Let us in the
next place consider the *nature* of this service. To *serve God*, what is it, but to
love what is *infinitely lovely*; to *follow* the
conduct of *infinite wisdom*, and to repose
our *confidence* in *that* being whose *goodness*
is as *boundless* as his *power*? to *serve God*,
'tis to pursue the great *end* of our *creation*,
to act consonant to the *dignity* of our *nature*, and to *govern* our *lives* by the dictates of an *enlightened reason*. How wisely
has our *church* in one of her *collects* expressed her *notion* of the *nature* of *God's
service? whose service is perfect freedom*. The
devil maintains his dominion over us, by

infa-

infatuating our *underſtandings*, by *enfeebling*
and *fettering* our *wills*, by *deluding* and *cor-
rupting* our *affections* : but on the quite contrary, the more *clear* and *impartial* our *underſtandings*, the more *free* and *abſolute* our
wills, the more *unbyaſs'd* and *rational* our *affections*, the *fitter* are we to *worſhip God*;
nay indeed, we *cannot* worſhip him at all
as we *ought* to do, *unleſs* our ſouls be *thus*
qualified. Therefore is the *ſervice of God*
called a *rational ſervice*, λογικὴ λατρεία :
and the *word of God* is called ἄδολον γάλα,
ſincere milk; to ſignify to us, that in the
ſervice of God all is *real* and *ſolid* good. Such
is the *Perfection* of *our natures*; the *might*
and *joy* of *the Spirit*; the *protection* and
conduct of *Providence*; and all the great and
precious *promiſes* of *God in Chriſt* are *Yea*
and *Amen*. But in the *ſervice* of *ſin* all is
cheat and *impoſture* ; and under a pompous
ſhew of *good*, the *preſent* is *vanity*, and the
future, repentance; but ſuch a *repentance* as
does not *relieve*, but *increaſe* the ſinners
miſery.

This is *enough* to be ſaid of the *nature*
of *God's ſervice :* and by the *conceſſions*
I made my *objector* about the *beginning* of
this *head*, I am *reſtrained* from taking notice of the *more glorious effects* of it : yet
ſome there are, very *great* and *good* ones, that
fall *not* within the compaſs of the *objection*,
which

which I will but juſt *mention.* The *firſt* is·
reſt. While *religion* regulates the *diſorder,*
and reduces the *extravagance* of our *affecti-*
ons, it does in effeĉt *lay a ſtorm,* and *compoſe a*
mutiny in our *boſoms.* Whilſt it *enlightens* our
minds, and teaches us the true *value,* that is,
at leaſt the comparative *worthleſneſs* of
worldly things, it *extinguiſhes* the *troubles*
which *preſent* diſappointments and loſſes,
and *prevents* thoſe *fears* which the proſpeĉt
of *future* changes and revolutions is wont
to create in us. A *mind* that is truly *en-*
lightened, and has no *ambition* but for *im-*
mortality and *glory,* whoſe *humility* with reference to theſe *temporal* things is built upon a *true* notion of the *nature* of them;
this ſoul has entered *already* into its *reſt.* This
is the *doĉtrine* of our *Lord* and *Maſter,* Matt.
xi. 28, 29. *Come unto me all ye that labour and*
are heavy laden ; that is, all ye that are oppreſſed by the *weight* of your own *cares*
and *fears,* that are *fatigued* and *toiled* in the
deſigns and projeĉts of *avarice* and *ambi-*
tion, and I will give you reſt. Take my yoke up-
on you, and learn of me, for I am meek and low-
ly in heart ; and ye ſhall find reſt unto your ſouls.
I need not, I think, here ſhew, that the
more we *fear* and *ſerve God,* the *more* we *love*
and *admire him,* the *more clear* is the *under-*
ſtanding, and the *more pure* the *heart* : for
the *more* we converſe with *ſolid* and *eternal*
                                        good,

good, the more *insignificant* and *trifling* will
temporal things appear to us ; and, the *more*
the mind *rejoyces in the Lord, the oftner*
'tis *rapt up* into *heaven*, and, as it were,
transfigured into a *more glorious* being, by
the *joy of the spirit*, and the *ardors* of *divine love* ; the more *flat* and *insipid* are all
earthly and *carnal* satisfactions to it. *Another effect* that attends our *shaking off* the
dominion of sin, and our *devoting* our selves
to the *service of God*, is our being *purified*
from *guilt*. The *stains* of the *past* life are
washed off by *repentance* and the *blood* of
Jesus; and the *servant* of *God* contracts no
new ones by *wilful* and *presumptuous* sin. *Now*
therefore he can *enter* into *himself*, and
commune with his own *heart*, without any
uneasiness; he can *reflect* upon his *actions*,
and *review* each *day* when it is *past*, without inward *regret* or *shame*. To *break off*
a *vicious* course; to *vanquish* both *terrors*
and *allurements*, when they persuade to that
which is *mean* and *base* ; to be *master* of
one's *self*, and *entertain* no *affections*, but
what are *wise*, and *regular*, and *such* as one
has reason to *wish* should daily *increase*
and grow *stronger*; *these* are things so far
from meriting *reproach* and *reproof* from
one's *own mind*, that they are sufficient to
support it against *all reproaches* from *without*.
Such is the *beauty*, such the *pleasure* of a
well established *habit* of *righteousness*, that

S   it

It does *more* than *compensate* the *difficulties* to which either the *attainment* or the *practice* of it can expose a man. *Lastly,* He that is *free* from *guilt,* is *free* from *fear* too. And indeed *this* is the *only* way to get *rid* of *all* our *fears;* not by *denying* or *renouncing God,* with *atheists;* but by *doing the things that please him.* He that is truly *religious,* is the *only* man who upon *rational* ground is raised above *melancholy* and *fear:* for *what* should he *fear? God is* his *glory,* his *boast,* his *joy,* his *strength;* and, if *God be for him, who can be against him? neither things present, nor to come; neither life, nor death, can separate him from the love of God in Christ Jesus.* There is *nothing* within the bounds of *time* or *eternity* that he needs *fear. Man* cannot *hurt* him; he is *encompassed with the favour and loving-kindness of God, as with a shield.* But if *God* permit him to *suffer* for *righteousness* sake, *happy* is he; this does but *increase* his *present joy,* and *future glory.* But what is most *considerable, death* itself cannot *hurt* him, *devils* cannot *hurt* him; *the sting of death is sin, and the strength of sin is the law; but thanks be to God, who giveth us the victory through our Lord Jesus Christ. For there is no condemnation to them who are in Christ Jesus, who walk not after the flesh but after the Spirit.* These *considerations* prove the *present* condition of a *servant of God happy:*

happy

happy in *comparison* of the *loose* and *wicked*; but in *comparison* with what he *shall* be *here-after*, he is infinitely *short* of the *joy* and *glory* of his *end*. In *this* respect indeed he is *yet* in a *state* of *tryal* and *trouble*, of *discipline* and *probation*; in *this* respect his *perfection* and *happiness* do but just *peep* up above the *ground*; the *fulness* and *maturity* of *both* he *cannot* enjoy till he come to *heaven*. And *this* is,

§. 4. The *last fruit* of *Christian liberty*. That *heaven* will confist of *all* the *blessings*, of *all* the *enjoyments* that *human* *nature*, when raised to an *equality* with *angels*, is *capable* of; that *beauties* and *glories*, *joys* and *pleasures*, will as it were, like a *fruit-ful* and *ripe* harveft *here*, grow up *there* in *all* the *utmost plenty* and *perfection* that *Omnipotence* itfelf will e'er produce, is not at all to be *controverted*. *Heaven* is the *master-piece* of *God*, the *accomplishment* and *confummation* of *all* his wonderful *defigns*, the *last* and *most endearing* expreffion of *boundless love*. And hence it is, that the *Holy Spirit* in *fcripture* defcribes it by the *most taking* and the *most admired* things upon *earth*; and yet we cannot but think that this *image*, tho' drawn by a *divine pencil*, mot fall infinitely *short* of it: for what *temporal* things can yield *colours* or *meta-phors ftrong* and *rich* enough to *paint heaven* to the *life*? *One* thing there is indeed,

S 2   which

which ſeems to point us to a *juſt* and *adequate notion* of an *heaven*; it ſeems to excite us to *ſtrive* and *attempt* for *conceptions*
of what we cannot *graſp,* we cannot *comprehend*; and the *labouring* mind, the *more* it
diſcovers, concludes ſtill the *more behind*; and
that is, *the beatific viſion. This* is that,
which, as *divines* generally *teach,* does *conſtitute heaven*; and *ſcripture ſeems* to *teach*
ſo *too.* I confeſs, I have often *doubted,*
whether our *ſeeing God* in the *life to come,*
did neceſſarily *imply* that *God* ſhould be the
immediate objeēt of our *fruition:* or only,
that we ſhould *there,* as it were, *drink* at
the *fountain-head*; and being *near* and *dear*
to *him* in the *higheſt degree,* ſhould ever
flouriſh in his *favour,* and *enjoy* all good,
heap'd up, preſs'd down, and running over. I
thought the *ſcriptures* might be eaſily *reconciled* to *this* ſenſe; and the *incomprehenſible
glory* of the *divine Majeſty* inclined me to
believe it the moſt *reaſonable,* and moſt eaſily *accountable. Enjoyment,* and eſpecially
where an *intelligent* Being is the *objeēt* of
it, ſeemed to *imply* ſomething of *proportion,*
ſomething of *equality,* ſomething of *familiarity.* But ah! *what proportion,* thought
I, *can* there ever be between *finite* and *Infinite?* what *equality* between a *poor creature* and his *incomprehenſible Creator?* What
eye ſhall gaze on the *ſplendors* of his *eſſential beauty,* when the very *light he dwells in*

is

is *inacceſſible,* and even the *brightneſs* he *veils* himſelf *in,* is too *dazling* even for *cherubs* and *ſeraphs,* for ought I know, to behold? Ah! *what familiarity* can *there* be between this *eternal* and *inconceivable Majeſty,* and *beings* which he has formed out of *nothing?* and when on this occaſion I reflected on the *effects* which the *preſence* of *angels* had upon the *prophets,* and ſaw *human nature* in *man ſinking* and *dying* away, becauſe unable to ſuſtain the *glory* of one of their *fellow-creatures,* I thought myſelf in a manner obliged to *yield,* and ſtand *out* no *longer* againſt a *notion,* which, though *differing* from what was generally *received,* ſeemed to have *more reaſon* on its ſide, and to be *more intelligible.* But when I called to mind, that *God* does not diſdain, even while we are in a *ſtate* of *probation* and *humility,* of *infirmity* and *mortality,* to account us not only his *ſervants* and his *people,* but his *friends* and his *children;* I began to *queſtion* the *former* opinion: and when I had ſurveyed the *nature* of *fruition,* and the various *ways* of it a little more *attentively,* I wholly *quitted* it. For I obſerved, that the *enjoyment* is *moſt tranſporting,* where *admiration* mingles with our *paſſion:* where the beloved *Object* ſtands not upon the ſame *level* with us, but *condeſcends* to meet a *virtuous* and *aſpiring,* and *ambitious affection.* *Thus* the happy *favou-*

rite

rite enjoys a *gracious master :* and *thus the*
child does with *respectful love* meet the
tenderness of his *parent :* and the *wisdom*
and *virtue,* which sometimes raises some
one happy *mortal above* the *common* size and
height of *mankind,* does not surely *diminish,*
but *increase* the *affection* and the *pleasure*
of his *friends* that enjoy him. *Again,* the
nature of *enjoyment* varies, according to
the various *faculties* of the *soul,* and the
sense of the *body.* One way we enjoy *truth,*
and *another goodness : one* way *beauty,* and
another harmony : and so on. These things
considered, I saw there was no necessity,
in order to make *God* the *object* of our
fruition, either to *bring him* down to any
thing *unworthy* of his *glory,* or to *exalt* our
selves to a *height* we are utterly *uncapable*
of. I easily saw, that we, who *love* and
adore God here, should, when we enter into his *presence, admire* and *love* him *infinitely*
more. For *God* being *infinitely amiable,* the
more we *contemplate,* the *more clearly* we
discern his *divine perfections* and *beauties,*
the *more* must our *souls* be *inflamed* with
a *passion* for *him :* And I have no reason to doubt, but that *God* will make
us the most gracious *returns* of *our love,*
and express *his* affections for *us,* in such
condescensions, in such *communications* of
himself, as will transport us to the *utmost*
degree that *created* beings are *capable* of.

Will

Will not *God*, that *sheds abroad his love in our hearts* by his *Spirit here*, fully *satisfy it hereafter?* Will not *God*, who *fills us here* with the *joy* of his *Spirit*, by I know not what *inconceivable* ways, *communicate* himself in a more *ravishing* and *eostatick* manner to us, when *we* shall *behold him as he is*, and *live* for ever *incircled* in the *arms* of his *love* and *glory?* Upon the whole then, I cannot but believe, that the *beatifick Vision* will be the *supreme* pleasure of *heaven:* yet I do not think that this is to *exclude* those of an *inferior* nature. *God* will be there, not only *all*, but *in* all. *We shall see him as he is*; and we shall *see* him *reflected*, in *angels*, and *all* the *inhabitants* of *heaven*; nay, in *all* the various *treasures* of that *happy place*: but in far more *bright* and *lovely* characters than in his *works* here *below.* *This* is a *state*, now, that answers *all ends*, and *satisfies all appetites*, let them be never so *various*, never so *boundless. Temporal good*, nay a *state accumulated* with all temporal goods, has still something *defective*, something *empty* in it: *That which is crooked cannot be made straight, and that which is wanting cannot be numbred.* And therefore *the eye is not satisfied with seeing, nor the ear with hearing: but all things are full of labour; man cannot utter it.* And if *this* were *not* the *state* of *temporal* things, yet that *one* thought of *Solomon*, that *he* must *leave*

S 4 them,

them, makes *good* the *charge* of *vanity and
vexation:* and the *contrary* is that which
compleats *heaven* ; namely, that it is *eternal.* Were *heaven* to have an *end,* that *end*
would make it *none* - *That death* would be
as much *more intolerable* than *this* here, as
the *joys* of *heaven* are *above* thofe of *earth.*
For the *terror,* and the *evil* of it, would
be to be eftimated, by the *perfection* of
that *nature* and *happinefs* which it would
put an *end* to. To *dye* in *paradife,* amidft
a *crowd* of *fatisfactions,* how much *more intolerable* were this, than to *dye* in thofe *ac-
curfed regions* that breed continually *briars*
and *brambles, cares* and *forrows?* And now,
I doubt not, but every one will readily ac-
knowlèdge, that an *heaven,* were it *believed,*
were *fuch* a *fruit* of *Chriftian Liberty, fuch*
a *motive* to it, as *none* could *refift.* Did I
believe this, have I heard *one* fay, I would
quit my *trade,* and all *cares* and *thoughts* of
this world ; and *wholly* apply my felf to get
that *other* you talk of. There was no *need*
of going *thus* far : but this fhews *what* the
natural influence of this doctrine of a *life
to come* is ; and that it is generally owing to
infidelity, where 'tis *fruftrated* and *defeated.*
What is in *this* cafe to be *done?* What
proof, what *evidences,* àre fufficient to beget *faith* in *him,* who rejects *Chriftianity*
and all *divine revelation? He that bears not
Mofes and the prophets, Chrift* and his *apoftles,*

ſtles, neither will he believe though one roſe from the dead. This *doctrine* of a *life to come* was generally *believed* by the *Gentile* world.. It was indeed very much *obſcured*, but never *extinguiſhed*, by the *addition* of many *fabulous* and *ſuperſtitious* fancies ; ſo *ſtrong* was the *tradition* or *reaſon*, or rather *both*, on *which* 'twas *built*. The *Jews* univerſally *embraced* it. The general *promiſes* of *God* to *Abraham and his ſeed*, and the ſeveral *ſhadows* and *types* of it in the *Moſaic* inſtitution, did *confirm* them in the *belief* of a *doctrine*, which I do not doubt, had been *tranſmitted* to them even from *Enoch, Noah*, and *all* their pious *anceſtors*. Nor muſt we look upon the *Sadducees* amongſt the *Jews*, or the *Epicureans* amongſt the *Gentiles*, to be any *objection* againſt this *argument* of a *life to come*, founded in *tradition* and the univerſal *ſenſe* of *mankind*: becauſe *they* were not only *inconſiderable*, compared to the *body* of the *Jewiſh* or *Pagan* world, but alſo *deſerters* and *apoſtates* from the *philoſophy* and *religion* received. To what end ſhould I proceed from the *Gentile* and *Jew* to the *Chriſtian?* Were *Chriſtianity* entertained as it *ought*, the very *ſuppoſal* of any *doubt* concerning *a life to come* would be *impertinent*. *Here* we have numerous *demonſtrations* of it. Not only the *fortune* of *virtue* in *this* life, which is often very *calamitous*, but even the *origin* and *nature*
of

of it, do plainly evince a *life to come*. For to *what* end can the *mortification* of the *body*, by *abstractions* and *meditations*, be enjoyned, if there be *no life to come*? What need is there of *renovation*, or *regeneration*, by the *Word* and *Spirit of God*, were there *no life to come*? One would think, the *common* end of this *natural* life might be well enough *secured* upon the *common* foundation of *reason* and *human laws*. What should I here add, the *love of God*, and the *merits* of *Jesus*? from *both* which we may derive many *unanswerable* arguments of a *life to come*. For though, when we reflect upon it, it appears as much above our *merit*, as it is above our *comprehension*; yet when we consider, that *eternal life is the gift of God through Jesus Christ our Lord*; what less than an *heaven* can we expect from an *infinite merit* and *almighty love*? The *love of God* must be *perfect* as *himself*: and the *merits* of *Jesus* must be estimated by the *greatness* of his *Person*, and his *sufferings*. He that cannot be wrought upon by these and the like gospel arguments, will be found, I doubt, *impenetrable* to all others. 'Tis in *vain* to argue with *such* a one from *natural topicks*: and therefore I will *stop* here.

I should now pass on to the *third* thing, the *attainment* of *Christian Liberty*: but this *chapter* is grown much too *big* already: and

and to the conſideration of the *fruit* of *this liberty*, which I have ſo long inſiſted on, nothing *more* needs to be added, but the obſervation of thoſe *rules*, which I ſhall lay down in the *following* chapters. For *whatever* advice will *ſecure* the ſeveral *parts* of our *liberty*, will conſequently ſecure the *whole*. I will therefore *cloſe* this *chapter* here; with a brief *exhortation*, to endeavour after *deliverance* from *ſin*. How *many* and *powerful motives* have we to it? Would we free our ſelves from the *evils* of *this* life? let us dam up the *ſource* of them, which is *ſin*. Would we ſurmount the *fear* of *death*? let us *diſarm* it of its *ſting*, and that is *ſin*. Would we *perfect* and *accompliſh* our *natures* with all *excellent* qualities? 'tis *righteouſneſs* wherein conſiſts the *image of God*, and *participation* of the *divine nature*: 'tis the *cleaning our ſelves from all filthineſs of the fleſh and ſpirit, and the perfecting holineſs in the fear of God*, that muſt *transform us from glory to glory*. Would we be maſters of the moſt glorious *fortunes*? 'tis *righteouſneſs* that will make us *heirs of God, and joint-heirs with Chriſt*: 'tis the *conqueſt* of our *ſins*, and the *abounding in good works*, that will make us *rich towards God*, and *lay up for us a good foundation for the life to come*. Are we ambitious of *honour*? let us free our ſelves from the *ſervitude* of *ſin*.

'Tis

'Tis *virtue* only, that is truly *honourable*
and *praise-worthy :* and *nothing* surely can
entitle us to so *noble* a *relation :* for this
allies us to *God.* For, as our *Saviour*
speaks, *they* only are the *children of Abraham, who do the works of Abraham*; the
children of *God,* who *do* the *works* of
God. These are *they,* who are *born a-
gain: not of the will of the flesh, or of the
will of man*; *but of God.* These are *they,*
who are *incorporated into the body of Christ*;
and being *ruled* and *animated* by *his Spirit,*
are *entitled* to all the blessed *effects* of *his
merit* and *intercession.* These are *they,* in
a word, who have *overcome,* and *will,* one
day, *fit down with Christ in his throne*;
*even as he also overcame, and is set down
with his Father in his throne,* Rev. iii. 21.
Good God! how *absurd* and *perverse* all
our *desires* and *projects* are! we complain
of the *evils* of the *world*; and yet we
hug the *causes* of them, and *cherish* those
vices, whose *fatal* wombs are ever big
with numerous and intolerable *plagues.*
We *fear death,* and would get *rid* of this
fear, not by *disarming,* but *sharpening* its
sting; not by *subduing,* but *forgetting* it.
We *love wealth* and *treasure :* but 'tis that
which is *temporal,* not *eternal. We receive honour of one another*; *but we seek
not that which comes from God only.* We
are fond of *ease* and *pleasure*; and at
the

the ſame time we *wander* from thoſe *paths* of *wiſdom*, which alone can *bring* us to it. For, in a word, 'tis this *Chriſtian Liberty* that makes men *truly free :* not the being in bondage to *no man,* but to *no ſin :* not the doing what we *liſt,* but what we *ought.* 'Tis *Chriſtian Liberty* that makes us *truly great,* and *truly glorious :* for this alone renders us *ſerviceable* to *others,* and *eaſy* to our *ſelves ; benefactors* to the *world,* and *delightſome* at *home.* 'Tis *Chriſtian Liberty* makes us *truly proſperous,* truly *fortunate ;* becauſe it makes us *truly happy, filling us with joy and peace,* and *making us abound in hope, through the power of the Holy Ghoſt.*

C H A P. IV.

Of liberty, as it relates to original ſin. The nature of which conſidered chiefly with re-ſpect to its corruption. How far this dif-temper of nature is curable. Which way this cure is to be effected.

WHatever difficulties the doctrine of original ſin really be involved in, or ſeem at leaſt to ſome to be ſo, they will not concern me, who am no further obliged to conſider it, than as it is an impediment of Perfection : for though there be

be much difpute about original fin, there
is little or none about original *corruption*
on; the *reality* of this is generally acknowledged, though the *guilt*, the finful-
nefs or immorality of it, be controverted.
And though here be diverfity of opinions
concerning the effects of original *corrup-*
tion in eternity; yet there is no doubt at
all made but that it incites and inftigates
us to actual fin, and is the feed-plot of
human folly and wickednefs. All men,
I think, are agreed, that there is a byafs
and ftrong propenfion in our nature towards the things of the world, and the
body: that the fubordination of the body
to the foul, and of the foul to God, wherein confifts righteoufnefs, is fubverted and
overthrown: that we have appetites
which clafh with, and oppofe the commands of God; not only when they threaten violence to our nature, as in the cafes of confeffion and martyrdom, but
alfo when they only prune its luxuriancy and extravagance: that we do not
only defire fenfitive pleafure, but even
to that degree, that it hurries and tranfports us beyond the bounds that reafon
and religion fet us: we have not only
an averfion for pain, and toil, and death;
but to that excefs, that it tempts us to
renounce God, and our duty, for the fake
of carnal eafe, and temporal fafety. And
finally,

finally, that we are so backward to entertain the belief of revealed truths, so prone to terminate our thoughts on, and confine our defires within this vifible world as our portion, and to look upon our felves no other than the mortal and corruptible inhabitants of it; that this makes us felfifh and fordid, proud and ambitious, falfe, fubtle, and contentious, to the endlefs difturbance of mankind and our felves. That this, I fay, is the ftate of nature; that this is the corruption we labour under, all men, I think, are agreed: and no wonder; for did a controverfy arife about this, there would be no need to appeal any farther for the decifion of it, than to one's own experience; this would tell every one that thus it is in fact; and reafon, if we will confult it, will tell us why it is fo: for what other than this can be the condition of man, who enters the world with a foul fo dark and deftitute of divine light, fo deeply immerfed and plunged into flefh and blood, fo tenderly and intimately affected by bodily fenfations; and with a body fo adapted and fuited to the things of this world, and faftned to it by the charms of pleafure, and the bonds of intereft, convenience and necef-fity? This account of original corruption agrees very well with *that* St. *Paul* gives

us

us of it, *Rom.* vii. and elſewhere: and
with that aſſertion of our *Lord* and *Maſter,*
on which he builds the neceſſity of *regeneration* by *water* and the *Holy Spirit,* John
iii. 6. *That which is born of the fleſh, is fleſh;
and that which is born of the Spirit, is Spirit.*
Having thus briefly explained what I
mean in this chapter by *original ſin,* I am
next to conſider theſe two things.

1. How far this diſtemper of nature is
curable.
2. Which way this cure is to be effected.

As to the firſt enquiry, I would not be
underſtood to proceed in it with a regard
to all the *regenerate* in general, but only
to the *perfect*; for the ſtrength of original
ſin cannot but be very different in new
converts, or babes in grace, and in ſuch
as are advanced to an habit of righteouſneſs. This being premiſed, I think, I
may on good ground reſolve, that original ſin in the *perfect* man, may be ſo far
reduced and maſtered, as to give him but
very *rare* and *ſlight* diſturbance. This ſeems
to me evident from the great change that
muſt be wrought in him who is converted
from a ſinner into a ſaint; *If any man be in
Chriſt, he is a new creature: old things are*
paſt

paſt away, behold all things are become new,
2 Cor. v. 17. And it is hard to conceive this
new nature, without new propenſions and
inclinations, not only different from, but
repugnant to our former original and corrupt ones ; or at leaſt we muſt ſuppoſe this
new creation ſo far to have reformed and
corre&ed the man, that original corruption
has loſt the ſtrength and force which before
it had. This will be more clear yet, if we
obſerve never ſo ſlightly, the ſeveral parts
of this great change. Firſt, The ſoul of an
excellent perſon is filled with an unfeigned
and habitual ſorrow for, and deteſtation of
all ſin; *I hate,* ſaith the *Pſalmiſt, every falſe
way.* And how inconſiſtent is the ſtrength
and heat of corrupt propenſions, with the
tears and averſions of a true penitent? how
tame is the body, how pure the mind, when
the man is poſſeſſed with a firm and holy indignation againſt ſin, when he diſſolves in
the pious tenderneſs of a contrite ſpirit !
next, the ſoul of a good man is poſſeſſed
with an ardent love of *God,* and of *Jeſus*;
with a firm belief, and a ſteddy hope of a
bleſſed eternity ; with enlightened eyes he
beholds the vanity of all earthly things, and
admires the ſolidity, the weight, and duration
of heavenly glory : *He is riſen with Chriſt,*
and therefore *ſeeks thoſe things that are above,
where Chriſt ſits on the right hand of God:
He has ſet his affeĉtions on things above, and*

T   *not*

*not on things on the earth; for he is dead, and
his life is hid with Christ in God.* And
muft we not now fuppofe fuch a one cleanfed
and purified from all corrupt affections,
when the very bent of his foul is quite
another way? muft we not fuppofe the
force and ftrength of depraved nature, over-
powered and fubdued by thefe heavenly affections? how mortified muft fuch a man
be to the world and to the body? how feeble
is the oppofition, that inferiour nature can
raife againft a mind invefted with fo abfolute
and foveraign authority, and endowed with
light and ftrength from above? Laftly, The
perfect man has not only crucified the inordinate and finful lufts and affections of
the body, but has alfo obtained a great
maftery, even over the *natural appetites* of
it; how elfe can it be that his *defires* and
hopes are in *heaven*; that he *waits for the
Lord from thence*; that he defires to be *dif-
folved* and *to be with Chrift*; and *groans* to
be rid of the *corruptible tabernacle* of the
body? he that is thus above the *body*, may
certainly be concluded to be in fome degree
above even the moft *natural appetites.*
He that has fet himfelf free in a great meafure even from his averfion to death, and
in his affection at leaft very much loofened
the bond, the knot, that unites foul and
body, may certainly very reafonably be
                                        prefumed

perſumed to be much more above all covetous, ambitious, or wanton inclinations.
Theſe are the grounds, on which I attribute
to the perfect man ſo high a degree of freedom from original ſin as I do in the propoſition laid down.

2dly, But yet I do not in the leaſt think,
that the moſt perfect man upon earth can ſo
extinguiſh the ſparks of original corruption,
but that if he do not keep a watch and
guard upon himſelf, they will gather ſtrength
and revive again: and the reaſon of this is
plain; becauſe it has a foundation in our
very nature. The diſpute concerning the
exiſtence of original corruption in us after
baptiſm, or regeneration, is, methinks, a
very needleſs one: for if it be about the
notion we ought to entertain of it, that is,
whether it be properly ſin or not, this
is a contention about words; for what
ſignifies it by what name we call this
remainder of original pravity, when all
grant, that the ſtain and guilt of it is
waſhed off and pardoned? But if it be
about the force and efficacy of it, this
indeed is a controverſy of ſome moment;
but a very fooliſh one on one ſide: for
to what purpoſe can it be, to ſay a great
many ſubtil and puzling things againſt a
truth, that every man feels and experiments

at

at one time or other? Upon the whole then, I may thus defcribe the liberty of the perfect man with refpect to original fin: he has *mortified* it, though not utterly *extirpated* it; he has *fubdued* it, though not *exterminated* it; and therefore he is not only free from finful and inordinate lufts and affections, but alfo, in a far greater meafure than other men, from thofe infirmities and irregularities, which are, as it were, the ftruglings and ebullitions of original fin, not yet fufficiently tamed. He has advanced his victory very far, even over his natural appetites; he has no ftronger inclination for the body, or for the world, and the things of it, than fuch as becomes a man that is poffeffed with a deep fenfe of the vanity of this world, and the bleffednefs of another. The world is in a high degree crucified to him, and he counts all things but dung and drofs in comparifon with the excellency of the knowledge of Chrift Jefus his Lord: His forrows and his joys, his defires and his fears, be the occafion never fo juft or lawful, pafs not the modeft bounds of a wife moderation. He defires without impatience, cares and contrives, hopes and purfues, without anxiety or follicitude; he is cautious without fear and pufillanimity; he is fad without dejection or defpondency, and pleafant without vanity. All this indeed fhews
him,

him, not only to have conquered fin and
folly, but in a great meafure alfo his natural propenfion to them. But after all,
this happy creature muft remember, that
he is ftill in the body ; in the body, whofe
appetites will foon pafs beyond their due
bounds, if he be indulgent or carelefs : he
muft remember that he is not immutably
holy, his underftanding is not fo clear and
bright, but that it may be deceived; nor
the bent of his affections fo ftrongly fet upon good, but that they may be perverted;
and therefore he muft be fober and vigilant,
and fear always. Thus have I ftated the
curablenefs of our original corruption. And
as I think I have plainly the countenance of
fcripture; fo I do not fee, that I in the leaft
clafh with that claufe in the ninth article of
our church, which affirms concerning original fin thus : *And this infection of nature
doth remain, yea, in them that are regenera-
ted, whereby the luft of the flefh, called in
greek* Φεόνημα σαρκός, *which fome do expound
the wifdom, fome the fenfuality, fome the affection, fome the defire of the flefh, is not fubject to the law of God.* For this muft not
be underftood furely, as if the flefh did always luft againft the fpirit in the regenerate,
but only that the regenerate themfelves
are liable and obnoxious to thefe luftings;
which, on fuppofal that the perfect man

T 3   were

were here thought upon by the compilers of this article, imports no contradiction to any thing I have delivered. The truth is, I have afferted no more concerning the curablenefs of original corruption, than what is neceffary to fecure the *interest* of *holinefs*, as well as the *honour* of the *Word* and *Spirit*. I have too often had occafion to obferve, that the ftating our obligation to reduce original corruption too laxly, minifters not a little to the carnal confidence of fupine and carelefs perfons. How greedily do fome imbibe, and how fond are they of this notion, that the flefh, even in the regenerate, does always luft againft the Spirit? And the next thing is, to look upon their darling errors, as unavoidable infirmities, flowing from the incurable diftemper of original fin. To the end therefore, that under colour and pretence of the impoffibility of a perfect cure and reftitution of our nature to perfect innocence and unfpotted purity, we may not fit down contented in an impure ftate, and never advance to thofe degrees of health and innocence, which we may, and ought actually to arrive at ; I think fit here, to guard the doctrine of original fin with this one general caution.

That we be very careful not to miftake contracted, for natural corruption ; not to miftake a fuper-induced nature, defaced by

all

all the flime and mud which popular errors and fashions leave upon it, for original nature, or nature in that state in which
it enters the world. 'Tis, I doubt, a very hard thing to find but one arrived at
any maturity of years, in whom nature is
the fame thing now that it was in the
womb or the cradle; in whom there are
no worfe propenfions than what neceffarily
flow from the frame and compofition of
his being. Alas! our original depravation,
be it what it will, is very betimes improved by falfe principles and foolifh cuftoms;
by a careless education, and by the blan-
difhments and infinuations of the world:
and every man is fo partial to himfelf, that
he is very willing to have his defect and
errors pafs under the name of natural and
unavoidable ones, becaufe this feems to
carry in it its own apology. This is a fatal error, and continues men in their vices;
nay, gives them peace in them too, to
their lives-end: for why fhould not a man
forbear attempting what he defpairs of
effecting? To prevent which, I earneftly
defire my reader to confider, that all who
have treated this doctrine of original fin
with any folidity or prudence, do carry
the matter as far at leaft, as I have done:
they teach not only, that original corruption may be *pruned* and *lopped*, but that

it

it may be *cut down, mortified,* and *dried up.* That, since no man can assure himself how far he may advance his conquest over his natural corruption, and the interest of every man's safety and glory obliges him to advance it as far as he can; he must never cease fighting against it, while it fights against him. That, since every sin is so far mortal as it is voluntary, and has as much guilt in it as freedom, every man ought to be extremely jealous, left he be subject to any vicious inclination, that is in reality the product, not of nature, but of choice. And lastly, since tho' much less than habitual goodness may constitute a man in a state of grace; yet nothing less can produce Perfection, or a constant assurance of eternal happiness: therefore no man ought to acquiesce, while he sees himself short of this; and every man should remember, that his goodness ought to consist in a habit of those virtues to which he is by nature the most averse. I have now dispatched my first enquiry, and resolved how far original sin is curable. The next is,

§. 2. How this cure may be effected. And here 'tis plain what we are to aim at in general: for if original righteousness consists, as I think it cannot be doubted, in the

the fubordination of the body to the foul, and the foul to God; and original corruption, in the fubverfion of this order; then the cure muſt confiſt in reſtoring this fubordination, by the weakning and reducing the power of the body, and by quickning and ſtrengthning the mind, and ſo re-eſtabliſhing its foveraignty and authority. The ſcriptures accordingly let us know that this is the great defign of religion, and the great bufinefs of man, 1 *Cor.* ix. 25. *And every man that ſtriveth for the maſtery, is temperate in all things. Now they do it to obtain a corruptible crown, but we an incorruptible.* And this St. *Paul* illuſtrates and explains by his own example, in the following Words: *I therefore ſo run, not as uncertainly; ſo fight I, not as one that beateth the air: but I keep under my body, and bring it into ſubjection.* The preference given to the cares aud appetites of the body, or of the mind, is the diſtinguiſhing character which conſtitutes and demonſtrates man either holy or wicked: *They that are of the fleſh, do mind the things of the fleſh; and they that are of the Spirit, the things of the Spirit,* Rom. viii. 5. And the threats of the goſpel belong to the ſervants of the fleſh, its promifes to the ſervants of the Spirit: *For if ye live after the fleſh, ye ſhall dye; but if ye through the*
Spirit

Spirit do mortify the deeds of the body, ye shall live, Rom. viii. 13. *He that soweth to his flesh, shall of the flesh reap corruption; but he that soweth to the Spirit, shall of the Spirit reap life everlasting,* Gal. vi. 8. I grant that in these places and elsewhere very commonly, as by the spirit is meant the mind enlightened and aided by the grace of God; so by the body or flesh is meant our inferior nature; not just such as it proceeds out of the womb, but as it is further depraved by a carnal and worldly conversation. However, since *original sin* is the seed or root of *voluntary* or customary corruption, these texts do properly and directly enough serve to the confirmation of the doctrine for which they are alledged. This then is the great duty of man, this is the great end which he is always to have in his eye, the mortifying the body, and entirely subjugating it to the reason of the mind. Here the Christian warfare must begin, and here end; for he, who has crucified the body with the lusts and affections thereof, has entred into rest, as far as this life is capable of it: he, that lays the foundation of morals here, does build upon a rock; and he, that here pushes his success to the utmost point, has reached the highest round in the scale of Perfection, and given the finishing strokes

to

to holiness and virtue. This I say then; he that will be free, muft lay down as a general rule to himfelf, from which he muft refolve never to fwerve, that he is by all rational and poffible methods to diminifh the ftrength and authority of the body, and increafe that of the mind. By this we ought to judge of the conveniencies or inconveniencies of our worldly fortunes; by this we are to determine of the innocence or malignity of actions; by this we are to form and eftimate our acquaintance and converfation, and by this we are to judge of the bent and tendency of our lives; by this we are to regulate our diverfions; by this we may refolve of the nature and degree of our pleafures, whether lawful, whether expedient, or not: and in one word, by this we may pafs a true fentence upon the degrees and meafures of our natural affections. There are many things that are in their own nature indifferent enough, that prove not fo to me; and there is fuch a latitude in the degrees and meafures of duty and deviations from it, that it is a very hard matter in feveral cafes to define nicely and ftrictly what is lawful or unlawful: but I am fure, in all cafes this is a wife and fafe rule, that we are to aim at the ftrengthning the authority of our minds, and the

weakning

weakning the force and power of our carnal appetites. By confequence, every man
ought to examine himfelf, by what arts,
by what practices the light of his underftanding comes to be obfcured, the authority of his reafon weakened, and the tendernefs of his confcience to be too much
blunted and worn off: and when he has
difcovered this, he muft avoid thefe things
as temptations and fnares; he muft fhun
thefe paths, as thofe that lead to danger
and death; and whatever he finds to have
a contrary tendency, thefe are the things
that he muft do, thefe are the things that
he muft ftudy, contrive, and follow. How
happy would a man be, how perfect would
he foon grow, if he did conduct himfelf by
this rule? How little need would he have
of outward comforts; how little value
would he have for power and honour, for
the ftate and pride of life? How little
would he hunt after the pleafures of fenfe?
What peace fhould he maintain within,
when he fhould do nothing that were repugnant to the reafon of his mind? What
joy and hope would he abound with, when
he fhould have fo many daily proofs of his
integrity, as the living above the body
would give him? And how would all this
ftrengthen and exalt the mind; what flights
would it take towards heaven, and how
invincible would it prove to all temptations?

tions? Happy and perfect that man, who has the kingdom of God thus within him, whose life is hid with Christ in God! when Christ, who is his life shall appear, he also shall appear with him in glory. This is a comprehensive rule, and if well pursued, sufficient of its self to do the work I am here aiming at: but that it may be more easily reduced to practice, I think it not amiss to take a more particular view of it: and then it may be resolved into these two:

1. We must lay due restraints upon the body.

2. We must invigorate and fortify the mind, partly by the light of the gospel, and the grace of the Holy Spirit; and partly by accustoming it to retire and withdraw itself from the body.

§. 1. As to the restraints we are to lay upon the body, what they are, we easily learn from the scriptures: for first these expresly forbid us to gratify the lusts and affections of the flesh; and that not only because they are injurious to our neighbour, and a dishonour to our holy profession, but also because they have an ill influence upon the strength and liberty, the power and authority of the mind. *Dearly beloved, I beseech you as strangers and pilgrims,*

grims, *abstain from fleshly lusts which war against the soul*, 1 Pet. ii. 11. And who-ever enters into the account of things, will easily discern this to be true ; there is a deceitfulness in sin, a sensuality in lust : who sees not that there is more attraction in the pride and ostentation of life, than in the simplicity and plainness of it? That there is more temptation and allurement in riot and luxury, than in frugality and a competency? That the imagination of a *Solomon* himself cannot but be wretchedly abused, if he give it leave to wander and wanton in variety? In a word, if the mind follow a carnal or worldly appetite and fancy in all its excesses and debau-ches, it will soon find it self miserably in-slaved and intoxicated; it will be whol-ly in the interest of the body, and wholly given up to the pleasures of it. Secondly, Tho' the scripture do not prohi-bit some *states* or *conditions* of this life, which seems as it were more nearly *allied* to, or at least-wise at less distance from the *lusts of the flesh*, than others are; yet it forbids us to *covet* and *pursue* them. Thus St. *Paul*, Rom. xii. 16. *Mind not high things.* The apostle does not here oblige any man to degrade himself be-neath his birth, or to fly from those ad-vantages which God's providence and his own merits give him a just title to ; but

certainly

certainly he does oblige the Chriſtian not to aſpire ambitiouſly to great things, nor fondly to pride himſelf in ſucceſſes of this kind. So when a little after he commands us *in honour to prefer one another,* certainly he does not teach how to talk, but how to act; not how to court and compliment, but to deport our ſelves conſonant to thoſe notions with which charity towards our neighbour, and humility towards our ſelves ought to inſpire us. Thus again, we are not forbidden to be rich; no man is bound to ſtrip himſelf of thoſe poſſeſſions which he is born to, or to ſhut out that increaſe which God's bleſſing and his own diligence naturally bring in : but we are forbid to *thirſt after riches,* or to *value* our ſelves upon them, and commanded to be content with thoſe things that we have; and if God bleſs us with wealth, to enjoy it with modeſty and thankfulneſs, and diſpenſe it with liberality, 1 *Tim.* vi. 6, 7, 8, 9, 10. *Godlineſs with contentment is great gain* ; *for we brought nothing into this world, and it is certain we can carry nothing out* ; *and having food and raiment, let us be therewith content. But they that will be rich, fall into temptation, and a ſnare, and into many fooliſh and hurtful luſts, which drown men in deſtruction and perdition. For the love of money is the root of all evil, which while ſome coveted after, they have er-*
red

*red from the faith, and pierced themselves
through with many sorrows.* ver. 17, 18, 19.
*Charge them that are rich in this world, that
they be not high-minded, nor trust in uncertain
riches, but in the living God, who giveth us
all things richly to enjoy. That they do good,
that they be rich in good works, ready to diftribute, willing to communicate : laying up
in store for themselves a good foundation against
the time to come, that they may lay hold on
eternal life.* And to multiply no more instances of restraints of this or the like nature, thus we ought to stand affected towards *praise* and *reputation, interest* and
power, beauty, strength, &c. We must
neither be too intent upon them, nor enjoy
them with too much gust and satisfaction ; for this is that disposition which appears to me to suit best with the spirit and
design of the gospel, and with the nature
of such things as being of a middle sort,
are equally capable of being either temptations or blessings, instruments of good or
evil.

3*dly,* The scripture regulates and bounds
our *natural* and *necessary* appetites, not so
much by *nicely* defining the *exact* degrees
and measures within which nature must be
strictly contained, as by exalted *examples*
of, and *exhortations* to a *spiritual, pure,*
and *heavenly* disposition. Thus our Lord
and Master seems to me to give some
check

check to the ſtream of natural affeċtion, and to call off his diſciples from it, to the conſideration of a ſpiritual relation ; *Mark* iii. 34, 35. *And he looked round about on them which ſat about him, and ſaid, behold my mother and my brethren : for whoſoever ſhall do the will of God, the ſame is my brother, and my ſiſter, and mother.* To which words of our Lord I may join thoſe of St. *Paul, Henceforth know we no man after the fleſh---yet now henceforth know we him no more,* 2 *Cor.* v. 16. The anſwer of our Lord to a diſciple who would have deferred his following him, till he had buried his father, *Matth.* viii. 21. and to him who begged leave to go and bid farewel firſt to his relations and domeſticks, *Luke* ix. 61. does plainly countenance the doċtrine I here advance; and ſo does St. *Paul,* 1 Cor. vii. 29. ſo often cited by me. Not that our Saviour or his apoſtles did ever account our natural affeċtions *vicious* and *impure* ; for 'tis a vice to be without them, *Rom.* i. 31. Not that they went about to diminiſh or abate, much leſs to cancel the *duties* flowing from them : no; they only prune the *luxuriancy* of *untaught* nature, and correċt the *fondneſſes* and *infirmities* of *animal* inclinations. Our natural affeċtions may entangle and enſlave us, as well as unlawful and irregular ones, if we lay no reſtraint upon them. Religion indeed makes them

U   the

the feeds of virtue, but without it they eafily betray us into fin and folly. For this reafon I doubt not, left under pretence of fatisfying our moft natural and importunate appetites, we fhould be enfnared into the love of this world, and entangled in the cares of it, our Saviour forbids us to take thought for to-morrow, even for the *neceffaries* of to-morrow, *what we fhall eat, and what we fhall drink, and wherewithal we fhall be cloathed,* Matth. vi. Thefe are the reftraints laid upon the body in fcripture; which if any man obferve, he will foon difcern himfelf as far purified and freed from original corruption, as human nature in this life is capable of. And that he may;

§. 2*dly,* He muft fortify and invigorate the mind. And this muft be done two ways. Firft, By poffeffing it with the knowledge of the gofpel, and the grace of the Spirit. Secondly, By withdrawing it often from the body. As to the former branch of this rule, the neceffity of it is apparent: fince the ftate of nature is fuch as has before been defcribed, we ftand in need not only of *revelation* to *enlighten* us, but alfo of *grace* to *ftrengthen* us; of the former to excite us to exert all the force and power we have; of the latter to enable us to do that which our natural force never can effect. It cannot be here expected that

I fhould

I fhould treat of the operation of the Spirit, and the ways of obtaining it, grieving, and quenching it; this would demand a peculiar treatife. I will here only obferve, that it is the work of the Spirit to *repair*, in fome degree at leaft, the *ruins* of the *fall*; to *rectify nature*; to *improve* our *faculties*, and to *imprint* in us the *divine Image*: that meditation and prayer, and a careful conformity to the divine will, obtain and increafe the grace of the Spirit: that negligence and prefumptuous wickednefs grieve and extinguifh it. As to the knowledge of the gofpel, I fhall not need to fay much here. I have confidered this matter in the chapter of *Illumination*, and will only obferve, that the doctrines of the gofpel are fuch, as, if they be thoroughly imbibed, do effectually raife us above a ftate of *nature*, and fet us free from the *power* and *prevalence* of our original corruption. Were we but once perfuaded, that we are ftrangers and pilgrims upon earth : that all carnal gratifications do war againft the foul: that our fouls are properly our felves, and that our firft cares are to be for them: that God is himfelf our foveraign good, and the fountain of all inferior good : that our perfection and happinefs confift in the love and fervice of him: that we have a mighty Mediator, who once died for us, and ever lives to make interceffion for us : that *a*

kingdom

kingdom incorruptible and undefiled, and that fadeth not away, is *reserved in heaven* for all meek, faithful, and holy souls: were we, I say, but once thoroughly perfuaded of thefe truths, with what vigour would they impregnate our minds? How clear would be the convictions of confcience? How uncontroulable the authority of reafon? How ftrong the inftincts and propenfions of the mind towards righteoufnefs and virtue? Thefe would alienate the mind from the world and the body, and turn the bent of it another way; thefe would infpire it with other defires and hopes, and make it form different projects from what it had before; *old things are done away, and all things are become new.* The fecond branch of this fecond particular rule is, that we muft accuftom our felves to retire frequently from the commerce and converfation of the body. Whether the eating the forbidden fruit did open to the mind new fcenes of fenfuality which it thought not of, and fo called it down from the ferenity and heights of a more pure and contemplative life, to participate the turbulent pleafures of fenfe, immerfing it as it were by this means deeper into the body, I pretend not to judge. But 'tis certain a too intimate conjunction of the mind with the body, and the fatisfactions of it, does very much debafe it. 'Tis our great unhappinefs,

happiness, that the soul is always in the sen-
fes, and the senses are always upon the
world ; we converse with the world, we
talk of the world, we think of the world,
we project for the world ; and what can
this produce, but a carnal and worldly frame
of spirit ? We must meditate heavenly
things ; we must have our conversation in
heaven; we must accustom our selves to
inward and heavenly pleasures, if we
will have heavenly minds : we must let no
day pass, wherein we must not withdraw
our selves from the body, and sequester
our selves from the world, that we may
converse with God and our own souls. This
will soon enable us to disdain the low and
beggarly satisfactions of the outward man,
and make us long to be set free from the
weight of this corruptible body, to breathe
in purer air, and take our fill of refined and
spiritual pleasure. I have insisted thus long
on the cure of original sin, not only because it is the *root* of all our *misery*, but also because there is such an *affinity* between
this and the sin of infirmity, which I am
next to speak to, that the same remedies
may be prescribed to both ; so that I am
already eased of a part of the labour,
which I must otherwise have undergone in
the following chapter.

I am now by the laws of my own method obliged to consider the *effects* of this

branch

branch of *Chriſtian Liberty* in the *perfect*
man, and to ſhew what influence it has upon his happineſs. But having, *ſect*. 1. *ch*. 4.
diſcourſed at large of the ſubſerviency of
Perfection to our happineſs ; and in *ſect*. 2.
chap. 3. of the happy effects of Chriſti-
and liberty in general, I have the leſs need
to ſay much here on this head: yet I cannot wholly forbear ſaying ſomething of it.
The conqueſt over original corruption,
ſuch as I have deſcribed it, raiſes man to
the higheſt pitch of Perfection that our nature is capable of ; makes him approach
the neareſt, that mortality can, to the *life*
of angels, and plants him on the mount
of God, where grace, and joy, and glory,
ſhine always on him with more direct and
ſtrong rays. Now is virtue *truly lovely*,
and *truly happy* ; now the aſſurance of the
mind is never interrupted, its joy never
overcaſt ; it enjoys a perpetual calm within,
and ſparkles with a peculiar luſtre that
cannot be counterfeited, cannot be equal-
led. Some faint and partial reſemblance, I
confeſs, of this virtue, or rather of this
ſtate or conſummation of it, have I, tho'
very rarely, ſeen in ſome maſterly ſtrokes
of nature. I have obſerved in ſome, that
ſweetneſs of temper ; in others, that coldneſs and abſolute command over themſelves,
with reſpect to the pleaſures ; and in ſeveral,
that innate modeſty and humility, that natural

tural indifference for the power, honour, and grandeur of life, that I could scarce forbear pronouncing, that they had so far each of them escaped the *contagion* of original corruption, and could not but bless and love them. But, after all, there is a vast difference between these *creatures* of *nature*, and those of *grace*: the Perfection of the one is confined to this or that particular disposition; but that of the other is in its degree universal: the Perfection of the one has indeed as much charm in it as pure nature can have; but the other has a mixture of something divine in it; it has an heavenly tincture, which adds something of *sacredness* and *majesty* to it, that nature wants: the Perfection of the one is indeed easy to its self, and amiable to others; but the Perfection of the other is joy and glory within, and commands a veneration as well as love from all it converses with. Blessed state! when shall I attain thy lovely innocence! when shall I enter into thy divine rest! when shall I arrive at thy security, thy pleasure!

CHAP.

CHAP. V.

Of liberty, *with respect to sins of* infirmity. *An enquiry into these three things,* 1.*Whether there be any such sins,* viz. *Sins in which the most perfect live and die,* 2. *If there are, what they be; or what distinguishes them from damnable or mortal sins.* 3. *How far we are to extend the liberty of the perfect man in relation to* these *sins.*

THIS is a *subject,* wherein the very *being* of holiness or virtue, the *salvation* of man, and the *honour* of God, are deeply interested: for if we allow of such sins for *venial,* as really are not so, we destroy the notion, or evacuate the necessity of holiness; endanger the salvation of man, and bring a reflection upon God as a favourer of impiety. On the other hand, if we assert those sins *damnable,* which are not really so, we miserably perplex and disturb the *minds* of men, and are highly injurious to the *goodness* of God; representing him as a severe and intolerable master. But how important soever this subject be, there is no other, I think, in the compass of divinity, wherein so many writers have been so unfortunately engaged; so that it is over-grown with dispute and controversy, with confusion and obscurity, and numberless absurdities and contradictions,

ons. This I have thought neceffary to obferve in the entrance of my difcourfe, not
to infult the performances of others, or to
raife in the reader any great expectation
for my own ; but indeed for a quite contrary reafon, namely, to difpofe him to a
favourable reception of what I here offer
towards the rendring the doctrine of fins
of infirmity intelligible, and preventing the
differvice which miftakes about it do to religion.

By fins of infirmity, both *ancients* and
moderns, papifts and *proteftants,* do, I think,
underftand fuch fins as are confiftent with
a ftate of grace and favour; and from
which the beft men are never intirely freed
in this life, though they be not imputed
to them. This then being taken for granted, I fhall enquire into thefe three
things.

1. Whether there be any fuch fins,
fins in which the moft perfect live and
dye.

2. If there are, what thefe be. What it
is that diftinguifhes them from *damnable*
or *mortal* ones.

3. How far we are the extend the *liberty*
of the perfect man in relation to *thefe.*

1. Whether there be any fuch. That
the beft men are not without errors, without defects and failings, and that not only
in their paft life, or unregenerate ftate,

but

but their beft, and moft perfect one, is a truth which cannot, one would think, be controverted: for what *underftanding* is there, which is not liable to *error?* What *will,* that does not feel fomething of *impotence,* fomething of *irregularity?* What *affections,* that are merely human, are ever *conftant,* ever *raifed?* Where is the *faith,* that has no *fcruple,* no *diffidence;* the *love,* that has no *defect,* no *remiffion;* the *hope,* that has no *fear* in it? What is the *ftate,* which is not liable to *ignorance, inadvertency, furprife, infirmity?* Where is the *obedience,* that has no *reluctancy,* no *remifnefs,* no *deviation?* This is a truth, which, whether men will or no, they cannot chufe but feel; the confeffions of the holieft of men bear witnefs to it. And the pretenfion of the *Quakers,* to a finlefs and perfect ftate, is abundantly confuted by that anfwer one of the moft eminent of them makes to an objection, which charges them with arrogating and affuming to themfelves infallibility and perfection, *viz. That they were fo far infallible and perfect, as they were led by the Spirit of God.* For what is this, but to *defert* and *betray,* not defend their caufe? 'Tis plain then, as to matter of fact, that the moft *perfect* upon earth are not without frailties and infirmities; and fuch infirmities, as difcover themfelves in actual flips and errors.

errors. But the queftion is, whether
thefe are to be accounted *fins* ? I muft
confefs, if we ftri&ly follow the language
of the fcripture, we fhould rather call
them by fome other name ; for this does
fo generally underftand by fin, a deliberate tranfgreffion of the law of God, that
it will be very difficult to produce *many*
texts wherein the word *fin* is ufed in any
other fenfe. As to *legal* pollutions, I have
not much confidered the matter. But as
to *moral* ones, I am in fome degree confident, that the word fin does generally fignify fuch a tranfgreffion as by the gofpel covenant is punifhable with death
and *rarely* does it occur in any other fenfe:
I fay *rarely* ; for, if I be not much miftaken, the fcripture does *fometimes* call thofe
infirmities, I am now talking of, fins. But
what if it did not? 'Tis plain, that every deviation from the law of God, if it
has any concurrence of the will in it, is
in ftri& fpeaking *fin :* and 'tis as plain
that the fcripture does frequently give us
fuch defcriptions and chara&ers, and fuch
names of thefe fins of infirmity, as do
oblige us both to ftrive and watch againft
them, and repent of them. For it calls
them fpots, errors, defe&s, flips, and
the like. But, what is, laftly, moft to
my purpofe, it is plain, that this diftin-
&ion of fins, into mortal and venial, or
fins

fins of infirmity, has its foundation in exprefs texts of fcrupture. Numerous are the texts cited to this purpofe : but he that will deal fairly muft confefs, that they are moft of them improperly and impertinently urged, as relating either to falls into temporal calamity; or to mortal, not venial fins; or to the fins of an unregenerate ftate; or to a comparative impurity, I-mean the impurity of man with refpect to God; a form of expreffion frequent in *Job.* I will therefore content myfelf to cite three or four, which feem not liable to thefe exceptions, *Deut.* xxxii. 4. *They have corrupted themfelves; their fpot is not the fpot of his children : they are a perverfe and crooked generation.* Here two things feem to be pointed out to us plainly : *Firft,* that the children of God are not without their fpots. *Secondly,* That thefe are not of the fame nature with thofe of the wicked, in comparifon with thofe wilful and perverfe tranfgreffions, the children of God are, elfewhere, pronounced blamelefs, without offence, without fpot, *Pfalm* xix. 12, 13. *Who can underftand his errors? cleanfe thou me from fecret faults : keep back alfo thy fervant from prefumptuous fins, let them not have dominion over me; then fhall I be upright, and I fhall be innocent from the great tranfgreffion.* Here again the *Pfalmift* feems to me to place

upright-

uprightnefs in freedom from deliberate or mortal fin, and to admit of another fort of tranfgreffions, in which even upright men flip fometimes. Nor does the *Pfalmift* here only affert venial fins; but he feems to me to fuggeft the fprings and fources of them, namely, fome fecret difpofitions in our nature to folly and error, which he prays God to cleanfe and free him from more and more; *Cleanfe thou me from fecret faults.* The word *fault* is not in the original; but fomething of that kind muft be fupplied to render the fenfe intire in our language. The words of *Solomon, Prov.* xx. 9. feem to relate to this corruption lurking in us, and never utterly to be extirpated; *Who can fay I have made my heart clean, I am pure from my fin?* For if this fhould be applied to mortal fin, every one fees, that it will contradict a hundred places in fcripture, which attribute to righteous men, purity of heart, and deliverance from fin. Laftly, *James* iii. 2. we are told plainly, that *in many things we offend all,* πταίομεν ἅπαντες, not finners only, but righteous and upright men, have their defects and flips. And accordingly there is not any life which we have the hiftory of in fcripture, how excellent foever the perfon be, but we meet with fome of thefe recorded; as will appear from thofe feveral inftances

ces I fhall produce, when I come to defcribe the nature of thefe fins. And certainly, when *David* fays of himfelf, *My
fins are more in number than the hairs of my
head:* he that fhall interpret this place of
mortal or prefumptuous fins, will both
contradict the fcriptures, which acquit
him, except in the matter of *Uriah,* and
highly wrong the memory of *David,* making him a prodigy of wickednefs, inftead of a faint. Nor does *that* make
any thing againft me, which he adds in
the next words, *My heart fails me ;* or *that*
in the foregoing verfe, *Mine iniquities
have taken hold upon me, fo that I am not
able to look up.* For I do not affirm that
the *Pfalmift* here has regard only to fins
of infirmity exclufively of others : no ; he
reckons all together, and fo difcerns the one
aggravated by the other ; and the guilt of
all together very far enhanced. Nor do
I, *fecondly,* intereft myfelf here in that
difpute between proteftants and papifts,
whether fins of Infirmity are not damnable in their own nature, though not imputed under the covenant of grace ? Nor
do I, laftly, examine what a vaft fheap
of fins of Infirmity may amount to, though
the guilt of this or that alone were not fo
fatal. I have then, I think, proved the
matter in queftion ; having fhewed, both
from the experience of mankind and the
fcrip-

fcripture, that the beft men have their
infirmities and defe&s; and that thefe
may properly enough be called fins. I think
it fuperfluous to prove, that they confift
with a ftate of falvation; fince 'tis not by
any, that I know of, denied; and may be
eafily enough made out, from what I have
already faid. I am now to enquire,

§. 2. What thefe fins be; and how diftinguifhed from mortal or damnable ones.
To this purpofe we may diftinguifh human a&ions (under which I comprife both
internal and external) into three forts;
voluntary, involuntary, and mixt.

§. 1. There are a&ions properly and
truly voluntary; fuch are thofe deliberate
tranfgreffions of a divine law, which
man commits in oppofition to the dire&
remonftrances of confcience; he knows
the a&ion is forbid; he fees the turpitude and obliquity of it; he is not ignorant of the punifhment denounced againft
it, and yet he ventures upon it: this is
plainly mortal, damnable fin; and I cannot think, that any circumftance or pretence whatever can render it venial. And
therefore I muft be pardoned, if I cannot
be of their opinion, who fuppofe, that
the fmallnefs of the matter, the relu&ancy
of confcience, or the length and force
of a temptation, can fo foften and miti-
gate

gate a voluntary tranfgreffion, as to diminifh it into a fin of Infirmity. 1. As
to the fmallnefs of the matter. Some cannot but think thofe tranfgreffions venial,
which are, for the matter of them, fo
flight and infignificant, that they feem to
be attended by no mifchievous confequence, nor to offer any difhonour to God,
nor injuftice to man. But I doubt this
notion of venial fin has no folidity in it;
for either men perform fuch actions deliberately, or indeliberately; knowing them
to be finful, or believing them to be innocent. Now, if we perform any action
deliberately, and knowing it to be finful,
we never ought to look upon this as a *little*
fin, much lefs a *venial* one. The reafon
of this is plain. The firft notion that
every man has of fin, is, that it is forbidden by, and difpleafing to God; and then
to do that deliberately, which we know
will provoke God, is an argument of a
fearlefs and irreligious heart, a heart deftitute of the love of God, the love of
righteoufnefs, and heaven. But if a man
tranfgrefs in a *trifling inftance indeliberately*;
this alters the cafe; for the matter not
being of importance enough to excite the
intention and application of the mind;
and there being confequently no malignity of the will in an action, where there
was no concurrence of the judgment, I
cannot

cannot but think, this may very well pass
for an human infirmity; for all the fault
that can be here laid to the charge of man
is, incogitancy or inadvertency; and that
too as excufable a one as can be. Laftly,
where the matter of an action is very
trifling and inconfiderable, and draws after
it no ill confequence, either with refpect
to God or man; in this cafe, if a man
judge it no fin, I cannot think it is, any
to him; though by a nice and fcrupulous
conftruction, it may fall within the compafs of fome divine prohibition. The diftinction of the fchoolmen is good enough
here; it is befides the law, but not againft
it: or it is againft the letter, but not
the defign and intention of the law
of God. I cannot think that it is confiftent with the infinite goodnefs of God,
to punifh fuch things as thefe with eternal mifery, or that it can become a man
of fenfe ferioufly to afflict his foul for
them. I cannot for my life perfuade
my felf, that I fhould provoke God, if
paffing through a field of my neighbour's corn or peafe, I fhould pull off an
ear or cod; or paffing through his or-
chard, fhould eat an apple. The notion
I have of God, and the great end and defign of his laws, will not fuffer me to entertain fuch trifling, weak, and fuperftitious fancies, And here I cannot but take

X notice

notice of two things, which very much
perplex the minds of fome good people ;
that is, an idle *word*, and *jeſting :* concerning both which, 'tis very plain, that
fuch are miſerably miſtaken; and that
they are no fins at all, unleſs unreaſonable and fuperſtitious ſcruples make them
fo : this, I fay, on fuppofition that by
idle word, they mean *only* fuch talk, as
does not tend to edification; and by jeſting, only *that* which is innocent and divertive. By an idle word (*Mat.* xii.) our Saviour plainly means a blaſphemous word,
if that faying of our Saviour, of every *idle
word*, &c. be to be limited and confined
by the fenfe of the context : for the occafion of the affertion of our Lord, was
the blaſphemy which the *Jews* belched out
againſt his miracles. Or if our Lord here,
on this occafion, advances a general doctrine, then, by an idle word, we muſt
underſtand a wicked one, proceeding
from a corrupt and naughty heart ; and
tending as directly to promote impiety,
as gracious and wholfome difcourfe does
to promote edification. This is evident
from *ver.* 25. *A good man, out of the
good treafure of the heart, bringeth forth
good things*; and an *evil man, out of the
evil treafure, bringeth forth evil things.*
And *ver.* 37. *for by thy words thou ſhalt be
juſtified, and by thy words thou ſhalt be con-*
demnned.

demned. By *jesting*, *Eph.* v. 4. the apoftle underftands the *modish raillery* of the
Greeks, which was generally made up of
prophaneness and *wantonness* ; or brisk and
fharp ironies. This is plain, both from
the company we find it in αἰσχρότης κỳ μω-
ϱολογία, filthiness and foolifh fpeaking ;
and from the character given it in common with the other two, Τα ἐκ ἀνήκοντα,
being the very fame that is given the moft
infamous and vileft lufts and paffions.
Rom. i. 28. *Things not convenient* is a di-
minutive expreffion, implying fuch things
as contain much turpitude and wickednefs in them. *Beza,* as appears by his
notes, reads ἢ, not κỳ, in this place, foolifh
fpeaking, *or,* not *and,* jefting ; which (as
he obferves) makes jefting the fame thing
with foolifh fpeaking, or buffoonry. And
juftifies that jefting, which confifts in a
pleafant and divertive facetioufnefs from
1 *Kings* xviii. 27. 2 *Kings* iii. 23. *Ifa.* xiv.
11.

2. Some think, that the mere reluctancy and oppofition of confcience againft
fin, is fufficient to conftitute a fin of Infirmity. And this has received no fmall
countenance from fuch an interpretation
of *Rom.* vii, as makes holinefs to be nothing
elfe but a viciffitude of defires and actions, repugnant to one another. But at
this rate no man's fins would be damning
X 2   but

but his whose conscience were seared; and
when one's heart did condemn one, God
would be sure to acquit one : which agrees
very ill with St. *John, If our heart condemn
us, God is greater than our heart, and knoweth all things,* 1 *Joh.* iii. 21. No man, unless arrived at a reprobate sense, can do
that which is evil, without reluctancy;
for his conscience will forbid him, as long
as it has the least degree of tenderness
in it; and restrain him as far as it has
power. And as to *Rom.* vii. it has been
abundantly considered; and, I think,
sufficiently proved to belong to those,
who are the servants of sin; as *Rom.* viii.
does to those who are set free. St. *Austin*
indeed tells us, that he understood that
chapter at first as the *Pelagians* did, for a
person under the law, and under the
power of sin; but that he found himself
constrained afterwards to understand it of
St. *Paul* himself. I will not examine the
solidity of his reasons: 'tis enough to
me, that his change of opinion does religion no harm: for he is so far from making a state of holiness to consist with acts
of deliberate sin against conscience, that
he will not excuse so much as rebellious
motions and appetites, if consented to.
All that he contends for, in a good man,
from this chapter is, that lapsed nature
will sometimes exert itself, even in the best

men, in diforderly and diftempered appetites.

3. Others, laftly, will have thofe fins,
into which we fall, either overpowered by
the ftrength, or wearied out by the affi-
duity or length of a temptation, pafs for
Infirmities. But this opinion has as little
ground as the two former. I can find no
fcripture that countenances this notion.
There are indeed fome of great reputation, who have promoted it. But, I think,
the words of St. *Paul* make againft it, 1 *Cor.*
x. 13. *There hath no temptation taken you,*
but fuch as is common to man; but God is
faithful, who will not fuffer you to be tempted
above that you are able; but will with the tem-
ptation alfo make a way to efcape; that ye may
be able to bear it. The defign of which
words is certainly to encourage Chriftians againft the biggeft temptations, by
an affurance of relief from God, proportionable to our neceffities; and confequently muft imply, that if we yield to
a temptation, 'tis our own fault. God
expects we fhould ftand firm under the
higheft trials. *Be thou faithful unto death,*
and I will give thee a crown of life, Rev.
ii. 10. *To him that overcometh will I grant*
to fit with me in my throne, even as I alfo
overcame, and am fet down with my Father in
his throne, Rev. iii. 21. *But whofoever fhall*
deny me before men, him will I alfo deny

before

before my Father which is in heaven, Mat.
x. 33. If therefore, by fins of Infirmity,
men mean, such as are confistent with the
state of grace, *i. e.* such as good men may
frequently fall into, without forfeiting the
peace of conscience, and the favour of
God, I cannot possibly think, that any
deliberate sin can be such, upon the
score of the temptation; or that any
of those fins, reckoned in the catalogue,
Gal. v. and *Eph.* v. can be such on the
account of the violence or perseverance
with which they attack us. But, secondly, if by fins of Infirmity, they mean
such fins as righteous men are liable to; I
know not what they are from which they
are exempted. But if, lastly, by fins of
Infirmity, they mean such, for which God
is more easily intreated; then there is no
question to be made, but that there is a
difference in fins; which is to be estimated
by the different measures of grace and
knowledge; by the different degrees of
deliberation and surprize; and by the
force or weakness, the continuance or
shortness, of a temptation: and, finally,
by the different effects and tendencies of
fins. To all which, I do not question,
but that the spirit has regard in those directions, which it gives us, for our behaviour
towards such as fall, *Gal.* vi. 1. *Brethren, if
a man be overtaken in a fault, ye which are*
spiri-

spiritual, restore such a one in the spirit of meekness ; considering thy self, lest thou also be tempted. And of some have compassion, making a difference : and others save with fear, pulling them out of the fire, Jude 22, 23.

§. 2. A Second sort of actions are such as we call involuntary ; that is, those wherein we exercise no deliberation, no choice. Some have reduced sins of infirmity to this head, but with what colour of reason any one may judge. For since action truly *involuntary*, are neither the objects of the understanding nor will, 'tis hard to conceive what morality there can be in them. The grounds on which this opinion is built are such as these. First, the measure, say they, of good and evil is the law of God; but involuntary and unavoidable actions are not a proper subject of laws : for to what purpose is it to prescribe rules, or to propose rewards and punishments to such actions, as are no way subject to our choice? Secondly, They tell us, 'tis inconsistent with the goodness of God, and the riches of gospel grace, to impute those things to a man as damnable sins, which fall not within the compass of his power or deliberation. Now, I must confess, I am so far from denying any actions, that can lay a just claim to this apology, to be venial,

X 4   that

that I cannot forbear thinking that they
are not finful : for *where there is no law,
there is no tranfgreffion.* But how does
this way of arguing for the excufablenefs
of involuntary tranfgreffions, confift with
thofe other doctrines which they maintain concerning them; namely, that we are
bound to repentance for them; that thefe
fins are not venial in their own nature,
but only thro' the favour of God? For the
law, taken in its rigour, denounces death
againft all fin in general, without limita-
tion or exception ; fo that if God fhould
judge rigoroufly, even involuntary fin
would fall under that fentence, *The wages
of fin is death.* This, I muft confefs,
feems to me very incoherent. For if an
action be of that nature, that it cannot
properly be the matter or fubject of a law,
how can it fall under the condemnation of
law ? If it be of that nature that it is incapable of any moral regulation, nor fubject to the influence of reward or punifhment, how can it be, mere matter of
grace that a man is not damned for it ?
In a word, if an action be truly and
properly involuntary, it can by no means
be fin; and if it be voluntary, it is fubject to the regulation of laws: 'tis a
proper inftance of deliberation and freedom, and capable of rewards and punifhments. And the truth is, the one needs
no

no apology, and the other is not capable of any; the one is a mortal fin, and the other no fin at all. And therefore, we muft look for venial fin in fome other fpe-cies of action.

§. 3. The laft clafs of actions are thofe which are of a mixt nature; partly volun-tary, and partly involuntary: and here, I think, we muft place fins of infirmity, by whatever names we may call them. For thefe furely, if they are to be ranked (as by all they are) amongft actual fins, muft be fuch actions as have in them, fomething of voluntary, fomething of in-voluntary, much of human frailty, and fomething of finful; much of unavoidable, and fomething of moral obliquity. Thefe are the trangreffions which the fcripture feems to me, to intend by errors, defects, flips, motes, the fpots of God's children; and thefe certainly, if any, muft be the fins that confift with a ftate of grace. For thefe do not imply a deliberate wick-ednefs in the will, much lefs an habitual one; nay, they do not include in them any *wickednefs* at all, ftrictly fpeaking, but are truly the effects of human frailty, and the unhappy circumftances of this mortal life. Thus then I defcribe a venial fin; it has in it fo much of voluntary as to make it fin, fo much of involuntary as to make it frail-ty;

ty; it has so much of the will in it, that
it is capable of being reduced; and yet so
much of necessity in it, it is never utterly
to be extirpated: it has something in it
criminal enough to oblige us to watch
against it, and repent of it; and yet so
much in it pitiable and excusable, as to
intitle us to pardon under the covenant of
grace. And thus I distinguish venial from
mortal sin: mortal sin proceeds from a
heart, either habitually corrupted, or deceived and captivated for the time; but
venial sin results from the imperfections
and infelicities of our nature, and our state.
Mortal sin is truly voluntary and deliberate
in the rise and birth of it, and mischievous
and injurious in its consequence: but venial sin is very far indeliberate in its beginning, and, if not indulged, almost
harmless in its effects: deficiency is, as it
were, the essence of the one, malignity of
the other; in the one we see more of frailty, in the other more of wickedness: in
the one something nearly allied to necessity, in the other to presumption: the one
is the transgression of the law of Perfection, the other of the law of Sincerity; the
one is repugnant to the letter, the other
to the design and end of the law; the one
is a violation of God's commands, taken in
the most favourable construction, the
other a violation of them in a rigorous
one.

one. That this was the notion of St. *Auſtin*, St. *Jerome*, and others, who impugned the ſinleſs Perfection of the *Pelagians*, is very plain. 1. From the diſtinction they made between Κακία and αμάρτημα, *Crimen* and *Peccatum*, i. e. between wickedneſs and defects, between crimes and faults; for this is plainly the ſenſe wherein they uſed theſe words. And next from thoſe very clear and lively deſcriptions of venial ſin, which occur frequently in St. *Auſtin*; after whom, 'tis well known, others writ. Such is that * *through ignorance or infirmity, for want of exerting out utmoſt ſtrength againſt concupiſcence, we are drawn away by it to ſome unlawful things; and the worſe we are, ſo much the more and the oftener; but the better we are, ſo much the leſs and the ſeldomer do we give way to it.* And thus † St. *Jerome* imputes venial ſin, to our not making uſe of our utmoſt ſtrength and diligence. I might content my ſelf with having given this general deſcription of ſins of infirmity, did I not know, how ill a talent ſome have at applications of generals to any particular caſe; and how little ſatisfactory ſuch account

* ——— *Fit per Ignorantiam vel Infirmitatem non exertis adverſus eam totis viribus voluntatis, eidem ad illicita etiam nonnulla cedamus, tanto magis & crebrius quanto deteriores, tanto minus & rarius quanto meliores ſumus.* Tom. 7. *De* Peccat. Rem. p. 689.

† *Hoc & nos dicimus, poſſe Hominem non peccare, ſi velit, pro tempore, pro loco, pro imbecillitate corporea, quamdiu intentus eſt Animus, quamdiu chorda nullo vitio laxatur in Cithara. Dial.* 3. *adv.* Pelag. p. 201.

count is to the weak and fcrupulous. For
the fake of thefe therefore, I think fit to
be a little more diftinct and particular on
this argument. In venial fins then, two
things muft be confidered.

    1. The matter of it.
    2. The manner of committing it.

    1. As to the matter, I conceive it ought
to be *flight* and *inconfiderable*. There is no
room for a venial fin in things of a crying
provoking nature ; as in adultery, idolatry, murther ; for in thefe, the injuftice
and wickednefs, with refpect to God and
man, is palpable and formidable ; and can
never, for ought I fee, be extenuated by
any circumftances into fins of infirmity.
But when I fay, the matter of the fin of
infirmity muft not be deteftable and crying provocation, I do not mean to extend
this to the firft *tendencies* and *difpofitions*
even towards fuch fins. Thus tho' adultery cannot be a venial fin ; yet the firft fal-
lies of the defire, the firft glances and
wandrings of the eye, may. And the
fame thing may be faid of the firft motions
towards any other fin.
    2. As to the next thing to be confidered
in a venial fin, that is, the *manner* of com-
mitting it, it muft proceed from *ignorance*,
frailty, or *furprife*.

                         1. From

1. From *ignorance.* By ignorance I do not mean that which is utterly *invincible,* but that which has some *defect,* some *frailty,* some *degree* of *negligence* in it. Of this kind, I take those errors to be, against which *David* prays, *Pfalm* xix. 12. *Who can understand his errors? cleanse thou me from secret faults.* He that considers human nature, and the power of education, the influences of prejudices which we suck in betimes, and such like, will easily acknowledge, that there may be such errors. When we have used a *moral diligence* in examining our lives, and trying our own hearts; yet considering the vast variety of duties we are to run through, no humble man can be confident, that he has omitted nothing, that he is mistaken in nothing. This I take to be the sense of *Solomon,* Prov. xx. 9. *Who can say, I have made my heart clean, I am pure from my sin?* And this I take to be the sense of St. *Paul,* 1 Cor. iv. 4. *For I know nothing by my self, yet am I not hereby justified: but he that judgeth me is the Lord.* There are mistakes and errors, which might indeed have been prevented or removed, by the *strictest* impartiality, and the *strictest* diligence. But alas! how often do good men fall short of both these? How common is it for good men to be too far transported by the best of principles, even zeal? How often do good

good men mix their errors in reproof and reprehenfion, and in one and the other, they difcern it not ?

2. *Surprife* and *inadvertency* is another thing that renders fin *venial.* The multitude of affairs and temptations, the fuddennefs and unexpectednefs of fome unufual temptation, or fomething of this kind, may betray a good man into fome flips or errors, in word or deed. This I take to be the cafe of *Sarah*, when fhe faid, *I laughed not :* of *Jonah*, when he replied upon God, *I do well to be angry*, *Jon.* iii. Of *David*, when he pronounced rafhly, *do thou and Zibah divide the land*, 2 *Sam.* xvi. 4. Of *Saul* and *Barnabas*, when they broke out into heat and anger. But that which was a fin of *infirmity* in the beginning, became, I doubt, a *deliberate* one in the end, when they parted from one another. Some extend this circumftance of furprize to excufe fins, which imply notorious wickednefs, and are of very ill confequence; but, I think, very erroneoufly. 'Tis true, thefe fins of furprize, whatever the matter of them be, are generally conceived to be much extenuated through want of opportunity to fummon our ftrength, and to make ufe of mature and fober deliberation; efpecially where the temptation is not *only fudden* but *violent* too. For in this cafe, the foldier

dier of Chrift, taken, as it were, in an ambufh, or blown up with a mine, feems to be loft and defeated before he difcerns his danger : I do not doubt then, but this fuddennefs of a temptation does very much diminifh the guilt of a fin. But we ought to remember too, that there are many things that do abate and take off from this excufe : as firft, it is not eafy to conceive how any thing, that is a direct wickednefs, that is a fin of a deeper dye than ordinary, on the account of its mif-chievous confequences, fhould make its approach fo filently, and fo fuddenly, that we fhould fall into it indifcernibly. Se-condly, The Chriftian is bound to fhun not only every evil, but every *appearance* of it ; and 'tis hard to imagine, that a fincere man, who does indeed ftrain at a *gnat*, fhould fwallow a *camel.* He that preferves the tendernefs of confcience, as he will have an *averfion* for *fmall fins* ; fo will he have an *horror* for *great ones.* Thirdly, The mind of a Chriftian ought to be pof-feffed and awed by the fear of God; and *that* not a flight and tranfient, but a deep and lafting one. The *Pfalmift* was not content to fay, *I am afraid of thy judg-ments* ; but, to exprefs how thoroughly this fear had feized him, he adds, *my flefh trembleth for fear of thee*, Pfal. cxix. And certainly, this fear is a fort of impenetra-

ble

ble armour, which extinguishes all the fiery darts of the devil. In vain is the suddenness, or the briskness of a temptation, unless we first lay aside this shield. Fourthly, We are bound to be always on our watch and guard; and therefore, if we relax our discipline, if we live secure and careless, if we rashly cast our selves upon dangers, our sin then will be but the consequence of our folly; and therefore one error cannot be an excuse, or an apology, for another. I think therefore, the apology of surprize should be confined and limited to *flight* offences; it cannot properly have room in *great* ones, or if it have, it may be urged in *mitigation* of our punishment; but never, I doubt, for *total impunity.*

3. Lastly, Venial sin has its rise from the defects and imperfections of our *nature*, and the disadvantagious circumstances of our *state.* Here come in the failures and defects in the *measures* and *degrees* of duty; if these can be properly reckoned for sins: I say, if they can; for I do not see that this is a good argument: we are bound to the highest degree of love by that law. *Thou shalt love the Lord thy God with all thy heart*; therefore whatsoever falls short of the highest and most absolute degree of love, is a sin: for at this rate, whatever were short of

Per-

Perfection, would be fin. We muft love, nothing better than God, nothing equal to him: this will conftitute us in a ftate of fincerity. What is farther required is, that we are bound to *aim* at, and *purfue* after the higheft and moft perfect degrees of love; but we are not bound under pain of *damnation* to *attain* them. But on the other hand, I readily grant, that our falling fhort in the degrees of faith, love, hope, and the like, may be properly reckoned amongft fins, when they fpring from the defects of vigilance and induftry: and if thefe defects be fuch as can confift with fincerity, then are the imperfections or the abatements of our virtues, pardonable; and then only. Here again fall in *omiffions, wandring thoughts, dulnefs* and *heavinefs* in duty, the fhort *titillations* of fome *irregular fancies, forgetfulnefs,* flight and fhort *fits* of *envy, difcontent, anger, ambition, gaiety* of mind. Thus we find the difciples falling afleep when they fhould have prayed, *Mat.* xxvi. and *David* praying *quicken thou me,* Pfal. cxix. Thus his foul too was often caft down, and difquieted within him, *Pfal.* xlii. 2 *Chron.* xxx. 18, 19. *Job* curfed the day of his birth. In fhort, our natures are *human,* not *angelical*; and our ftate is fo full of variety of accidents, that they are too apt to difcompofe the mind, and divert it from its great end. The ebbs and flows of blood and

Y   fpirits,

spirits, and an unlucky conftitution, or a diftemper ; the multitude or confufion of affairs; the violence or the length of trials; the eafe and flattery of profperity; the wearinefs of. the body, or of the mind ; the incommodioufnefs of fortune, rough- nefs of converfation; thefe, and a thoufand other things, are apt to produce defects and failures in our obedience, fhort difor- ders in our affections; and fuch emotions and eruptions as abundantly prove the beft to be but men ; and the higheft Perfection, if it be but human, to be wanting and de- fective. I think I have now omitted no- thing neceffary to form a true notion of the fin of infirmity. My next bufinefs there- fore is, to confider,

§. 3. How far the *liberty* of the perfect man, in refpect of *venial fin*, ought to be extended. There is great affinity between venial and original fin; and therefore the perfect man's liberty, as it relates to the one and the other, confifts in much the fame degrees, and is to be attained by the fame method; fo that I might well enough dif- mifs this fubject, and pafs on to mortal fin. But reflecting on the nature of man, how prone we are to fin, and yet how apt we are to think well of our felves, I judge it neceffary to guard the doctrine of venial fin by fome few rules, which may at once ferve serve to secure our sincerity, and point out the Perfection we are to aspire to. 1*st*, then, If we would prevent any fatal event of sins flowing from *ignorance*, we must take care, that our ignorance it self be not *criminal*; and that it will not be, if our hearts be sincerely disposed to do our duty, and if we use moral diligence to know it: if we be impartial, humble, and honest, and have that concern for the knowledge and practice of our duty, that is in some sort proportionable to the importance of it. The ignorance that arises from natural incapacity, or want of sufficient revelation, is *invincible*; and therefore *innocent*, John ix. 41. *Jesus said unto them, if ye were blind, ye should have no sin ; but now ye say, we see ; therefore your sin remaineth:* and xv. 22. *If I had not come and spoken unto them, they had not had sin: but now they have no cloak for their sins.* This rule must be understood of *necessary* knowledge in general; and more *legible* and *conspicuous* lines of duty : both which notwithstanding, there may be room for sins of infirmity to enter, where mortal ones cannot; there may be imperfect dispositions of mind, and latent prejudices; there may be instances of duty of a slighter moment ; there may be several circumstances, and small emergencies that may either be without the aim, or escape the discovery of a mo-

Y 2 ral

ral fearch, that is, of a human one; which, tho' it be without *hypocrify*, is not yet without more or lefs *frailty*. As to Perfection; it differs in this, as it does in other cafes, from fincerity, only in the degrees by which it is advanced above it. He that will be perfect, muft fearch for wifdom as for hid treafures: his delight muft be in the law of the Lord, and in his law muft he meditate day and night: his thirft of truth muft be more eager and impatient, his diligence more wakeful, more circumfpect, more particular, more fteady and conftant, than that of the beginner; or of one who is no farther advanced, than fuch meafures of faith and love, as are indifpenfably neceffary to fincerity, will carry him. 2*dly*, Sins that are occafioned by *furprize* and *inadvertency*, will not prove deftructive, if the *inadvertency* it felf be in a manner *innocent*: that is, firft, there is no room for inadvertency in compleat acts of crying fins. Secondly, there is no pretence for inadvertency, if we had any mifgivings within, or warnings without concerning that particular fin, into which we fell afterwards; much lefs if we cherifh ill motions till they grow too ftrong for us. And laft of all, if we repeat the fame fin frequently and contemptuoufly. And to this I may add; he cannot be faid to fin through furprize, who throws him-

felf

felf into the way of temptation, even tho'
he be confcious of his own infirmity. 3*dly*,
As to thofe moral defects which flow from
natural infirmity ; they will not deftroy us,
if the infirmity it felf be pardonable.
There are infirmities, which we acquire ;
infirmities, which grow ftronger by indulgence ; infirmities, which continue merely
becaufe we do not take pains to fubdue
them : our moral defects muft not flow
from thefe kinds of infirmities ; but from
fuch as, confidering human nature, and the
ftate of this world, 'tis impoffible utterly
to root out. Thefe moral defects will do
us no harm; if, firft, we take care to
fettle in our minds the habits of thofe virtues that are directly oppofite to them.
Secondly, If we watch and fight againft
our natural infirmities; and endeavour to
reduce our appetites, even our natural appetites, within ftrict and narrow bounds.
Thirdly, If we wafh off the ftains of our
flips and defects by a general repentance :
for upon the notion I have here given of
venial fin, repentance appears to be very
neceffary : for I require in them fomething of voluntary, fomething of freedom ; enough to make an action finful,
tho' not to prove the heart corrupt or
wicked. And becaufe the degrees of voluntary and involuntary are not fo eafily
diftinguifhable from one another, 'tis plain

our

our best security against any ill consequence of our defects and frailties, is a godly sorrow. And therefore I wonder not if *David* charge himself more severely than God does, *My sins are more in number than the hairs of my head.* This was a confession that became the humility and solicitude of a penitent ; that became the reflections of a wise and perfect man, and the corruption of human nature ; the alloy of human performances ; the slips and defects, the interruptions, neglect, and deviations of the best life.

C H A P. VI.

Of liberty, *as it imports freedom or deliverance from* mortal sin. *What mortal sin is. How the perfect man must be free from it. And which way this* liberty *may be best attained ; with some rules for the attainment of it.*

HERE I will inquire into three things ;.

1. What mortal sin is ; or what kind of sins they be, which are on all hands acknowledged to be inconsistent with a state of grace and favour.

2. How

2. How far the perfect man muſt be ſet free or delivered from this kind of ſins; or how remote he is from the guilt of them.

3. Which way this liberty may be beſt attained.

§. 1. The firſt thing neceſſary is, to ſtate the notion of that ſin, which paſſes under the name of *mortal, wilful, preſumptuous,* or *deliberate* ſin: for theſe in writers are equivalent terms, and promiſcuouſly uſed to ſignify one and the ſame thing. *Sin* (ſaith St. *John*, 1 *Ep.* iii. 4.) *is the tranſgreſſion of the law.* This is a plain and full definition too of ſin: for the law of God is the rule of moral actions; 'tis the ſtandard and meaſure of right and wrong, of moral good and evil. Whatever is not within the compaſs of the law, is not within the compaſs of morality neither: Whatever cannot be comprehended within this definition, cannot have in it the entire and compleat notion of ſin; or, which is all one, it cannot be ſin, in a ſtrict, proper, and adequate ſenſe of the word. Hence St. *John* in the ſame verſe tells us, that *whoſoever ſinneth, tranſgreſſeth the law.* And St. *Paul.* Rom. iv. 15. *Where there is no law, there is no tranſgreſſion.* Sin then muſt always ſuppoſe a law; without which there can be

Y 4   neither

neither vice nor virtue, righteoufnefs nor
wickednefs : for thefe are nothing elfe
but the violation or obfervation of the
law of God ; or habits and ftates refulting from the one or the other. But this is
not all : two things more muft be remar-
ked, to render this definition, which the
apoftle gives us of fin, clear and full. Firft,
The law muft be *fufficiently revealed.* Secondly, The tranfgreffion of it muft be
truly *voluntary.*

1. By fufficient revelation of a divine
law, every one underftands, that the law
muft be fo publifhed to the man who
is to be governed by it, that the *authority*
and *fenfe* of it may be, if it be not his
own fault, rendered evident to him. If
the divine authority of any rule or precept be doubtful and uncertain, the obligation of it will be fo too : and it is as neceffary that the fenfe of the law fhould be
evident, as its authority. The law, that
is penned in dark and ambiguous terms,
is, properly fpeaking, no law at all; fince
the mind of the Lawgiver is not fufficiently made known by it. Whatever is neceffarily to be forborn or done by us, muft be
fully and clearly prefcribed in the law of
God ; and if it be not, it can never be neceffary. Men through weaknefs or defign
may enact laws that are but a heap of
letters, a croud of dubious *Delphick*
fenten-

fentences: but God can never do fo, becaufe this is repugnant both to his wifdom
and goodnefs, and to the very end of a law
too, which is to be a rule, not a fnare;
'tis *to give underftanding to the fimple*; to
be *a light to our feet, and a lamp to our
paths*; not like an *Ignis fatuus*, to betray
us into brakes and precipices, and ruin, and
death.

2. The tranfgreffion muft be a *voluntary*
one. And this imports two things: 1. A
knowledge of the law. 2. Confent to the
breach of it. Firft, As to the knowledge
of the law. All that I have to fay here
in a few words, is, that ignorance of the
law excufes a tranfgreffion, when it is it
felf excufable; but if the ignorance it felf
be criminal, the effect of it muft be fo
too. We muft never think of excufing
our fins, by alledging an ignorance into
which, not our own incapacity, or any other
reafonable caufe, but neglect or contempt
of the truth, or fome other vicious luft or
paffion, has betrayed us. Secondly, As to
the confent of the will; this is neceffary
to demonftrate any action finful or virtuous; without this the mind will be no
partner in the fin, and by confequence
cannot be involved in the guilt of it.
Whatever we cannot help, is our misfortune, not our fault; actions merely natural, or merely forced, can neither be good
nor

nor evil. The concurrence of reafon and choice is indifpenfably neceffary to the morality of an action. All this is plainly taught us by St. *James* i. 14, 15. *But every man is tempted, when he is drawn away of his own luft, and enticed. Then when luft hath conceived, it bringeth forth fin; and fin when it is finifhed, bringeth forth death.* Which words do certainly imply, that the fpring and principle of fin is within our felves; that 'tis our natural corruption that entices and allures us; and 'tis our confent to its enticements that gives being to fin, and defiles us with guilt.

From all this now put together 'tis eafy to conclude what fort of a defcription we are to form of *mortal fin*: 'tis fuch a tranfgreffion of the law of God, as is *vicious* in its *original, deliberate* in its *commiffion*, and *mifchievous* in its *tendencies* or *effects*: the heart is corrupted and mifled by fome luft or other, and fo confents to the breach of the moral law of God, a law of eternal and immutable goodnefs: or if the fin confifts in the breach of any pofitive law, it muft yet imply in it fome moral obliquity in the will, or in the tendency of the action, or both. So that prefumptuous, or mortal fin, call in by what name we will, is a *deliberate* tranfgreffion of a *known* law of God, tending to the *difhonour* of God, the *injury*

ry of our *neighbour*, or the *depravation* of
our *nature.* Such are thofe fins which the
prophet *Ifaiah* exhorts thofe who will repent, to ceafe from. And fuch are thofe
we have a catalogue of, *Eph.* v. *Gal.* v.
and elfewhere : *Now the works of the flefh
are manifeft, which are thefe, adultery, fornication, uncleannefs, lafcivioufnefs, idolatry,
witchcraft, hatred, variance, emulations,
wrath, ftrife, feditions, herefies, envyings,
murders, drunkennefs, revellings, and fuch
like.* Thefe are the fins, of which, as of
fo many members, the body of fin confifts:
thefe conftitute the old man : thefe are
fometimes called, *the filthinefs of the flefh
and fpirit, ungodlinefs, wickednefs, iniquity,
the lufts of the flefh, worldly lufts,* and fuch
like. Thefe and the like fins have, as I
faid, in them very apparent fymptoms of
malignity and mortality : they are always the effect of fome carnal and worldly lufts, prevailing over the law of the
mind ; and they imply a contempt of
God, injuftice to our neighbour, and fome
kind of defilement and pollution of our
nature. And that thefe are the plain indications of fuch a guilt as excludes a man
from heaven and the favour of God, is
very plain from the account which the
fcripture gives us both of the origin and
influence of fin; from the care it takes to
fortify the heart againft all infection ;
from

from the conftant reprefentations it makes us of the fhamefulnefs and the mifchief of fin, even in reference to this world as well as the other. I cannot fee any thing further neceffary to the explication of deliberate or prefumptuous fin, unlefs it be here fit to add, that it is mortal, though it proceed no further than the heart : there is no need at all that it fhould be brought forth into action, to render it fatal and damnable. This is evident, not only from the nature of divine worfhip, which muft be entire, fincere, and fpiritual; and therefore can no more be reconciled to the wickednefs of our hearts, than of our actions ; but alfo from the exprefs words of our Saviour, *Out of the heart proceed fornication, adultery, theft*, &c. And elfewhere he pronounces the adultery of the *heart damnable*, as well as that of the *body*, Mat. v. 28. *But I fay unto you, that whofoever looketh upon a woman to luft after her, hath committed adultery already with her in his heart.*

§. 2. I am next to give fome account of the liberty of the perfect man, in reference to the fin I have been difcourfing of. I fhall not need to ftop at any general or preliminary obfervations ; as, that abftinence from fin regards all the commandments of God alike ; and to do otherwife,

wife, were to mutilate and maim religion, and to diſhonour God, while we pretend to worſhip and obey him : for the breach of any ſingle commandment is a manifeſt violation of the majeſty and authority of God, whatever obſervance we may pay all the reſt : *For he that ſaid, Do not commit adultery ; ſaid alſo, Do not kill. Now if thou commit no adultery, yet if thou kill, thou art become a tranſgreſſor of the law,* Jam. ii. 11. That the reſtraints man is to lay upon himſelf, relate no leſs to the *luſts* of the *ſoul* than the *actions* of the *body : Except your righteouſneſs exceed the righteouſneſs of the Scribes and Phariſees, you ſhall by no means enter into the kingdom of heaven,* Matth. v. 10. That to begin well will avail us little, unleſs we finiſh well too. Univerſality, ſincerity, and perſeverance are generally acknowledged to be eſſential and indiſpenſable properties of ſaving, juſtifying faith. Theſe things therefore being but juſt mentioned, I proceed to the point to be enquired into and reſolved.

1. To be free from the *dominion* and *power* of mortal ſin, is the firſt and loweſt ſtep; this is indiſpenſable to ſincerity, and abſolutely neceſſary to ſalvation : *Let not ſin reign in your mortal bodies, to fulfil the luſts thereof,* Rom. vi. 12. And the advancing thus far does, I acknowledge, conſtitute man in a ſtate of grace : for

in fcripture men are denominated righteous or wicked, not from fingle acts of
vice or virtue, but from the prevalence
and dominion, from the habit or cuftom
of the one or the other : *Know ye not, that*
to whom ye yield your felves fervants to obey,
his fervants ye are to whom ye obey; whether
of fin unto death, or of obedience unto righ-
teoufnefs? Rom. vi. 16. But then I muft
here add two remarks, by way of caution. 1. We muft not prefume too foon
of victory over an habitual fin. An evil
habit is not foon broken off; nor is it an
eafy matter to refolve, when we have fet
our felves free from the power of it.
Sometimes the temptation does not prefent itfelf as often as it was wont, or not
with the fame advantage; fometimes one
vice reftrains us from another; fometimes
worldly confiderations, or fome little
change in our temper, without any thorough change in our minds, puts us out of
humour for a little while with a darling
fin; and fometimes the force and clear-
nefs of conviction, produces fome pious
fits, which, though they do not utterly
vanquifh a luft, do yet force it to give
way, and retreat for a while, and *inter-*
rupt that love which they do not *extin-*
guifh : all this may be, and the work not
yet be done, nor our liberty yet gained.
If therefore we fall, though but now and
                                        then,

then, and though at fome diftance of time, into the fame fin, we have great reafon to be jealous of its power and our fafety : nay, though we reftrain our felves from the outward commiffion of it ; if yet we feel a ftrong propenfion to it; if we difcern our felves ready to take fire on the appearance of a temptation ; if we are fond of approaching as near it as we can, and are pleafed with thofe indulgences which are very near a-kin to it, we have reafon to doubt that our conqueft is not yet entire. nay, the truth is, we cannot be on good grounds affured that we are mafters of our felves, till we have a fettled averfion for the fin which before we doated on, and fhun the occafions which before we courted, till we be poffeffed of a habit of that virtue which is a direct contradiction to it ; and take as much pleafure in the obedience, as ever we did in the tranfgreffion of a divine command.

2dly, Thefe are fome fins of that provoking nature, fo criminal in their birth, and mifchievous in their confequences, that one fingle *act* or *commiffion* of one of thefe is equivalent to a *habit* of others ; fuch is murther, idolatry, perjury, adultery ; thefe cannot be commited without renouncing *humanity* as well as *Chriftianity* ; without refifting the inftincts and impulfe of nature, as well as the light of the gofpel,

fpel, and the grace of the Spirit. We muft break through a great many difficulties and terrors, ere we can come at thefe fins; we muft commit *many* other, in order to commit one of thefe ; we muft deliberate long, refolve defperately, and in defiance of God and confcience ; and what is the *effect* of habit in other inftances, is a neceffary *preparative* in thefe, that is, *obduration.* In this cafe, therefore, the unhappy man, that has been guilty of any one of thefe, muft not look upon himfelf as fet free, when he is come to a refolution of never repeating it again; but then when he loaths and abhors himfelf in duft and afhes; when he has made the utmoft reparations of the wrong he is capable of ; when, if the intereft of virtue require it, he is content to be oppreffed with fhame and fufferings: when, in one word, a long and conftant courfe of mortification, prayers, tears and good works have wafhed off the ftain and guilt.

2. We muft be free, not only from a *habit*, but from fingle *acts* of deliberate prefumptuous fin. The reafon is plain ; mortal fin cannot be committed without wounding the confcience, grieving the fpirit, and renouncing our hopes in God through Chrift, for the time at leaft. *The wages of fin is death*, is true, not only of habits, but fingle acts of deliberate fin.

Death

death is the penalty, the fanction of every
commandment ; and the commandment
does not prohibit habits only, but fingle
acts too. Nor is there indeed any room
to doubt or difpute here, but in one cafe ;
which is, if a righteous man fhould be taken off in the very commiffion of a fin,
which he has fallen into. Here, indeed,
much may be faid, and with much uncertainty. But the refolution of this point
does not, as far as I can fee, minifter to
any good or neceffary end ; and therefore
I will leave it to God. In all other cafes,
every thing is clear and plain; for if the
fervant of God fall into a prefumptuous fin,
'tis univerfally acknowledged, that he cannot recover his ftation but by repentance.
If he repent prefently, he is fafe ; but if
he continue in his fin, if he repeat it, he
paffes into a ftate of wickednefs, widens
the breach between God and his foul, declines infenfibly into a habit of fin, and
renders his wound more. and more incurable. 'Tis to little purpofe, I think, here
to confider the vaft difference there is in
the commiffion, even of the fame fin, between a child of God, and a child of wrath ;
becaufe a child of God muft not commit it
at all : if he do, tho' it be with reluctancy ; tho' it be, as it were, with an imperfect confent, and with a divided foul; tho'
the awe of religion and confcience feems

Z

not

not utterly to have forſaken him, even in the midſt of his ſin; tho' his heart ſmite him the very minute it is finiſhed, and repentance and remorſe take off the reliſh of the unhappy draught; yet ſtill 'tis ſin; 'tis in its nature damnable: and nothing but the blood of Jeſus can purge the guilt.

3. The perfeɛt man may be ſuppoſed, not only aɛtually to abſtain from mortal ſin, but to be advanced ſo far in the mortification of all his inordinate affeɛtions, as to do it with *eaſe* and *pleaſure*, with *conſtancy* and *delight*. For it muſt reaſonably be preſumed, that his viɛtory over ungodly and worldly luſt, is more confirmed and abſolute; his abhorrence of them, more deep and ſenſible, more fixt and laſting, than that of a beginner or babe in Chriſt. The regenerate at firſt fears the conſequence of ſin; but by degrees he hates the ſin it ſelf. The purity of his ſoul renders him now incapable of finding any pleaſure in what he doted on before; and the love of God and virtue raiſeth him above the temptations which he was wont to fall by: *Old things are paſt away, and all things are become new.*

4. Laſtly, The perfeɛt man's abſtinence is not only more *eaſy* and *ſteady*, but more *intire* and *compleat* alſo than that of others: he has a regard to the end and deſign

defign of the law; to the perfection of his nature; to the purity and elevation of his foul; and therefore he expounds the prohibitions of the law in the moft enlarged fenfe, and interprets them by a fpirit of faith and love. He is not content to refrain from actions directly criminal, but fhuns every appearance of evil; and labours to mortify all the difpofitions and tendencies of his nature towards it; and to decline whatever circumftances of life are apt to betray the foul into a love of this world, or the body: he has crucified the world, and the body too. That pleafure, that honour, that power, that profit, which captivates the finner, tempts, and tries, and difquiets the novice, is but a burthen, a trouble to him: he finds no guft, no relifh in thefe things. He is fo far from intemperance, fo far from wantonnefs, fo far from pride and vanity, that could be without any difadvantage to the intereft of religion; he would imitate the meannefs, the plainnefs, the laborioufnefs, the felf-denial of our Saviour's life; not only in difpofition and affection of his foul, but even in his outward ftate and deportment; and would prefer it far above the pomp and fhew of life. In one word, he inquires not how far he may *enjoy* and be *fafe*, but how far he may *deny* himfelf and be *wife*: he is fo far from

defiring

defiring forbidden fatisfactions, that he is unwilling and afraid to find too much fatisfaction in the natural and neceffary actions of an animal life. I need not prove this to any one who has read the foregoing chapters : for it is what I have been doing throughout this treatife. It is nothing, but what is confonant to the whole tenour of the fcripture ; and to the example of the beft times. And 'tis conformable to what the beft authors have writ, who have any thing of life and fpirit in their works ; or have any true notion of the great defign of the Chriftian religion, which is an heavenly converfation. Let any one but caft his eyes on St. *Bafil*, or any other after him, who aimed at the fame thing I now do, the promoting holinefs in the world in the beauty and perfection of it ; and he will acknowledge, that I am far from having carried this mater too high. I will quote but one or two paffages of St. *Bafil* ; (a) his defcription of the perfect man with regard to his felf-denial runs thus. He is one that confults the *neceffities*, not the *pleafure* of his nature ; and feems to grudge the time which he beftows on the fupport and nourifhment of a corruptible body. He is fo far from looking upon eating and drinking, &c. as an enjoyment, that he rather accounts it a task or troublefome fervice.

(a) Μόλις ἢ ἐπ μικρον τ ἀναγκαίων ἀπτόμενον. Καὶ ὡς λιτυργίαν ἐπαχθῆ ἀποτελούντα τῇ φύσει, ἢ δυσχεραίνοντα μὲν τῷ καιρῷ τῆς ἀεὶ ταῦτα διατριβῆς. Ὅροι κτ' πλάτος. p. 454.

service which the frailty of his nature demands at his hands. Nor was this great man more severe against the lusts of the flesh, than against those other branches of the love of the world, the lust of the eyes, and the pride of life. (*b*) All vanity and affectation of praise and respect; all the oftentation (*faith he*) and shew of life, is utterly unlawful for a Christian. And all this is directly consonant to his gloss (*c*) on those words of St. *Paul, They that use the world as not abusing it.* Whatever is beyond *use* is *abuse*; directly consonant to his definition of temperance. (*d*) That it is the extirpation of sin; the extermination of unruly passions, and the mortification of the body, extending even to the *natural* appetites and affections of it.

I know not what scruples or mistakes the doctrine I here advance concerning this part of my perfect man's liberty, may be encountered with: but I am confident, I have given no just occasion for any. I do not say of the perfect, with *Jovinian*, that they cannot fall; but I say, that they may, and ought to stand; and, if it be not their own fault, will do so. I do not affirm of them, as the hereticks in *Vincen-*

Z 3
tius

(*b*) Ἡ κενοδοξία, κỳ ἡ ἀνθρωπαρέσκεια, κỳ τὸ πρὸς ἐπίδειξιν τι ποιεῖν, ὅλως ὅπῃ παντὸς πράγματ⊙ Χριστιανοῖς ἀπηγόρευται. p. 456.

(*c*) Παράχρησις δὲ ἐστὶν ἡ ὑπὲρ τ Χρειαν δαπάνη. p. 457.

(*d*) Ἐστὶν ὂν ἡ Ἐγκράτεια, ἁμαρτίας ἀναίρεσις, παθῶν ἀπαλλοτρίωσις, σώματος νέκρωσις, μέχρι κỳ αὐτῶν φυσικῶν παθημάτων τε κỳ ἐπιθυμίων. pag. 445.

tius Lyrinenſis did of their party, that are
privileged from ſin by a peculiar grace
and tranſcendent favour; but I affirm,
that they ſhall not want grace to preſerve
them from it, unleſs they be wanting to
themſelves. I do not go about to maintain, that God ſees no ſin in his children ;
but I maintain, that mortal ſin, is not the
ſport of his children. But do not I in
this fall in with the *Papiſts,* who aſſert
the poſſibility of keeping the commands
of God? I anſwer, that taking them in
the ſenſe, in which they themſelves in the
conference at *Ratisbone* defend this doctrine, I do. They there tell us, that, when
they talk thus, they take the law or commands of God, not in a ſtrict and rigid,
but in a favourable and equitable, *i. e.* a
goſpel conſtruction : and this is ſo far
from being heterodox, that *Davenant* accounts it a plain giving up the queſtion in
controverſy. But am I not run into the
error of the *Pelagians* and *Quakers ?* I anſwer, if the one or the other aſſert, that
the perfect man paſſes thorough the whole
courſe of life without falling into any ſin ;
or, that in the beſt part of life, he is im-
peccable, and not ſubject to ſin (as in the
heat of diſputation their adverſaries ſeem
ſometimes to faſten on them) I am at a
wide diſtance from them. But if they
teach,

teach, that the perfect man has grace and strength enough to forbear wilful sin, and that many actually do so, I am, I must confess, exactly of their mind. But then I am, at the same time, of the same mind with St. *Austin*, and St. *Jerome* too ; for they teach the very same doctrine : for they never contended about the possibility of freedom or deliverance from *mortal* sin, but only from *venial.* St. *Jerome* * shall explain his own sense, *Etenim absque vitio, quod græce dicitur* Κακί·, *hominem posse esse aio :* Ἀναμάϱτητοι, *id est, sine Peccato, esse nego.* Which is the same thing that St. *Austin* commonly admits ; that man may be *fine Crimine*, but not *fine Peccato*; without mortal, but not without venial sin. And in this, they are certainly of the mind of the scripture ; which every-where represents the perfect man, as holy, blameless, undefiled, without spot, walking with God : and, in one word, as free from sin. If any man can reconcile these texts, which are very numerous, with mortal sin, I will not say in the best state of the best men, but a state of sincerity and regeneration, I will acknowe ledge my mistake. But till then I connot but think, the doctrine I advance, necessary to establish the true notion of holiness, and convince us of our obligation to it. This doctrine

* *Dial. Secund. ad Pelag.* p. 189.

is

is again neceffary to wipe off thofe afperfi-
ons and calumnies the *Quakers* caft upon
our Church; as if it held, that the regenerate themfelves may continue in their fins;
nay, cannot be freed from them. Our
Church teaches indeed (*Artic.* 4.) that the
moft perfect men are never utterly exempt
from defects, failings, and human infirmities; and I believe they themfelves are not
confident enough to teach otherwife: only
they will not call thefe infirmities fins: and
and then the whole controverfy is reduced
to this; we agree in the thing, but differ in
the name: and in this difference, we are
not only on the humbler, but the fafer fide
too: for acknowledging them fins, we fhall
be the better difpofed fure, to be forry for
them, to beg pardon for them, and watch
againft them.

The fruit of this liberty has been fufficiently accounted for in *chap.* 3. And therefore I proceed.

§. 3. To propofe fome rules for the attainment of it.

1. The mind muft be grounded and
rooted in the faith; it muft be thoroughly
convinced and perfuaded of thefe great articles of the Chriftian religion, That there
is a God, and fuch a God, a holy, juft,
omnifcient, and omnipotent one; the in-
carnation,

carnation, suffering and glory of the blessed Jesus; a judgment to come, and the eternal rewards and punishments of another life. The firm belief of these things does naturally promote these two effects. 1. It will awaken a sinner out of his lethargy and security; it will disturb him in his sinful enjoyments, and fill his mind with guilty fears, and uneasy reflections. And when the man finds no rest, no security in his sins, this will naturally oblige him to endeavour the conquest of them. But then we must not stifle and suppress these thoughts; we must give conscience full liberty; we must hear the dictates of our own minds patiently; and consider seriously those terrible truths, which they lay before us; till we go from this exercise deeply impressed with such notions as these: that our sins, sooner or later, will certainly bring upon us temporal and eternal misery: that nothing but sincere righteousness can produce true and lasting happiness: that it is a dreadful danger to dally too long with indignation, or presume too far on the mercy of a just, and holy, and almighty God: that the neglecting the great salvation, tender'd by the gospel, and procured by the blessed Jesus; the slighting the blood of the covenant, and grieving the Holy Spirit (all which we do by wilful sin) is a guilt, that will sink down the

obstinate

obftinate finner into the loweft hell; and render his condition more intolerable than that of *Tyre* and *Sidon*, *Sodom* and *Gomorrah*. 2. The fecond effect of the firm belief of thefe gofpel truths, is, that it begets in us a contempt of this world, and all the things of it. To him that believes; how fhort is time compared to eternity? how falfe, how empty are the pleafures of fin, compared with thofe of heaven? how infignificant the efteem or love of man to that of God? how worthlefs are all our worldly hopes and pretenfions in refpect of an intereft in Jefus? Now the foul, that is once thoroughly poffeffed with thefe notions, what will it not do, what will it not fuffer, rather than fall fhort of, or forfeit its crown? In what ftate will it not be contented; nay, in what ftate will it not abound in joy, whilft it holds faft the ftedfaftnefs of its hope, and is fecure of the love of Jefus? Here begins that purity of heart, which is the fountain of true Epicurifm; that greatnefs of mind, which alone is true honour and fortitude. But, that faith may have thefe effects upon us, it muft not be only a *true*, but a *lively* faith: therefore my

2. Second Rule, or, if you pleafe, another branch of the former rule, fhall be this. They that will be free indeed, muft not only believe the great truths of the gofpel,

gofpel, but muſt frequently and ſeriouſly ponder them, till they have imprinted in themſelves as clear, diſtinct and perfect *idea's* of them as we are capable of. This will ſoon mortify the appetites of the body, correct our falſe opinions of worldly things : and baffle all the ſophiſtry and confidence of luſt. A lively faith, is a faith that imparts the moſt clear and natural, the moſt full and enlarged notions of its objects; a faith, that not only looks upon the articles of our creed as true, but beholds them in a manner as preſent; and ſo repreſented and drawn to the life, that they fill the ſoul with great and moving conſiderations. This faith does not only believe that there is a God; but it beholds him, and walks before him as preſent ; it ſees him arrayed in all his glory, and in all his majeſty, in all the power and all the terrors, in all the beauties and all the graces of the divine Nature : it does not only believe, that there are rewards and puniſhments ; but is extremely ſenſible of the terrors of the one, and attractions of the other; and looks upon both as at the door. It does not only acknowledge a Mediator; but takes a full view of the miſery of that ſtate, wherein we lay thro' ſin; and of the bleſſedneſs of that, into which we are tranſlated by the redemption, which is in Jeſus. It contemplates this Mediator in

all

all the several steps of condescension and humiliation; in all the tenderness and transports of his passion; in all the melancholy scenes of his sufferings, and the bright and chearful ones of his glory. This is the faith that sets us free.

3. We must not stop in faith, till it be made perfect in love. We must meditate divine truths till they have fired our souls; till they have enkindled our affections; till we be possessed by an ardent love of God, of Jesus, of righteousness, and of heaven; till all our other desires and passions be converted into, and swallowed up of love; till God becomes the center of our souls; and in him we rest, in him we glory, and in him we rejoyce. O love! how great and glorious are the things that are said of thee! 'tis thou who dost impregnate and animate faith itself: 'tis thou who dost surmount the difficulties of duty, and make the yoke of Christ easy, and his burden light: 'tis thou, who dost cast out fear, and make religion full of pleasure: 'tis thou, that dost make us watchful against temptations, and impatient under the interruptions of duty: 'tis thou, that makest us disrelish the pleasures of this world, and long to be dissolved and to be with Christ. Here is the liberty of the sons of God. Blessed are they, even in this world, who attain it. But one caution

I

I muſt here add, that our love muſt not be a *flaſh*, a *fit*; but a ſteddy and well-ſetled affection; an affection that has the *warmth* of *paſſion*, and the *firmneſs* of *habit*. We muſt therefore, by repeated meditations and prayers, daily nouriſh this flame of the altar, and not ſuffer it to go out.

4. We muſt never be at reſt, till we have poſſeſſed our minds with a perfect *hatred* of the ſin which we are moſt ſubject to: The love of God, his long-ſuffering and forbearance, the ſufferings of Jeſus, the ſtruglings of the ſpirit, the peace and pleaſure of holineſs, the guilt and vexation, the ſhame and puniſhment of ſin, its ill influence on our preſent perfection and happineſs, on our peace and hopes, are proper topicks to effect this. A thorough hatred of ſin, once ſetled and rooted in us, will produce that ſorrow, that indignation, that watchfulneſs, that zeal, which will remove us far enough, not only from the ſin, but alſo from the ordinary temptations to it; and place us almoſt without the danger of a relapſe.

To this fourth rule, I ſhould add this other: that when once a man has reſolved upon a new courſe of life, whatever difficulties he finds in his way, whatever baffles he meets with, he muſt never quit the deſign of virtue and life; he muſt never give over fighting till he conquer:
the

the reafon is plain, for he muft either *conquer* or *die*. But this belonging rather to perfeverance in virtue, than the beginning of it, therefore I but juft mention it.

5. It will not be imprudent in this moral, as in phyfical cures, to obferve diligently, and follow the motions and tendencies of nature. Where there are feeds of generofity and honour; the turpitude and fhame of fin, the bafenefs and ingratitude of it, the love of God and of Jefus, and fuch like, are fit topicks to dwell upon. Where fear is more apt to prevail, there the terrors of the Lord are the moft powerful motives: and fo whatever the frame and conftitution of nature be, it will not be difficult to find arguments in the gofpel adapted to it, which will be fo much the more *prevalent*, as they are the more *natural*.

6. Laftly, We muft ufe all means to obtain the Spirit of God; and to increafe and cherifh his influence: we muft ask, and feek, and knock, *i e*. we muft pray, and meditate, and travel with patience and with importunity, that our heavenly Father may give us his Holy Spirit: and, when we have it, we muft not grieve it by any deliberate fin; nor quench it by fecurity or negligence, by fenfual freedoms and prefumption; but we muft cherifh

every

every motion, improve every defire and paffion that it works in us; we muft fhun every appearance of evil; we muft prefs on towards perfeftion; we muft watch unto prayer; we muft fpend the time of our fojourning here in fear; we muft rejoyce and glory in the Lord; and we muft wait for the bleffed hope, and the glorious appearance of the great God, and our Saviour Chrift Jefus. And now I have finifhed what I had to fay on this fubjeft, of the perfeft man's liberty as it relates to mortal or. wilful fin: I have fhewed what this fin is; and how far man may be freed from it, referring the reader to *chap. 4.* for the fruit of this freedom. I have here, laftly, given that advice which I thought moft ferviceable to the attainment of it. And through this whole chapter, I have had regard, not only to perfeftion, but fincerity; it being indeed improper to do otherwife, fince we cannot arrive at the one, but through the other. For fincerity is Perfeftion in its infancy or non-age; and Perfeftion is nothing elfe but fincerity cultivated by meditation and difcipline, and cherifhed by the the influence of heaven. And now let no man's heart fail him, while he contemplates the difficulties which block up the way to his liberty. The way indeed is fteep, and the top is high; but ferenity

and

and happiness, security and glory dwell
there. Many indeed are the temptations
which would forbid our ascent, and thrust
us down; but we are armed all over; they
cannot hurt us; the Spirit supports and encourages us; and nothing but our cowardise and inconstancy can prevent our success: *Watch ye, stand fast, quit ye like men,
be strong;* and then you shall be sure to
conquer and enter into rest.

C H A P. VII.

*Of unfruitfulness, as it consists in idleness.
Idleness, either habitual or accidental.
Considerations to deter men from the sin of
idleness.*

UNfruitfulness is a fit subject to conclude
a discourse of *liberty* with, or begin
one of *zeal*; for lying, like a tract of
ground, between two bordering kingdoms, it may indifferently be laid to either.
As it implies a direct opposition to spiritual life and sincerity, it naturally falls in
under the consideration of zeal: as it implies a servile subjection to some vile lust
or other, it naturally falls in under the
consideration of liberty: so that by al-
lotting it this place, I shall at once compleat my reflections on the argument of
liberty,

Barrenness, or unfruitfulness, may in general best be understood by comparing it with a state of *wickedness:* from which, as it is usually distinguished in the notion of the vulgar, so does it really differ on many accounts. The one has in it an air of *defiance*, the other of *unconcernment* for religion ; the one *forgets* God, the other *contemns* him ; the one has no *relish* nor *savour* of that which is *good*, the other finds too much *gust* and *pleasure* in that which is *evil* ; the one makes us by degrees *enemies*, the other *strangers* to God. In short, there is little doubt to be made, but that the *omission* of a *duty*, and the *commission* of a *crime*; *lukewarmness* in that which is *good*, and *eagerness* and *confidence* in that which is *evil*, may, and generally do, differ very widely in the degrees of guilt: from hence it is (the sinner being always a partial and indulgent judge of himself) that it is not unusual for many, who seem to have some abhorrence of wickedness, to be far enough from apprehending much evil, or much danger in unfruitfulness. This is a fatal error; it frustrates the great design of religion, and robs it of its truest honour, good works. For what can religion effect by that man, who retains nothing of it but the bare form and profession, and dares promise himself not only impunity, but a

A a   heaven,

heaven, in an ufelefs and uprofitable life?

Unfruitfulnefs, if more particularly enquired into, confifts in two things; a *neglect* of *duty*; or a *lifelefs* and *unprofitable* performance of it. The former I will call *idlenefs*; the latter *lukewarmnefs*, *coldnefs*, *formality*; and treat of each in order; of the former in this, and of the latter in the following chapter. And becaufe each of them are encumbered with miftakes and errors, which arife not only from felf-love and partiality, but alfo from fhallownefs of judgment, joined with tendernefs of confcience; I fhall endeavour fo to manage this fubject, as neither to difcourage the weak, nor embolden the carelefs.

§. 1. Of idlenefs. The omiffion of a duty may be either *habitual*, or *occafional* and *accidental*: and accordingly the cafe of omiffion may be very different.

1. An *habitual omiffion* of duty cannot confift with fincerity: a general neglect of duty defeats the main end of religion, which is to honour God, adorn our holy profeffion, and promote the good of human fociety; all which can never be attained but by following after righteoufnefs, and abounding in the fruits of it. By
this

this rule, an *idle,* though *innocent,* life, must neceſſarily be accounted *irreligious* and *vicious,* being a flat contradiction to our excellent profeſſion. He, who does not pray, nor meditate, nor purſue any end of charity, though he be otherwiſe civil and regular in his life; yet becauſe he does not work righteouſneſs, becauſe he is ſo far from imitating the zeal and charity of the bleſſed Jeſus, that he acts directly repugnant to both ; therefore muſt he not be looked upon as a diſciple of Jeſus, but as an alien and a ſtranger. He, whoſe life is ſpent in *vanity* or *drudgery,* in pleaſure or buſineſs, though his pleaſure be not *impure,* nor his buſineſs *unjuſt* ; yet is he, before God, a criminal, becauſe unprofitable ; he has received the grace of God in vain ; the light of the goſpel has riſen upon him in vain ; and he has ſerved no intereſt of virtue or religion in his generation ; and therefore he will be excluded heaven, with the *ſlothful ſervant, who hid his Maſter's talent in a napkin,* Luke xix. 20.

2. The caſe of an *accidental* or *occaſional* omiſſion of duty, is very different from that of *habitual* neglect of it; an *occaſional omiſſion* may be, not only *lawful,* but *neceſſary* ; but the *neglect* of duty never can be either. The circumſtances of po-

ſitive

sitive duty, and the measures and degrees of moral good, are not strictly fixed and settled; and therefore a single omission, either in the one or the other, where-ever there is a sufficient reason for it, can neither grieve the spirit, nor frustrate the design of religion; nor consequently imply any . corruption in the heart. But then we must take care,

1. That our omission be not too frequent. We must always have regard, in this matter of duty, to the great end and designs of its injunction; we must take care that our omissions in moral duties be not so often, that either the honour of our religion, or the welfare of our neighbour, suffer by it. Nor must we so often omit instrumental duties, prayers, reading, the sacrament, and the like, as thereby to *abate*, or much less *extinguish*, our spiritual gust and fervour. Omission of duty, too often repeated, breeds a kind of indifference, or lukewarmness; and lukewarmness soon passes into coldness and insensibleness; and this often ends in a reprobate mind, and an utter aversion for religion.

2dly, We must endeavour some way or other to compensate the omission of a duty; to make up by charity, what we have defalked from devotion; or to supply by short ejaculations, what we have been forced

ced

ced to retrench from fixed and regular offices of prayer. And he that watches for opportunities, either of *improvement*, or *doing good*, will, I believe, never have reason to complain of the want of them: God will put into his hands either the one or the other; and for the choice, he cannot do better, than follow God's.

3*dly*, A single omission must never proceed from a *sinful motive*; from a love of the world, or indulgence to the body; *necessity* or *charity* is the only just and proper apology for it. *Instrumental* or positive duties may give way to *moral* ones; the religion of the *means*, to the religion of the *end*; and in moral duties, the less may give way to the greater. But *duty* must never give way to *sin*, nor *religion* to *interest* or *pleasure*.

Having thus briefly given an account, what omission of duty is, and what is not sinful; and consequently so settled the notion of idleness, that neither the careless, nor the scrupulous can easily mistake their case; I will now propose such *considerations* as I judge most likely to deter men from it; and such *advice* as may be the best guard and preservative against it.

1. The first thing I would have every one lay to heart is, that a state of idleness is a state of damnable sin. Idleness is directly repugnant to the great ends of God,

both

both in our creation and redemption. As
to our *creation*; can we imagine that God,
who created not any thing but for some
excellent end, should create man for none,
or for a silly one? The spirit within us is
an active and vivacious principle; our rational faculties capacitate and qualify us
for doing *good*; this is the proper work
of reason, the truest and most natural pleasure of a rational soul. Who can think
now, that our wife Creator lighted this
candle within us, that we might oppress
and stifle it by negligence and idleness?
That he contrived and destined such a
mind to squander and fool away its talents
in vanity and impertinence? As to our
redemption, 'tis evident both what the design of it is, and how opposite idleness is
to it. Christ gave himself for us, *to redeem
us from all iniquity; and to purify to himself a peculiar people zealous of good works,*
Tit. ii. 14. And this is what our regeneration, or sanctification aims at: *We are
God's workmanship, created in Christ Jesus unto good works, which God has before ordained,
that we should walk in them,* Ephes. ii. 10.
How little then can a useless and barren life
answer the expectations of God? What a
miserable return must it be to the blood of
his Son; and how utterly must it disappoint all the purposes of his Word and
Spirit? But what need I argue further?
the

the truth I contend for is the express and constant doctrine of the scriptures: is not *idleness* and *fulness of bread* reckoned amongst the sins of *Sodom?* What means the sentence against the *barren fig-tree, Luke* xiii. 7. but the destruction and damnation of the idle and the sluggish? The indignation of God is not enkindled against the barrenness of *trees,* but *men.* What can be plainer than the condemnation of the unprofitable servant, who perished because he had not improved his talent? *Mat.* xxv. 38. And how frequently does the apostle declare himself against the *idle* and *disorderly?* And all this proceeds upon plain and necessary grounds: our Lord was an example of virtue, as well as innocence; and he did not only refrain from *doing evil,* but he *went about doing good.* We can never satisfy the intention of divine precepts by *negative* righteousness: when God prohibits the *filthiness of the flesh and spirit,* he enjoins *the perfecting holiness in his fear:* when he forbids us *to do evil,* he at the same time prescribes *the learning to do well.* What need I multiply more words? Idleness is a flat contradiction to faith, hope, charity; to fear, vigilance, mortification; and therefore certainly must be a damning sin: *These* are all active and vigorous principles; but idleness enfeebles and dis-spirits, manacles and fetters us:

A a 4

These

Thefe are pure, ftrict, and felf-denying
principles; but idlenefs is foft and indulgent: *thefe* conquer the world and the body, raife and exalt the mind; but idlenefs
is far from enterprizing any thing, from
attempting any thing that is good; it pam-
pers the body, and effeminates and diffolves
the mind; and finally, whatever innocence
or inoffenfivenefs it may pretend to, it does
not only terminate in fin, but has its beginning from it; from ftupidity and ignorance, from vanity and levity, from foftnefs and fenfuality, from fome prevailing
luft or other.

2. Next after the *nature*, the *confequences*
of idlenefs are to be confidered; and if it
be taken in the utmoft latitude, there is
fcarce any fin which is more juftly liable
to fo many tragical accufations; for it is
the parent of *difhonour* and *poverty*, and of
moft of the *fins* and *calamities* of this mortal life. But at prefent I view it only as it
is drawn with a half face, and that the
much lefs deformed of the two: I confider it here as pretending to *innocence*; and
flattering it felf with the hopes of happinefs: and yet even thus, fuppofing it as
harmlefs and inoffenfive as it can be, yet
ftill thefe will be the miferable effects of it:
it will rob religion, and the world, of the
fervice due to both: it will bereave us of
the pleafure of life, and the comfort of
death;

death ; and send us down at last to a cur-
sed eternity. For where are the virtues
that should maintain the order and beauty
of human society ; that should relieve and
redress the miseries of the world? Where
are the virtues that should vindicate the
honour of religion, and demonstrate its divinity as effectually as predictions or miracles can do? Where are the bright examples that should convert the unbelieving part
of mankind, and inflame the believing part
with a generous emulation ? Certainly the
lazy Christian, the slothful servant, can
pretend to nothing of this kind. As to the
pleasure of life, if true and lasting, if pure
and spiritual, 'tis easy to discern from what
fountains it must be drawn. Nothing but
poverty of spirit can procure our peace, nothing but purity of heart our pleasure. But
ah! how far are the idle and unactive from
these virtues? Faith, love, and hope, are
the seeds of them : victories and triumphs,
devotion, alms, and good works are the
fruits of them : but what a stranger to these
is the drone and sluggard ? Then for the
comfort of death, it must proceed from a
well-spent life : he that sees nothing but a
vast solitude and wilderness behind him,
will never, like the *Israelites,* see a *Canaan*
before him. Life must be filled with
good works, or else death will look but
dark

dark and gloomy: when the conscience inquires every where after the effects of the Word, and the Spirit, and the blood of Jesus, and can discover in all the parts, in all the paths of life, no tracks of any thing but *fancy* and *fortune, humour* and *indulgence*; how will it shrink, and faint, and tremble! what pensive, melancholy doubts will damp and choak its hope! and how can it be otherwise? Alas! the mind of a Christian is sufficiently informed that every man shall receive according to what he has done in the body; God will judge every man according to his works; what then must become of him who has none to shew? If immortality and glory, if life and peace be the reward of *well-doing*, nay, of *patient continuance* in well-doing, what will become of the drowsy, the supine and careless, the sot and the sluggish, who have slept, and fooled, and trifled away life?

3. I might aggravate the guilt of idleness, by taking an estimate of the *talents* it wastes, the *obligations* it slights, and the *hopes* it forfeits. I might render man more jealous and apprehensive of falling into it, by observing how generally it prevails; which is a plain proof, either of the strength of the temptation, or of our propension; a plain proof either that there is I know not what secret magick in

the

the sin, or else that the cheat it imposes upon the world is a very clever, a very dexterous one. But I have said enough; and where the former considerations fail, these will hardly succeed: therefore I will now pass on from arguments to advice, which was the next thing proposed to be done.

And here my advice must have regard to two different sorts of persons. 1. To such as are born to plentiful or competent fortunes. 2. To such as are to raise their own, or to provide for the support and maintenance of themselves and their families, by their labour or industry in some calling or profession. To the former the best directions I can give, are these:

1. He that is master of his time, ought to devote the more to religion: *To whom God hath given much, of him much will be required:* Nor has such an one any excuse left, either for omission, or a hasty and cursory performance of duty, but one, one that will encrease his guilt, *i. e.* laziness, pleasure, or some sin or other. Such an one therefore ought to be constant and diligent in frequenting the publick assemblies of the church; his attendance upon prayers, sacraments, sermons, must be such as becomes a man, who, as it has pleased God, seems born not to provide for life, but only to live, only to improve and enjoy life, and carry on the noble designs of it; and as

becomes

becomes a man whofe good or ill example is of fuch vaft importance to the fervice or difiervice of religion. Nor muft fuch an one's attendance on the publick excufe him from the religious offices of the clofet, or his family ; he ought to abound in each : he may be more frequent in meditation and prayer, in reading and inftruction, and perform each with more juftnefs and folemnity than others can.

2. Perfons of fortune ought to be careful in the choice of intimates and friends. Converfation is not always a lofs, but fometimes a gain of time : we often need to have our forgetfulnefs relieved, our drowfinefs awakened by the difcourfes and reflections of our friends. If difcourfe were generally feafoned with grace, converfation would be the greateft blefling ; if with fenfe and reafon, innocence and prudence, it would be the moft agreeable entertainment of human life. But how mifchievous is the acquaintance which infects us with vanity and lightnefs of fpirit, which fhews us nothing but a gaudy outfide and a frothy foul ! whofe example binds men in civility to be foolifh, and makes confidence, and vice, and mis-fpence of time, a fafhion.

3. It were to be wifhed, that perfons of the beft rank, were ever bred up to fomething ; to fomething that might improve, to fomething that might amufe and innocently

cently engage their minds; to something
that might employ life, without incumbring
it. And yet, alas! what need I wish this?
How many excellent qualities are neceffary
to render a gentleman worthy of the ftation
where God has placed him? Let him purfue *thefe*. How many are the virtues, how
many the duties to which a Chriftian is obliged? Let him attend *thefe*. There is a
great deal requifite to make a good mafter,
a good husband, a good father, a good fon,
a good neighbour, a good parifhioner, an
excellent fubject, and an excellent friend;
and yet there are many other relations befides thefe. In a word, there is no man,
who, when he fhall appear before God, will
not be found to have omitted many duties;
and to have performed many other with lefs
care and diligence than he ought; and furely
fuch an one cannot juftly complain for want
of bufinefs. I doubt rather on the contrary, that whoever takes a juft and full
view of things, will have reafon to complain,
that life is fhort, and our work great; that
let us ufe all the diligence we can, and be
as frugal of our time as we will, we arrive much fooner at a maturity of years,
than of knowledge and virtue.

4. The diverfions of perfons of this
quality ought to be well regulated; fuch as
become the character of a *gentleman*, and
the dignity of a *Chriftian*; that is, they
must

must be neither *mean* nor *vicious.* But I have treated this and the foregoing heads more copiously in *human life*; to which I refer my reader.

As to such, in the next place, who are engaged in a profeſſion, I have particularly conſidered their ſtate in ſeveral places, and find little to add here, but only to mind them, that they may be guilty of idleneſs too; that their idleneſs is the more criminal, the leſs temptation they have to it. They may neglect the duties of their calling, I mean their ſecular calling; and if they be unfaithful and negligent in their temporal concern, it is not to be expected that they ſhould be more ſolicitous and induſtrious about their ſpiritual one. They may again ſuffer the cares of this life to thruſt out thoſe of another; and then they are truly idle and ſlothful ſervants to God, how induſtrious and faithful ſoever they are to the world: for life is but waſted and miſ-ſpent, if it makes not proviſion for *eternity*; and it matters little whether it be waſted in *pleaſure* or in *drudgery.*

CHAP.

CHAP. VIII.

Of Unfruitfulnefs, *as it confifts in* Lukewarmnefs *or* formality. *The caufes from
which Lukewarmnefs proceeds. The folly,
guilt, and danger of a* Laodicean *ftate.*

IN the former chapter I confidered that
part of Unfruitfulnefs which confifts
in the *omiffion* of duty: I am now to confider another part of it, which confifts in
too *perfunctory* a *performance* of it. Befides thofe who are truly unprofitable, becaufe they flight or neglect the duties of
religion; there is another fort of men,
who at the laft day will fall under the fame
character and condemnation; not becaufe they perform no duties, but becaufe their performance of them is depre-
ciated by Coldnefs and formality: men,
who make a fair appearance of religion,
and yet have no inward fpiritual life:
men, who do generally obferve the external duties of religion, but with fo little
guft, with fuch indifference and Lukewarmnefs, that they are neither acceptable to God, nor ufeful to themfelves. This
ftate of deadnefs may be confidered either more *generally*, as it runs through the
whole courfe of our lives and actions;
or more *particularly*, in this or that inftance
of religion.

1. When

1. When 'tis so general, that the bent and course of our lives is, for want of relish of the things of God, perverted and depraved; when we have no designs, drive on no ends, that are suitable to the *excellency* and *dignity* of our *nature*; to the *holiness* of our *profession*, and to the great and manifest *obligations* of God: when we have no joys or pleasures, no thirsts or appetites, that do truly become a Christian; when we make no progress, no advance towards our great end; when our discourses and employments have no tincture of the Spirit, and no tendency to edification. I think we may then boldly conclude, that this is a state of *carnality* and *death*. And that this want of relish in the general course of our lives, proceeds from a real want of a sincere faith, and true illumination. For were the mind once truly enlightened; were it once clearly convinced, firmly and habitually persuaded, of the beauty and excellency of the things of God; as we should have notions different from those of worldly carnal men, so would there consequently be a difference in the nature of our hopes and fears, of our desires and designs, of our joys and sorrows; and as necessarily in the main scope and tendency of our conversation. Whoever therefore finds this general stupidity in the

course

courfe of his life, let him not flatter himfelf in the performance of any of the duties of religion: he has a corrupt, carnal,
and blind heart; his performances proceed
not from true principles, and have not that
life and vigour in them that they ought;
they are as different from the performances
of a man truly regenerate and fanctified,
as the civilities and complements of a well-
bred acquaintance, from the fuftantial offices of a fincere and affectionate friend.
Nor can any man, who will take the leaft
pains to examine himfelf, be ignorant of,
or miftaken in the condition of his foul, if.
this be it. For whoever will act honeftly
and impartially, ought not to pafs a fentence of abfolution on himfelf, upon the
bare performance of fome relative, or inftrumental duties of religion; but he ought
to inquire, firft, what virtues he practifes,
which put him upon *expence, hazard,* or
travel; what works of piety or charity he
performs; and what proportion they bear
to his ability. Next, he ought to confider
the *defign* and *end* he propofes to himfelf in
all his religious performances; whether he
feek the honour of God, the welfare of
man, and his own improvement and
growth in goodnefs; or whether he does
this merely to acquit himfelf of a task,
and difcharge himfelf of what he takes

B b   for

for granted as a duty, tho' he finds no pleasure, no advantage in it. Thirdly, He must reflect upon the *frame* and *temper* of his mind in reference to these duties; what hunger and thirst he has for righteousness; what warmth, ardor, elevation, or earnestness of mind accompanies his performances; what peace and pleasure his reflection on them; or whether religion be not a burthen to him, or something to which custom only reconciles him. Lastly, He ought to examine what operation, what *influence* his religious performances have upon him. Prayer, hearing, reading, and such-like duties, do naturally tend to enlighten the mind, purify the heart, increase our love, strengthen our faith, and confirm our hope; and therefore, where this is not the effect of them, we may conclude, that they are not discharged in that manner and with that sincerity they ought. He therefore, that will examine himself aright, must not ask himself how often he reads, how often he hears, &c. and then rest there; but must ask himself what *effect* these performances have had upon his mind; which he will soon discern, if he demand of himself, what the bent and scope of his life is; how much he advances and improves in the conquest of any vice, and the attainment
ment

ment of any virtue ; what he loves, or
what he hates ; what esteem he has for
the things of God, and what for the things
of men. And, in a word, how he follows
after universal righteousness ; and how he
increases in purity of heart, and poverty of
spirit.

2. *Lukewarmness,* and *coldness,* may be
considered more *particulary,* as it discovers
it self in the performance of this or that
duty ; in hearing, reading, prayer, and
participation of the Lord's Supper. Now,
'tis certain, that there is a deadness in these
duties, which proceeds from a *carnal* and
unsanctified heart, and is a plain symptom
of a *state of sin :* and yet it is too common,
that they, who are subject to it, make little
reflection upon it, and are little concerned
for it. On the other hand, many complain of lifelesness in duty, where there
is no just ground for this complaint ; and
this is no small evil to such ; for it disturbs
the peace of their minds, damps the chearfulness and alacrity of their service, and
clogs and encumbers their religion with
needless doubts and scruples. Some have
gone about to set this matter right very
unskilfully ; and whilst they have, as they
thought, shunned *enthusiastic* raptures, and
irregular heats, have really betrayed the
cause of *true* and *solid fervency of spirit ;*
and talked of prayer, and such other du-

ties,

ties, in fuch a manner, as cannot but reflect difadvantageoufly on themfelves, a-
mongft fuch, as are moderately verfed
in the fcriptures, and have any experience
of the power of God's Word and Spirit
upon their fouls. But what furprizes me
moft is, that fome, of very deferved re-
pute, have taught, that the *feeking fpiritual pleafure in prayer,* is an *enemy to Perfection :* that *heat* and *ardor* of fpirit in
prayer, does often happen to the *weakeft*
Chriftians ; and very feldom to the *perfect.* But my bufinefs not being to combat the opinions of men, but to advance
truths in the moft charitable, and in the
moft effectual manner that I can : therefore, without taking notice of the motives
or reafons which have byaffed any on this
fubject, I will lay down two or three pro-
pofitions, which will, I hope, clear this
matter, and promote the defign I am now
carrying on.

1. then, *Lifelefnefs* or lukewarmnefs in
thefe duties muft never be *conftant.* There
is a vaft difference between *habitual* and
accidental coldnefs in duty ; the former is
the fymptom of worldly, carnal, and unregenerate minds ; but not the latter.
Many are the accidents which difturb
and indifpofe the body ; many are the
things which diftract and clog the mind :
from

from both which becaufe we fhall never be utterly free in this world; therefore our devotion will never be fo conftant and uniform, but that it will have its *interruptions* and *allays*; and dulnefs and lifelefnefs will fometimes feize upon the beft of Chriftians. But then, if this fpiritual deadnefs in religious exercifes be *fixed, conftant,* and *habitual,* it muft needs be a proof of a corrupt mind: for 'tis impoffible that there fhould be a true principle of grace within, which fhould never, or very rarely, fhew it felf in the fincerity and fervency of our devotion. How is it poffible that that man, who is generally flight and fuperficial in his confeffion, fhould have a true compunction and fincere contrition for fins? How is it poffible that he, who is generally indifferent, formal, and cold in his petitions, fhould have a juft fenfe either of his wants or dangers; or a true value for the grace and favour of God? The fum is, deadnefs in duty is either general or rare, common or accidental: if it befals us *commonly,* 'tis an argument of an unregenerate heart; if *rarely,* 'tis not. But if the returns of life and deadnefs in duty be fo frequent and unconftant, that 'tis impoffible to determine whether the one or the other prevail moft; then 'tis

B b 3   plain,

plain, that the state also of such a man is very dubious.

2. Duty must never be destitute of *sincerity*, tho' it may of *pleasure* and transport; it must never be without *seriousness* and concernment, tho' it may be very defective in the *degrees* of *love* and *ardency*: Thus in prayer, the tenderness and contrition of the soul, dissolved in love and sorrow, is a frame of spirit much above what the penitent commonly arrives at. But an aversion for sin, a firm resolution to forsake it, and a hearty desire to be enabled by the grace of God so to do, is what he must not want. So again, joy and transport, the ardor and exultancy of mind, is the effect of a clear understanding, an assured conscience, an heart inflamed with love, and a strict life: whoever therefore falls short in the one, will generally fall short in the other too. But every Christian, that is truly such, must have a true sense of his wants, a hearty desire to please God, a true notion of his goodness, and a steddy dependence upon it through Christ. And these things are sufficient to unite our hearts and our lips in the same petitions: to make us in earnest, in all the duties we perform, and careful to intend the main end of them.

3. The

3. The prayer of the *perfect* man is generally offered up with the *tendereft* and
moft *exalted* paffion ; and a holy pleafure
mingles it felf in every part of his office :
his petitions and praifes ; his confeffions,
deprecations and confidences, are all of
them expreffions of warm and delightful
paffions. And how can we well conceive
it otherwife? Muft not thofe *praifes* and
Magnificats be full of joy and tranfport,
which flow from a full affurance of the divine favour, from a long experience of his
love, and from the glorious profpect of a
bleffed eternity? Can thofe *deprecations*
and *confidences* want a heavenly calm and
tranquillity of fpirit, which reft upon the
Mediation of Jefus, the promifes of an
immutable God, and the pledge of his Spirit? Can thofe *confeffions* want contrition,
that have all the tendernefs that holy zeal
and the humbleft reflections can infpire
them with? which are poured forth by a
foul enlightened, purified, ftrong in the
faith, rooted and grounded in love; by a
foul confequently that has the livelieft fenfe
of the deformity and danger of fin, of the
beauty and pleafure of holinefs, of the infinite goodnefs of God, and of that love of
Chrift that paffeth knowledge? Can, finally, thofe *petitions* want defire and flame,

B b 4   which

which are offered up by a ſoul that hungers
and thirſts after righteouſneſs, that counts
all things but dung and droſs in compari-
ſon of Jeſus, that pants after God, that
longs to be diſſolved and to be with Chriſt?
And as we may thus, from the nature of
things, collect what kind of prayers thoſe
of the perfect man generally are; ſo may
we, from the example of the royal *Pſalmiſt*, and others, demonſtrate all this to be
no vain ſpeculation, but real matter of
fact. 'Tis true, *weight* and *dignity* of *matter*, *gravity* and *ſignificancy* of *expreſſion*,
are the character moſt conſpicuous in *publick* offices, in the beſt and moſt ancient
prayers: and particularly in the Lord's
prayer. We find in them few or no figures of ſpeech, no vehemence of expreſſion. But it is true too, that the devotion of a ſoul diſengaged, as it were,
from the body, retired from the world,
collected within it ſelf, raiſed by daily
contemplation, and accuſtomed to converſe
with heaven, flows naturally and eaſily.
Thoſe great *ideas*, which ſuch a prayer as
that of our Lord's compoſure preſent to
the mind, inflame the deſire, awaken all
the paſſions of the holy man, without
any labour of imagination, or artifice of
words.

Thus

Thus have I confidered the nature of lukewarmnefs; and fhewed how far the perfect man is removed from it. My next bufinefs is, to perfuade and exhort men to quit it; and become fincere and zealous. Only I muft, firft, take notice by the way, that befides idlenefs and lukewarmnefs, there is fometimes a third caufe or occafion of unfruitfulnefs; which deferves never to be flighted: that is, *ficklenefs, unfteadinefs,* or *inconftancy.* Many there are, who often purpofe, project, and refolve great matters; but never bring forth any fruit to perfection: what they build one day, they throw down another. They put on as many various moral forms, as *Proteus* in the poets does natural ones: fometimes they are in a fit of zeal; at other times nothing but coldnefs and bare form: fometimes they are in the camp of virtue; fometimes in that of vice. In a word, they halt, like the *Ifra-elites,* between *God* and *Baal*; and are divided and diftracted between a *fenfe* of *duty,* and the *love* of the *world* and the *body*; between the *checks* and incitements of *confcience* on the one hand, and fome foolifh *inclinations* on the other. This ftate I have had an eye to very often, nor fhall I forget it here; but fhall propofe fuch a method for the cure of lukewarmnefs and formality, as may be alfo of very good ufe to all fuch, as

fall

fall short of the main end of religion; being not truly and thoroughly changed; but are only *almost persuaded to be Christians:* and only not altogether *so far from the kingdom of heaven* as others. This being premised, I proceed, and,

1. I will inquire into the causes from whence lukewarmness, and all abortive attempts after virtue, flow.

2. I will shew the *folly*, *guilt*, and *danger* of a *Laodicean* state.

§. 1. Of the causes, &c. These are generally four.

1. Men finding themselves under great difficulties in coming up to holiness, in the true genuine and gospel-notion of it, have endeavoured to enlarge the way, and widen the gate that leads to life; and have therefore formed to themselves more soft and pliant notions of vice and virtue: such as may be more easily accommodated, either to their particular *inclinations*, or to the *modes* and *fashions* of the world, than those of Christ and the apostles can. Hence it is, that amongst such as pretend to some regard for religion, humility, poverty of spirit, self-denial, abstinence and mortification, are so far from being visible in their practice, that we seem

to

to have almoſt loſt the notion of them.
And the pride of life, and the luſt of the
eyes, are ſo univerſally practiſed, that
tho' we know, that theſe in St. *John* are
the names of vices, we ſcarce know
what the things themſelves are. We have
confounded the mears and bounds of vice
and virtue; and ſuch are the freedoms,
I will not ſay of thoſe who profeſs debauchery, but Chriſtianity, that if they
be conſiſtent with the ſanctity and purity
of the goſpel, 'twill be hard to determine
what exceſs is. And, in a word, how
many are there, who, making a profeſſion
of living by faith, and looking for the
bleſſed hope and the glorious appearance
of Chriſt, do yet live, as if all the buſineſs of life were to get and enjoy as much
of this world as they can; who, profeſſing
themſelves the diſciples of Chriſt, whoſe
heart was lowly, his fortune mean, and
his appearance humble, do yet lay out
their time, their labour, their wealth
on this one deſign, to make ſuch a ſhew,
ſuch a figure in the world, as may render them the gaze and envy of their
neighbours? And, as our indulgence to
our ſelves in theſe things, which relate
to the pride and vanity of life, and the
eaſe and appetites of the body, is very
great; ſo on the ſame ground, and for
the ſame reaſon, is our *zeal* for the intereſt

tereft of virtue, and the honour of God, very little, faint, and remifs. Converfation has very little favour, very little grace in it; and we are fo far from being refolute and induftrious to awe or fhame vice abroad, that we our felves fhould be almoft out of countenance, if we fhould be obferved to pay any particular refpect to religion or virtue in company. The government of our families is fo lax and eafy, that it favours more of coldnefs and indifferency, than fervency of fpirit. 'Tis true indeed, thefe I am fpeaking of do generally frequent the houfe of God; *and they fit before him as his people; and delight to hear his word:* But fo did the *Jews,* when God tells them, in the prophet *Ezek.* xxxiii. 31. *that their hearts went after their covetoufnefs:* And in the prophet *Ifaiah,* we have but an odd character of the morals of thefe people; of whom God faith, *Yet they feek me daily, and delight to know my ways :* Nay, further, *they delight in approaching to God,* Ifa. lviii. 2. Now though fuch, as I am fpeaking of, may not be guilty to this degree, fo as to be chargeable with open wickednefs; yet I am very much afraid, that even in this duty they but promote the cheat and impofture they put upon themfelves; and make their diligence in this point minifter to quiet their confciences in their *Laodi-*
cean

cean ftate; for 'twere eafy to prove, that fuch as thefe do more generally aim at the entertainment of the ear, than the refor- mation of the heart.   And we may fay of preachers now, as God did of *Ezekiel*; *And lo, thou art unto them as a lovely fong, of one that has a very pleafant voice,* Ezek. xxxiii. 32.. The mufick of the voice; the graceful- nefs of delivery; a flow of words; the furprize of novelty, and notion; the beauty of fentences; and the fparkling of wit and fancy, or an appearance of learning: thefe are, I doubt, too often the things that draw together and charm an auditory: and fo all are pleafed, but none converted or edified; for who fweats or blufhes, who trembles or grows pale at thefe fermons? Who goes away from them wounded or ftruck through, ferious and penfive, full of pious fears and devout defires?

2. A *Laodicean* ftate fprings from floth and pufillanimity, or the want of a tho- rough and well-grounded refolution.   This was one caufe of the *Ifraelites* fluctua- tion and uncertainty; they were indeed defirous of a *Canaan,* but were not forward to purchafe it, by tedious marches, ha- zardous encounters, and the hardfhip of hunger and thirft, and fuch like: they were ever and anon willing to have pre- ferred

ferred the dishonour and servitude of
Egypt, with security and fulness, before
a *Canaan* on these terms. And thus it is,
this day, with Christians of a *Laodicean*
spirit, and a doubtful staggering allegi-
ance. An heaven they would have, but
would not purchase it at too dear a rate ;
they would be accounted the disciples of
Christ, and share in the merits of his
sufferings; but they would not take up his
cross, in any sense, and follow him. But,
alas! *Israel* might as well have gained
their liberty, without going out of *Egypt*;
or a *Canaan*, without travel, and hardship,
and blood; as these, virtue, and heaven,
without watchfulness and industry : we
may as well hope to support and encrease
the health and strength of the body,
without food or exercise; as that of the
soul, without meditation and prayer : we
may as soon conquer our enemies without discipline, expence, and blows; as
master our corruptions, and become virtuous, without spiritual watchfulness, travel, or contention. There is indeed force
and efficacy enough in the word of God,
to enlighten the mind, and purify the
heart; if we would but frequently and
seriously read and meditate it. The grace
of the Spirit is sufficient to conquer our
corruptions, and strengthen and establish
us in faith and obedience, if we did but
                                    earnestly

earneftly and frequently pray for it; and cherifh and improve it, when obtained. The means which God has prefcribed are undoubtedly proper and fuitable, powerful and effectual, to the attainment, prefervation, and increafe of holinefs; and all his ordinances have a divine virtue and energy in them, if they be but duly and confcientioufly made ufe of. But if we do not watch; if we do not meditate; if we do not pray; if we expofe our felves to a vain and trifling converfation; if we indulge the body in all the eafe it is inclined to, and put our felves upon no duties, practife no difcipline that we have any reluctancy for; 'tis not to be wondered at, if our virtue be crazy and fickly, if our performances be cold and unedifying, our faith weak, our affections low and groveling, our life unfteddy and unprofitable, our religion deftitute of true pleafure, and our latter end of any rational comfort, or well-grounded confidence. 'Tis naturally to be expected that the foul of the fluggard fhould be like his field. *Prov.* xxiv. 30. *I went by the field of the flothful, and by the vineyard of the man void of underftanding; and lo, it was all grown over with thorns, and nettles had covered the face thereof, and the ftone wall thereof was broken down:* This is one plain caufe, and commonly the firft, of our

halt-

halting between *God* and *Baal*; namely, our idlenefs and floth in religion, joined with pufillanimity and cowardife, which moves us to decline all difficulties, and difables us to make a bold refiftance againft temptations : how criminal and guilty this muft render us in the fight of God, 'tis no difficulty to guefs. Is this the zeal, the revenge of an humble and active penitent? Is this to redeem the time, and efface the memory of our paft fins and provocations? Is this the converfation, that becomes the children of the light, and of the day? Is this our hunger and thirft after righteoufnefs? Is this our ambition, our paffion for an heaven? Finally, Is it thus we requite the mercies and obligations of God, and the love of Jefus, that paffeth knowledge? Shall fuch halting trimming Chriftians as thefe, think ye, ever be judged endued with a true and living faith, who exprefs in the whole tenour of their lives, fo much coldnefs and indifference for their falvation, which the Son of God thought worth the purchafing, by fo much travel and fo much forrow, fo much fhame and fo much blood?

3. A third caufe of our halting between *God* and *Baal* is fome degrees of infidelity. This was the cafe of *Ifrael* too. They

they were ever prone to idolatry; partly trained up to it in *Egypt,* and elfewhere;
partly being more capable of forming an
idea of a finite and topical God, than of
an infinite and univerfal one, *Jer.* xxiii. 23.
partly being fond of following the fafhions
of other nations. And, laftly, moved, partly by that great and long profperity, which
Egypt and other idolatrous nations enjoyed;
and no doubt, comparing it too with the
variety and uncertainty of their own fortune, and the frequent difappointment of
their expectations, *Hofea* ii. never laying
it to heart all the while; that the way to
fecure their profperity, was to change, not
their God, but their manners. I would
to God, this were not too lively a defcription of the ftate of too many Chriftians;
and that we could not trace our lukewarmnefs and ficklenefs in religion, too
plainly back to the fame fource or origin; namely, fome degrees of infidelity.
I wifh the profperity of the wicked do not
fomewhat undermine the belief of a providence: I wifh, whatever we talk of a
treafure in another world, we do not
now and then think it wifeft to have our
portion in this. I am afraid, that the decays and diffolutions of our nature in
death, the rottennefs and corruption of
the grave, and the variety of changes
and fortunes our very duft undergoes,

C c   may

may tempt us to some scruples and jealou-
sies about a posthumous life. But however it be in these points, I am too too well
assured, that we do often doubt, whether
virtue be the true blessedness of life ;
whether there be that pleasure in righteousness the scripture affirms there is. I
am confident, the notions of righteousness and holiness, with which the scripture furnishes us, are often blurred and
blotted by the maxims and customs of the
world ; and perswade my-self, that there is
scarcely one of those, that are *Laodiceans*
and trimmers in religion, that do not
flatter themselves, that God will not be as
severe as his threats ; and that he will receive them into heaven upon milder and
softer terms than the gospel proposes.
Some such kind of infidelity as this must
possess the heart, where-ever the life is so
infinitely below our profession. When *the
word preached doth not profit*, it is because it
is not *mingled* with a due measure of *faith
in those that hear it.* If we did truly believe the revelations of God ; if we did
see the promises of God as evident and present by faith, though distant in themselves, 'twere impossible but they must
move, but they must take us ; 'twere impossible but they must enkindle in us another sort of desire, and this desire would
soon produce another sort of endeavours,
ano-

another fort of life. When *Moses* beheld *Canaan* from *Pisga,* how paffionately did he defire to enter into *that* good land! When the difciples had feen Jefus afcend up into heaven, how were they tranfported with a defire of following him! how unfpeakable was their joy! how fervent their prayers! how lafting and enlarged their gratitude! *They returned to* Jerufalem *with great joy; and were continually in the temple praifing and bleffing God.* How does a profpect of gain captivate the covetous! How does the fancy or expectation of pleafure inflame the voluptuary! How does the fight of vanity and grandeur infect the proud! And the hope of glory fire the ambitious? What, hath the beauty and pleafure of holinefs no attraction? Has heaven no charms in it? Has the favour and love of God, and of Jefus, no force, no power in them? Surely we have not the face to deny, but that the promifes of God are great and precious ones; and if they raife no paffion in us, it muft not be through want of *excellence* and *lovelinefs* in *them,* but want of *faith* in *us.* And then judge you, how acceptable this kind of infidelity muft render us to God; what value can God have for a people whom no kindnefs can oblige, no arguments convince; with whom no miracles can gain belief; no affurances or

pro-

promifes find credit? Hell is the portion
of the *fearful* and *unbeliever*, Rev. xxi. 8.
And what dreadful judgments did over-
whelm *Ifrael,* as often as they thus halted
between God and idols! it did not excufe
them that they had fome fort of *veneration*
for the memory of *Mofes* and his *miracles*;
fincé this was not able to over-rule their
prejudice and *fuperftition*; that they retain
fome honour for *Abraham, Ifaac,* and *Ja-
cob,* and that *God* which was the *fear* of
their *fathers,* fince they had as much, or
more, for the *nations* round about them,
and their *gods* too. And whatever power
they did acknowledge in the God of heaven, or whatever benefit they did own themfelves to have derived from him, as I can
hardly think the memory of either was
utterly extinguifhed amongft them; all this
availed them nothing, while they made
their court to other gods too, and put
their truft in their patronage and protection. Though this be fufficient to make
us fenfible of the guilt of a *Laodicean* virtue and an uncertain halting faith; yet I
muft advance on, and obferve unto you a
worfe principle, if worfe can be, of this
deportment yet, which is,

4 The fourth fountain of this unfteadinefs and remifnefs in religion is,
fome remains of corruption; the prevalency

lency of some vicious passion or other.
Mens actions are the plainest indications
of their affections. If the life looks two
ways, we need not doubt but that the
heart does so too. This was that made
the young man in the gospel fluctuate so
between *Christ* and *mammon*; this was the
case of *Herod*; he had yielded, no doubt,
to the power and force of the *Baptist's rea-*
sons, if he had not been drawn back by the
charms of his *Herodias.* And this is the
case of every man who is but *almost* a
Christian; he is under the ascendant of
some silly or vile lust or other ; this is that
which spoils the taste of the hidden *man-*
na, and diminisheth the price of *Canaan.*
Without doubt men would apply themselves more vigorously to spiritual things,
were they not too fond of the body and the
pleasures of it ; they would certainly seek
the kingdom of heaven more earnestly,
and make a better provision than they do
for the other world, were they not too
much taken with this, and therefore too
apt to set up their rest on this side *Jordan.*
Now if this be so, what can we expect?
They only who *conquer,* are *crowned*; they
that *sow* to the *flesh* and to the *world,* can
reap nothing from these but *corruption.*
These kind of Christians, though peradventure they are not slaves to any *infamous*
and *scandalous* lusts, are yet entangled by

some

some other, not much less injurious, though not to *reputation*, yet to *purity of heart*; they are captivated to the world and flesh, though their chains seem better polished, and of a finer metal; they cannot mount upwards, they cannot conquer, being retarded and kept under, if not by the *strength* of *temptation*, yet by their own *softness* and *weakness*; and yet, why should I doubt but these are conquered by temptation? The more *innocent* the object of any one's passion is, generally the more *fatal*, because we are the more apt to *indulge* our selves in it. The causes of Lukewarmness being thus pointed out, 'tis evident what the cure of it consists in, namely, in forming just and correct notions of virtue and vice; in strengthening and confirming our faith, and in perfecting and compleating our reformation. I will now endeavour to possess the minds of men with an aversion and dread of this state of Lukewarmness, by shewing,

1. The folly.
2. The guilt; and,
3. The danger of it.

1. The folly. How reasonably may I here address myself to the lukewarm in the words of *Elijah* to the *Israelites*: *How long halt ye between two opinions? if the Lord be*

be God, follow him ; but if Baal, then fol-low him, 1 Kings xviii. 21. If you do in-deed believe, that your safety and happi-ness depends upon God, then serve him in good earnest ; but if you think this depends upon the world, the flesh, and the devil, then serve these ; if you really think that virtue and religion are the most solid and stable treasure, then strive sincerely and vi-gorously to possess your selves of them; but if you really think, that the ease and pleasure of the body, respect, and pomp, and state, is the proper portion and sove-raign good of man, then devote and offer up your selves to these. For what a folly is that life, which will neither procure us the happiness of this world, nor of ano-ther? To what purpose is it to listen only so much to conscience, as to damp and chill our pleasure ; and so much to pleasure, as to disturb the peace and repose of consci-ence? But indeed, as the words of *Elijah* were rather an *irony* than any real doubt, whether *Baal* or the Lord were God ; ra-ther a scornful derision of their folly and stupidity, than a serious exhortation to de-liberate, whether idolatry or the worship of the true God were to be chosen : I doubt not, but mine will seem to you to carry no other sound in them. The dispa-rity is so vast between God and the world, between religion and sensuality, covetous-

ness

ness and ambition ; between those hopes
and enjoyments we may reap from the one,
and those we can fancy in the other ; that
there is no place for doubting what choice
we are to make, or to which side we are
to adhere ; nay, in this we are more criminal than the *Israelites*, being self-con-
demned. The *Israelites* indeed, seem to be
at a loss, whether the Lord or *Baal* were
God ; they doubted under whose protection they might thrive best. But at this
day, whoever believes a God, knows very
well there is none besides him. Whatever
passion we have for the world, and the
things of it ; whatever spiritual idolatry
we are guilty of, our opinions are not yet
so far corrupted, as to attribute to them,
in reality, any thing like Divinity. Whilst
we dote on wealth, we at the same time
know that it makes it self wings and
flies away ; whilst on greatness and power, we know that 'tis but a piece of empty and toilsome pageantry. and often the
subject of misery and dismal tragedies,
not incident to a lower state ; whilst we
dote on pleasure, we are well assured that
'tis dishonourable and short, and intermix-
ed with fears, and shame, and torment ;
we know that nothing here below is able
to free our state and fortune from calamity, our mind from guilt, the body from
death, much less the whole man from a
miserable

miferable eternity. In one word, we
know that what we admire is vanity, and
what we worſhip is indeed an idol. This
being ſo, I will inſiſt no longer on this to-
pick; for ſince the world bears no compe-
tition with God in our opinion, tho' it often rivals him in our affections, we are not
to impute the halting of a *Laodicean* Chriſtian to any perſuaſion of omnipotence or
all-ſufficiency, or any thing like Divinity
in the things he dotes on, ſerves, and wor-
ſhips; but we muſt find out ſome other
reaſon of it. And that is generally this :
we are willing to believe, that our fond-
neſs for the world, and our indulgence to
the body, is conſiſtent enough with religion; that it is no violation of our faith,
nor provocation to God ; nor conſequently, prejudice to our eternal intereſt ; and
then 'tis no wonder if we blend and com-
pound religion and ſenſuality ; and ſtand
divided in our affections ; and conſequently halt in our ſervice between God and
the world. To prevent this, I will ſhew,

2. That this is a great *ſin*; which is
ſufficiently evident from this ſingle conſideration, that it fruſtrates the efficacy of
the goſpel and the Spirit, and entirely defeats the great deſign of the Chriſtian religion. For, 1. Religion has no effectual
influence upon the lukewarm himſelf; the
goſpel

gospel works no thorough change in him:
The sinner is not converted into a saint;
nor human nature perfected by participation of a divine one. 2. The *Laodiceans*
can never offer up to God any gift, any sacrifice worthy of him; nor render him
any service acceptable to him; the *kingdom of God is righteousness and peace, and
joy in the Holy Ghost,* Rom. xiv. *He that
in these things serveth Christ, is acceptable to
God, and approved of men.* But alas! these
men are almost utter strangers to these
things; a few faint and irresolute wishes,
formal and customary prayers, niggardly
and grumbling alms, and an attendance
upon God's word, rather out of spiritual
wantonness, than devotion; these are the
offerings they can make God; and will
God be better pleased with these, than he
was with those of *Israel,* that were deformed with maims and blemishes? *Mal.
i. 8. Offer now these to thy governour; will
he be pleased with thee, or accept of thy person?* saith the Lord of hosts: The *Magi,*
indeed, left their country, and offered *gold,
frankincense and myrrh to our Saviour,* Mat.
ii. *David would not sacrifice to God of that
which cost him nothing,* 2 Sam. xxiv. 24.
The primitive Christians offered up to God
prayers and tears, labours and travels;
nay, their honours, their fortunes, their
lives, their blood. But, alas! what have
these

these men to offer? They have not love enough to put them upon any expence; nor faith enough to put them upon any hardships, for the fake of God and virtue. *For tho' they think themselves rich, and increafed in goods, and to have need of nothing, yet are they poor, wretched, and miferable, and blind, and naked, Rev.* iii. 17. And shall these receive a crown of righteousness? Shall these share in the kingdom of Jesus? Shall these partake in the triumph of the last day? It can never be; they do nothing worthy of the gofpel, nothing worthy of the Spirit of God; nothing that can entitle them to the benefit of the Crofs of Christ.

3. The life of the *Laodicean* Christian will never do any credit to religion, or reflect any honour on the gofpel. No man will be ever able to difcern the beauty of holinefs, or the power and efficacy of divine truths, from the practice and converfation of fuch an one. Ah! had the carriage of the primitive times been fuch as his, I know not what *miracles* might have done, I am fure *examples* would never have made any profelytes. But the Chriftians then acted thofe virtues, which the *Pagan* only pretended to; and faith in Jesus atchieved thofe victories over the world, which the *Jews* (fo debauched and ftupid were

were they grown) did in the declenfion of
that ftate neither underftand nor pretend
to : this was that which made the world
admire and love Chriftianity. After thus
much faid of the effects of this fort of carriage ; I need fcarcely put any one in mind,
what will be the laft and faddeft effect of
it ; for if our Chriftianity be fuch, that it
neither truly fets us free from our bondage
to the world and flefh; nor inriches our foul
with true and folid virtues ; if it neither
promote the honour of God, nor the good
of man, it muft unavoidably follow, that
having no true title to God's favour, nor
any rational ground, on which to build an
affurance of it, we can reap no true comfort or pleafure from religion here, or any
reward from it hereafter. Alas! what
talk I of comfort and reward? *Diftrefs and*
anguifh muft take hold of the finners in Sion;
and fearfulnefs muft furprife the hypocrite:
and from the troubles and miferies of *this*
life, they muft go down into the everlafting torments of *another*. The fcripture is
plain; God will fpue them out of his
mouth, as he did the *Laodicean:* he will
fhut the *gate* of *heaven* againft them,
as againft the *foolifh virgins* that had
no *oil* in their *lamps :* and their hell
will have one torment in it, which is
incident to no others, that they had once
the hopes of heaven ; and it is no fmall
aggra-

aggravation of mifery to fall into it, even from the expectation of happiness.

This is not, as I obferved above, to be applied to accidental dulnefs or deadnefs in duty ; nor are the decays or abatements of love, which good men fometimes fuffer, immediately to be pronounced damnable. But yet *thefe* are to be put in mind of the danger they are in ; and recalled to their former zeal, in the words of the Spirit to the Church of *Ephefus* ; *Neverthele/s, I have fomewhat again/t thee, becau/e thou ha/t left thy fir/t love. Remember therefore from whence thou art fallen ; and repent, and do the fir/t works ; or el/e I will come unto thee quickly, and will remove thy candle/tick out of his place, except thou repent,* Rev. ii. 4, 5.

CHAP.

CHAP. IX.

Of Zeal. *What in general is meant by* Zeal; *and what is that perfection of holiness in which it consists. Whether the perfect man must be adorned with a confluence of all virtues; and to what degree of holiness he may be supposed to arrive.*

I Am arrived at the *last stage of perfection*, which I chuse to call a state of *zeal*; not only because the *scripture* seems to direct me to this expression, but also because it seems to me more full and proper than others, that may be, or are made use of for the same end. A state of *union* is an expression that better suits *another* life than *this.* For the lesson the *perfect* man is ever and anon to revolve in his mind, is, that the present life is a life of labour, and travel, and sufferings; the future one, of rewards, and crowns, and enjoyments. Then as to that other expression, the state of *love*, it suits my purpose well enough; but does not come up so justly and exactly to it, as the state of *zeal*; for I take *zeal* to be *love*, in the utmost elevation and vivacity that it is capable of.

And now, what a noble, what a fruitful *argument* am I entring upon? Methinks I feel my soul grow *warm*, and *in-*
kindle

kindle upon my approaching it; and my
firft views or contemplations of it infpire
me with defires of the fame nature with it
felf. I am concerned to fee my felf confined and limited by the laws of *method*; and
find my felf inclined to wifh, that I were
now to write, rather a juft *volume*, than a
few *pages*. Here the heroic *acts*, or, what
is more, the heroic *lives* of faints, martyrs, and confeffors, prefent themfelves to
my thoughts; here *human* nature, enriched, adorned, and elevated to the utmoft
degree, by a participation of the *divine*
one; here the power of *God's Word*, the
energy of the *Holy Ghoft*, the triumphs of
faith, and the extafies of *love*, would be
defcribed; here the different excellencies of
different *virtues*, and the different value of
good works, fhould be ftated and fettled,
and the various paths, in which men purfue the *heights* of virtue and the nobleft
defigns be examined, and folid piety and
true wifdom be refined from the alloys and
mixtures of enthufiafm, fuperftition, fancy, or whatever elfe they are disfigured
and debafed by. But this cannot *now* be
done, and it may be it could not at all be
done by *me*: no meafure of the *Spirit*,
peradventure, below that with which the
apoftles were infpired, is fufficient to treat
this argument as it requires. Befides, according

cording to my capacity, I have been all
along making this point. When, in the
firſt ſection, I ſtated the *notion* of *perfection*,
ſhewed by what ſteps we advanced to it,
what *means* we are to make uſe of, and
what would be the *fruit* of it, I did in effect deſcribe to my reader, the ſtate of *zeal*,
and marked out the path that leads to it.
When, in the *ſecond*, I labour to eſtabliſh
the true *liberty* of man, upon the overthrow
and extirpation not only of *mortal ſin*, and
of *idleneſs* and *lukewarmneſs*, but alſo, as
far as it might be, even of *ſin of infirmity*,
and *original corruption*; what elſe was I
doing, but proſecuting this one deſign,
namely, the implanting and propagating in
the world the ſtate of *zeal?* However,
ſomething there ſeems to me yet wanting
to *compleat* my undertaking; and that I am
to endeavour now. To which end I will
here diſcourſe of three things,

    1. What it is in general I mean by *zeal*.
    2. What is that *Perfection* of *holineſs* or
righteouſneſs, wherein it conſiſts And,
    3. Of the *efficacy* or *force* of this *holi-
neſs*, as it exerts it ſelf in *good works*. Of
theſe, the *two former* ſhall be the argument of *this*; the *third* of the *following*
chapter.

§. 1. Of

§. 1. Of *zeal* in *general,* what it is. I
do not exclude fome degrees of *zeal,* from
every period of the Chriftian's life ; fincerity cannot fubfift wholly without it. *The
hunger and thirft after righteoufnefs,* which
is the fubject of one of our Saviour's *Bea-
titudes,* muft be more or lefs in every
child of God. But it may fignify one
thing in the *infant,* another in the *adult*
Chriftian ; in the one, the conqueft of fin,
or rather of the reliques and remains of
former finful habits, and the attainment of
habitual goodnefs, is the *object* of this
hunger and thirft : in the other, it imports
a vehement defire of whatever is yet wanting to a farther accomplifhment and confummation of righteoufnefs *already* fixed
and eftablifhed ; the entire and ultimate
perfection of it in *heaven* ; and in the
mean time, the promoting the divine glory upon *earth,* whatever it coft him to do
fo. By a ftate of *zeal* then, I here mean
virtue or holinefs, not in the bud, or in
the bloffom, but in its full ftrength and
ftature, grown up, and ripe, and loaded
with bleffed fruits : I mean *that* holinefs
that is the refult of illumination, or clear-
nefs of judgment, of the ftrength and force
of holy refolution, and the vigour and
energy of holy paffions. In a word, I
mean that folid, fpiritual, and operative
D d religion,

religion, which may be felt and enjoyed
by us our felves, in the ferenity and tranquillity of confcience, the longings and
breathings of pious defires, the joys and
pleafures of a rational affurance; difcerned
by the world in our lives and actions, in
the modefty of our garb, in the plainnefs
and humility of all things elfe that per-
tain to the *port* of life; in the temperance
of our meals, the purity and heavenlinefs
of converfation, the moderation of our defigns and enjoyments, the inftruction of
our families, with a tender and indefatigable watchfulnefs over them; the conftancy of our attendance *upon*, and the de-
voutnefs of our deportment *in*, the publick worfhip of God; and finally, in the
activity and generofity of our charity: or,
to fpeak my thoughts in the language of
St. *Paul*, a ftate of *zeal*, is that perfection or maturity of holinefs, which abounds
in *the works of faith, the labour of love,
and the patience of hope, in our Lord Jefus
Chrift, in the fight of God, and our Father,*
1 *Theff.* i. 3. Now the end of all this is,
the advancing the glory of God: and
therefore *zeal* is well enough defcribed or
defined, by an ardent or vehement defire of doing fo. Now this is advanced
two ways: *firft*, by our *perfonal* and *inhe-
rent holinefs* : and, *fecondly*, by the fruit of
it,

It, *good works.* Of both which I will now
fpeak a little more particularly.

§. 2. Of that *perfection* of *holinefs* which
conftitutes the ftate of *zeal.* Here I will
inquire into *two* things.

1. Whether the *perfect* man muft be
poffeffed of *all* the treafures of goodnefs;
whether he muft be adorned by a confluence, and an accumulation of *all* virtues.

2. What *height* of virtue, what *degree*
of holinefs, he may be fuppofed to arrive
at.

1. Of the *extent* of righteoufnefs. It is
generally thought, that univerfality is as
effential and neceffary a property of gof-
pel-righteoufnefs, as fincerity and perfeverance: that there is an infeparable connexion and union, between *all* Chriftian
virtues; fo that he, who wants *any*, muft
be concluded to have *none:* this *want* being, not like a blemifh that diminifhes
the beauty, or a maim that weakens the
ftrength; but like a wound that diffolves
the frame and contexture of the natural
body. This opinion is partly built upon
reafon, which tells us, that there is a native luftre and beauty in all virtues; and
therefore there is no one in the whole fyf-

Dd 2   tem

tem of morality, but muſt be lovely and amiable to a good mar. Partly upon *ſcripture,* in which we find the Chriſtian repreſented, *as holy in all manner of converſation,* 1 Pet. i. 15. *Perfect in every good work,* Heb. xiii. 21. *As filled with all the fulneſs of God,* Eph. iii. 19. *As fruitful in every good work,* Col. i. 10. and exhorted in the moſt comprehenſive terms imaginable, to the practice of *every* virtue. *Finally, brethren, whatſoever things are true, whatſoever things are honeſt, whatſoever things are juſt, whatſoever things are pure, whatſoever things are lovely, whatſoever things are of good report; if there be any virtue, if there be any praiſe, think on theſe things.* To which may be added numerous texts, importing, that faith is a principle of *univerſal* righteouſneſs; and that the fear and love of God, do equally oblige us to *all* his commandments; and that the violation of *one* involves us in the guilt of *all.* And the reſult of all this ſeems to be plainly this, that the whole *chain* of graces is diſſolved and loſt, if there be but one *link* wanting. But at this rate, as the *ſincere* man muſt be endowed with *all* manner of virtues, ſo muſt the *perfect excel* in *all:* but the one and the other aſſertion, if we conſider things cloſely, ſeems to have in them inſuperable difficulties. There is a vaſt *variety* in the natures of men, in the ſtates and

and conditions of life, and in the kinds,
and degrees, as well as of the fanctifying.
as of the miraculous gifts of God. St
Paul tells us, *every man has his proper gift
of God*, 1 Cor. vii. 7. From whence it
feems naturally to be inferred, that every
man is not capable of attaining to an excellence and eminence in *every* virtue. Experience tells us, that there are different
kinds of *natures*, as well as *foils*; and that
fome kinds of *virtues*, like fome kinds of
feed, will thrive better in *one* than in *another*. Nor does *grace* alter the matter
much; fince it generally accommodates it
felf to *nature*. Laftly, it feems very hard,
that every man fhould have the virtues of
all men, of all ftates, of all capacities; every particular member, the virtues of the
whole Church; the beauty and ftrength of
the Church, as well as of the natural body,
or common-wealth, confifting, not in the
all-fufficiency of every member, but in
that variety of gifts and graces, that ce-
ments and unites, enriches and fupports the
whole. To come to the matter of *fact*; I
read of the *faith* of *Abraham*, the *meeknefs*
of *Mofes*, the *patience* of *Job*, the *love* of
Mary Magdalen, the *zeal* of St. *Peter*, and
the *labours* and *travels* of St. *Paul*; which
firmnefs and conftancy is too mean a name
for. Thefe virtues feem therefore, to
have been the *peculiar* excellencies of thefe

per-

perfons; and to have fhone in *them*, with more tranfcendent luftre, than any *other* : thefe feem to have been the virtues, for which grace and nature eminently qualified them; and to which the providence of God more immediately and directly called them. All this confidered, feems it not enough to come up to the *perfection* of *thefe* great men? May it not fuffice to excel in thefe virtues, which nature, grace, and providence prefcribed? May not the *perfect* be allowed to want, what he does not need? Would not one think, that, in many refpects, it were enough for him to be free from this or that vice, rather than to expect that he fhould be adorned with this or that virtue, which he has no ufe for? Efpecially, if by virtue we underftand ftrictly, fuch a habit as enables us to act eafily and delightfully. To adjuft this matter;

1. The *perfect* man muft, as I have proved before, not only be fet free from the dominion of fin, but alfo abftain even from a fingle act of prefumptuous wickednefs : he muft neither criminally *omit* a duty, nor deliberately *commit* any thing repugnant to it.

2*dly*, He muft be endowed with fpiritual wifdom and underftanding, with faith, hope, charity, with the graces which I will

call

call *universal,* becaufe neceffary and indifpenfable to all as Chriftians, abftracting
from their particular capacities and relations ; and *that* too in an *eminent* degree, fo
as to be *ftrong in the grace which is in Chrift
Jefus,* 2 Tim. ii. 1. This will render him
*holy in all manner of converfation, and tho-
roughly furnifhed to all good works.* Thefe
two things conftitute *univerfal* righteoufnefs, compleat the *perfect* man, and fully
fatisfy the texts alledged ; or, if *not,* what
follows *will.*

3*dly,* He muft excel in thofe virtues
which are moft *natural.* I call thofe virtues *natural,* to which grace and nature
moft powerfully difpofe and incline him ;
for *thefe* he feems to be defigned by God ;
thefe will foon grow up to maturity; and
much will be their fruit, and great their
beauty. I do not all this while fuppofe,
that the *perfect* man ought not fo far to fubdue and rectify his temper, as not only to
overcome the fin of his *conftitution,* but in
fome degrees poffefs the virtue that is
moft repugnant to it. But to expect him
to be eminent *here,* is, I doubt, too hard
and unreafonable. For *here,* when he has
beftowed much pains and travel, much care
and coft, his progrefs may not be fo much,
as where he beftowed *leaft.* But here I
muft add *two* cautions ; the *one* is, that

no man miſtake contracted *habits* for *nature*, and then conclude, that it will be impoſſible for him to attain the *perfection* of this or that virtue, through a natural incapacity. In the next place, let no man ſatisfy and content himſelf, in a weak and imperfect ſtate of *that* virtue, which is directly oppoſed to the ſin of his *conſtitution* ; but let him think, that *here*, if any where, his virtue muſt be always *growing* ; and let him not doubt, but that our Saviour's promiſe, as far as it can be accompliſhed on earth, belongs to his ſincere endeavours here ; *bleſſed are they that hunger and thirſt after righteouſneſs ; for they ſhall be filled,* Matth. v. 6.

4. The *perfect* man muſt be eminent in thoſe virtues which are moſt *neceſſary* : ſuch are thoſe which his particular ſtation and calling, or any other diſpenſation of providence he is under, requires of him. Whatever virtues may be more *delightful,* theſe are more *important* ; others may be more *natural,* theſe have more of *uſe* and more of *merit.* A man may fall ſhort of *perfection* in others, without either *diſparagement* or *guilt* ; but deficiency in theſe, can hardly eſcape *both.* Beſides, every thing is lovely in its *place,* and in its *time.* There is a *peculiar* grace and luſtre, that attends the virtues of a man's *ſtation,* that

is

is fcarcely to be found in any other. I
would, therefore, have my *perfect* man
truly great in his *own* bufinefs; and fhine
with a dazling luftre in his *own* fphere. To
this purpofe, furely, fpeaks the advice of
St. *Paul,* Rom xii. 6, 7, 8. *Having then
gifts, differing according to the grace that is
given to us, whether prophecy, let us prophefy
according to the proportion of faith: or miniftry, let us wait on our miniftring: or he that
teacheth, on teaching: or he that exhorteth,
on exhortation: he that giveth, let him do it
with fimplicity: he that ruleth, with diligence:
he that fheweth mercy, with chearfulnefs.*

5. Laftly, As there is different *guilt*
in fins, fo there is different *merit* in virtues: as amongft miraculous, fo amongft
fanctifying gifts, fome are more *excellent*
than others; and he is the *moft perfect
man,* who is enriched with the *moft perfect gifts.* The three heroic virtues of
the gofpel are *faith, love, humility.* Nor
do I prefumptuoufly, contrary to the apoftle, exclude *hope*; but comprehend it under *faith.* Of *faith* I have often had occafion to fpeak. *Humility* will make the
laft chapter of *this* fection; and therefore
I will only exhort to *love. Love* is the
nobleft fruit of illumination and faith,
the true fource and parent of joy and
peace,

peace. *Love* is the most pregnant seed of a divine life; 'tis the principle that animates, moves, and forms the whole body of righteousness: *love* is the bond of union and *communion with the Father and his Son Jesus* through the *Spirit*. And 'tis but fit, that what renders us most *like* God, should render us most *dear* to him too: and this *love* does; *for God is love.* In short, *love is the fulfilling of the law;* 'tis the beauty and perfection of a disciple of Jesus; and the great subject of praise and glory in the day of judgment. *Love* is the last round in the scale of *Perfection*; and therefore my *perfect* man must abound in this. What degrees of *love*, of *desire*, or *complacency* for the things of this *present* life, may consist with sincerity, what with *Perfection*, may be easily learned from several parts of this work. There is no doubt but the *perfect* man must *love* God to that *degree*, that he must always cleave to him; walk as always before him; ever meditate and contemplate on him and his works; contrive and study, labour and contend to please him: it must be an affliction to him to be divided from him but for a little while; and he must ever and anon, by day and night, break out into his praises, and rejoyce and glory in him. 2. He must love

love God to that degree, as that all things, in comparison of him, must appear blasted and withered, empty and contemptible, without pleasure, without beauty: and consequently he must so thirst after the *beatific vision*, after the presence and fruition of God, that he must earnestly *desire to be dissolved*, and pant and long to be dismissed from the *pilgrimage* of this *world*, and from the corruptible *tabernacle* of the *body*. Nor do I, lastly, doubt, but that this *love* is often sensibly *transporting* : 'tis a fire within, that strives to break out, and exert itself in the fruitions of heaven : 'tis a rich and mighty cordial, that raises nature above itself, and makes it all purity or glory.

Thus have I considered the *extent* or compass of the *perfect* man's *virtues*. And the *sum total* is: in some he must excel, because natural and easy ; in others, because necessary. Universal ones he *cannot* want; they are essential to Christianity ; others of a peculiar nature he *may*, unless his circumstances exact them : nor is this any diminution of his *perfection*. Patience, fortitude, moderation, vigilance, &c. are the virtues of earth, not heaven ; and yet none think the blessed inhabitants of that place imperfect, because not endowed with habits which they do not want.

Above

Above all, he that will be *perfect*, muft abound in thofe graces, which are for the moft *heroic* nature ; faith, love, and humility: for thefe are they, which moft effectually exalt man above *himfelf*, and above the *world*; which inflame him with a *zeal* for the honour of God, and the good of man; and enable him to furmount the difficulties, which he meets with in profecuting this glorious defign. I am next to enquire,

§. 2. To what *height*, to what *degrees* of virtue, the *perfect* man may advance. I have in part anticipated this enquiry already ; yet cannot forbear adding here *two* obfervations. *Firft*, That reafon and fcripture feem to prefs us on towards an endlefs progrefs in virtue. And yet, *secondly*, That both feem to propofe to us fuch a *ftate* of *perfection* as attainable, beyond which we cannot go ; that fo the *beginner* may not *defpair* of perfection, nor the *perfect abate* any thing of their vigilance, and their induftry. Such a degree of excellence, to which nothing can be added; fuch aheight, above which there is no room to foar, if apply'd to man and this world, is furely but an imaginary notion. To dream of *fuch* a *perfection*, were to forget our nature, and our ftate: no fagacity of judgment, no ftrength of refolution,

lution, no felicity of circumſtances, can ever advance us to *this* height. Such a *perfection* as this, that is incapable of any increaſe, belongs, I believe, to *God* alone : or, if we may allow it to *angels*, we muſt certainly deny it to *man :* in *whom*, one would think, the appetites of the body can never be ſo entirely ſubdued, that there ſhould be no place to extend his conqueſt, or render his victory more intire and compleat : and in *whom*, one would think, the Spirit of God ſhould never reſide in that meaſure, that there ſhould be nothing to be added to his fulneſs. 'Tis hard to conceive, how we ſhould ſtudy the ſyſtem of divine faith, how we ſhould daily reflect upon our lives and actions, without *growing* in ſpiritual wiſdom and underſtanding; 'tis hard to conceive, how we ſhould give God, the world, and our ſelves, repeated proofs of our integrity in the day of tryal, without *increaſing* our ſtrength and aſſurance : and love muſt naturally increaſe with theſe. Whence it is, that St. *Paul*, acknowledging himſelf not yet *perfect*, reſolves, *that forgetting thoſe things that are behind, and reaching forwards to thoſe things that are before, be would preſs on towards the mark, for the prize of the high calling of God, in Chriſt Jeſus*, Phil. iii. 13, 14. And St. *Auſtin* reſolves, *Pleniſſima charitas, quamdiu hic homo vivit, in nemine*

Of Zeal.

mine est : An *absolute plenitude of charity is
in no mortal upon earth.*

And yet, if we come to *fact* and *practice,* one would be tempted to think, that
the *disciples* of our Lord and Master,
had arrived at that state, wherein their
business was not to climb higher, but rather to make good the ground they had
gained. What could render St. *Paul's* victory over the body more compleat, who
assures us, *I am crucified with Christ?* And
again, *I am crucified to the world, and the
world is crucified to me ?* What could render the authority and dominion of *his*
mind more absolute, or its graces more
consummate and entire? Who could say
with truth, *'Tis not I who live, but Christ
who lives in me.* What would you have
added to that faith, and love, which
made *him* ready, *not only to be bound, but to
die at Jerusalem,* which made *him long to
be dissolved and to be with Christ ?* As to
those words of *his,* Phil. iii. 13. *forgetting
those things that are behind, and reaching forwards,* &c. *they* relate to his tryals and
performances, to his perils and conflicts;
not to his attainments: he does not here
deny himself to be *perfect,* though that
might well enough have become his modesty and humility; but only, that he
was not to look upon himself as already
at his goal, a conqueror and crowned;
there

there being much yet behind to do and
suffer, notwithstanding all that he had
passed through. This is the sense of his
ἐχ ὅτι ἤδη τετελέωμαι. which we render,
not as though I were already perfect. As to
St. *Austin*, I am wholly of his mind;
for he speaks *comparatively*, and does in
effect no more than affirm, that no man
living is as *perfect* in *this* world, as he
will be in *another*, which no man sure
can ever doubt———If we consult *rea-*
son, will it not be apt to tell us, that as
every *being* has its *bounds* set it, so has
every *perfection* too? That there is a *sta-*
ture, as of the *natural*, so of the *spiritual*
man, beyond which it cannot grow? That
as to *grace*, no more can be infused, than
our *natures* are capable of? Otherwise,
like too rich a cordial, it will not strengthen, but fire our natures; or, like too
dazling a light, it will not assist, but oppress our faculties. And does not the
parable of our *Master* countenance this,
Matth. xxv. 2. wherein he tells us, that
God gave to one five talents, to another
two, to another one, to every man according to his *ability.* By which one would
think our Lord insinuates, that the measures of *grace* are usually distributed in
proportion to the capacities of *nature*; and
that *he*, who improved his *two* talents into
four, arrived at his proper *perfection*, as
well

well as *he*, who improved his *five* into *ten* ;
it being as abfurd to expect, that the *perfection* of every man fhould be the fame,
as to expect, that all mens *bodies* fhould be
of the fame height, or their *minds* of the
fame capacity.

Reflecting on all this together, I cannot but be of opinion, that fome have
actually arrived at *that* ftrength of faith,
at *that* ardour of love, that they feemed
to have been incapable of any confiderable
acceffions in *this* life. But yet, new occafions may ftill demand new virtues ; which
were indeed before contained and included
in faith and love ; but no otherwife, than
as fruits and trees are in their feeds.
And fome degree of original corruption
may ftill be lurking in the moft fanctified
nature ; and fome venial defects and
imperfections or other, may ftill leave room
for the greateft of faints to extend his
conqueft. Befides, 'tis hard to determine
or fix the bounds of knowledge ; and
every new degree of light feems to make
way for more. So that after all, nothing
hinders, but that the *path of the perfect
man* may, as well with refpect to his
rigtheoufnefs as his *fortunes*, be *like the
fhining light, which fhineth more and more
unto the perfect day* ; I mean, the day of a
bleffed eternity.

The *motives* to *perfection*, the *fruit* of
it, the *means* and *methods* of attaining it,
laid down in the *first* section, will all serve
here : therefore I have nothing to offer of
this sort ; only, if I forgot to pay that deference to the *institutions* of *our church*,
which they justly deserve, I do it *now :* and
do earnestly perswade my *reader* to a strict
observance of them. I do not only think
this necessary to maintain a *face* of *religion*
amongst us, but also highly conducive to
true *perfection.* I am fully satisfied, that
there is a *peculiar* presence of God in his
publick ordinances ; that the devotion of
good men does mutually enflame and enkindle one another ; that there is an holy awe
and reverence seizes the minds of good men,
when they draw near to God in publick
worship ; and finally, that if the *offices* of
our *liturgy* do not affect our *hearts*, 'tis
because *they* are very much indisposed, and
very poorly qualified for the true and spiritual worship of God.

E e   C H A P.

CHAP. X.

Of Zeal, as it confifts in Good Works. That our own fecurity demands a Zeal in thefe good works; fo likewife do the good of our neighbour, and the glory of God, which are much promoted by good works.

AND now let not any one think, that I have taken pains to advance the illumination of a finner, to knock off his chains and fetters, to raife him as far as might be above the corruption of nature, and the defeats and infirmities of life; to fcatter thofe lazy fogs and mifts which hung upon his fpirits, and to enrich him with heroic virtues; let no man, I fay, fancy that I have laboured to do all *this*, that after all, my *perfect man* might *fit down* like an *Epicurean God*, and enjoy himfelf; might talk finely of folitary fhades and gardens, and fpend a precious life, fitted for the nobleft defigns, in a fluggifh retirement. No, no; as *virtue* is the perfection of human life, fo is *action* the perfection of *virtue:* and *zeal* is that principle of *action*, which I require in a faint of God. Accordingly, the fcriptures defcribe this great, this happy man, as *full of the Holy Ghoft, fervent in fpirit, zealous of good works.* Such a

one

one was *Moses, mighty in word and deed,* as well as *learned in all the knowledge of the Egyptians:* such an one was St. *Stephen,* as full of a divine ardour and irresistible fervency of spirit, as of an irresistible wisdom ; and such an one was the excellent *Cornelius, a devout man,* one that had transfused and derived the fear of God from his own bosom, throughout his family, and relations, and friends too; *one that gave much alms, and prayed to God always.* What need I multiply instances ? This is that which distinguishes the *perfect* man from all others ; the victories of faith, the labours of charity, the constancy and patience of hope, and the ardors of devotion.

Need I here distinguish a *zeal* of God, from the fierceness of faction, the cruelty of superstition, from the wakeful and indefatigable activity of avarice and ambition, from the unruly heats of pride and passion, and from the implacable fury of revenge ? It needs not; no foolish, no false, fantastick, earthly, or devilish principle can counterfeit a divine *zeal.* 'Tis a perfection that shines with such a peculiar lustre, with such a heavenly majesty and sweetness, that nothing else can imitate it ; 'tis always pursuing good, the honour of God, and the happiness of man : it *contends earnestly for the faith once*

de-

delivered to the saints; but it contends as
earneſtly too, to root out wickedneſs, and
implant the righteouſneſs of the goſpel in
the world. It is not eager for the *articles*
of a *ſect* or *party*, and unconcerned for *catholick* ones. When it preſſes for *reformation*, it begins *at home*, and ſets a bright
example of what it would recommend to
others. 'Tis meek and gentle under its
own affronts, but warm and bold againſt
thoſe which are offered to God. In a word,
though love fill its *ſails*, divine wiſdom
and prudence give it *ballaſt*; and it has no
heat, but what is tempered and refracted
by charity and humility.

 Need I, in the *next* place, fix or ſtate the
various *degrees* of *zeal*? Alas! it is not
requiſite; *zeal* being nothing elſe but an
ardent thirſt of promoting the divine
glory by the *beſt works*. 'Tis plain, the
more excellent the *work*, and the more it
coſt, the more perfect, the more exalted
the *zeal* that performs it. When, like
Mary, we quit the cumber and diſtracti-
on of this world, and chuſe religion for
our portion, then do we love it in good
earneſt. When with the *diſciples* we can
ſay, *Lord, we have forſaken all and followed
thee*, or are ready to do ſo; when we are
continually bleſſing and praiſing God;
when, if the neceſſities of Chriſt's church
require it, we are ready to call *nothing our
own* ;

own; when we are prepared, if the will of God be so, to *resist even unto blood*; when nothing is dear, nothing delightful to us, but God and holiness; *then* have we reached the *height* of *zeal*. In a word, *zeal* is nothing else but the *love of God* made *perfect* in us. And if we would see it drawn to the life, we must contemplate it in the blessed *Jesus*, who is the perfect pattern of heroic love. How *boundless* was *his love*, when the whole *world*, and how *transcendent* when a *world of enemies*, was the object of it! how indefatigable was *his zeal!* how wakeful! how meek! how humble! how firm and resolved! his labours and travels, his self-denial, prayers and tears, his silence and patience, his agony and blood, and charitable prayers poured out with it for his persecutors, instruct us fully, what divine *love*, what divine *zeal* is. And now, even at this time, *love* reigns in *him* as *he* reigns in *heaven*: *love* is still the predominant, the darling passion of *his* soul. Worthy art thou, O Jesus! to receive honour, and glory, and dominion! worthy art thou to sit down with thy Father on his throne! worthy art thou to judge the world, because thou hast *loved*, because thou hast been *zealous* unto death, because thou hast *overcome!* some there are, indeed, who have *followed* thy bright

E e 3 example,

example, tho' at a great diftance. Firft, martyrs and confeffors: next, thofe beloved and admired princes, who have governed their kingdoms in righteoufnefs; to whom the honour of God, and the good of the world, has been far dearer, than pleafure, than empire, than abfolute power, or that ominous blaze that is now called glory. And next follow,——— Hold! this is the work of angels, they muft marfhal the field of glory in the end of all things. O my God, may I at leaft be one, to fill the train of this triumphant proceffion of that bleffed day, when thou fhalt crown the zeal and patience of thy faints! Thus have I given a fhort account of *zeal*. I will now endeavour to kindle it in every breaft by fome few confiderations; which will at once evince the *neceffity*, and declare the *fruit* of it.

1. Our *own* fecurity and happinefs demand of us *zeal* fruitful in *good works*.

2. It is indifpenfable to the welfare and good of our *neighbour*.

3. It minifters moft effectually to the *glory of God*.

1. Our *own* falvation and happinefs depend upon it. For without *this*, we reject, or at leaft fruftrate the *counfels of God*,

againft

against our own souls; 'twas for this Chrift died, that *he might purify to himfelf a peculiar people zealous of good works.* This is the great end of our *election*; *God hath chofen us in Chrift before the foundation of the world, that we fhould be holy and without blame before him in love,* Eph. i. 4. which is to be explained by *Eph.* ii. 10. where God is faid to have *before ordained that we fhould walk in good works.* And the beginning of the *verfe* minds us, that 'tis for *this* end God imparts the light of his Word, and the vigour of his Spirit; and for *this* end he fanctifies and renews our nature; *We are his workmanfhip created in Chrift Jefus unto good works.* St. *Peter* tells us, that this is that which all the great and precious promifes of God immediately aim at: firft godlinefs, then life; firft virtue, then glory. What fhall I fay more? Our *Lord,* in his narrative of the laft judgment, and elfewhere; and his *apoftles,* in almoft innumerable places, have with great power, and great earneftnefs, inculcated *this* doctrine, that we fhall *be judged according to our works:* that immortality and glory is the portion, not of knowledge, but patience and charity; not of an orthodox belief and fpecious pretenfion, but of righteoufnefs and zeal; for the *incorruptible,* the *never-fading crown,* is *a crown of righteoufnefs.* Or, if men will be judged by their *faith*, which is not the language of the *gospel*, this does not alter the matter at all; since *faith* it self will be judged by its *works*. And as a happy *eternity* depends upon our *zeal*; so nothing elfe can give us any comfortable, any rational affurance of it in *this* life. The reason is plain; because 'tis *zeal* that is the only unqueftionable proof of our integrity; and *good works* are the fruit which alone can evidence the life and truth of our *faith* and *love*; *hereby we know, that we know him, if we keep his commandments*, 1 John ii. 3. *Yea, a man may say, thou haft faith, and I have works: fhew me thy faith without thy works, and I will fhew thee my faith by my works*, James ii. 18. Doft thou believe in *God?* Why art thou not *holy as he is holy?* Doft thou believe in *Jefus?* Why doft thou not *deny thy felf, take up thy crofs and follow him?* Why doft thou not walk as he walked? Doft thou believe a judgment to come? Why doft thou not *work out thy falvation with fear and trembling?* Why doft thou not *prepare to meet thy God?* Why art thou not *rich in good works,* that thou mayeft *lay up a good foundation againft the time to come, and lay hold on eternal life?* Nor are *good works* lefs neceffary to prove our *love*, than *faith*. Certainly, if we love holinefs, if we *hunger and thirft after righteoufnefs*, we fhall never live in a direct

rect contradiction to the strongest passions of our soul; we shall never refuse to gratify an inclination, which is not only fervent in us, but its gratification will procure us eternal rewards too. Certainly, if we *love God*, we cannot but seek his glory; we cannot but be desirous to maintain communion with him. And if so, do we know any *sacrifice* that is more acceptable to God than *good works?* Do we know any that he delights in more than *zeal?* Do we *love* the *blessed Jesus?* Are not *good works* the very test of this love which himself has appointed? *If a man love me, he will keep my commandments,* John xiv. 15. *Ye are my friends, if ye do whatsoever I command you,* John xv. 14. *The love of Christ,* saith the apostle, *constrains us* what to do, *to live not to our selves, but to him that died for us, and rose again,* 2 Cor. v. 15. What other returns can we make to Jesus? What other way can we express our gratitude to him? He sits on the right-hand of God; *all power is given him in heaven and in earth:* he does not himself need our ministry, nor want our service and charity; but hear what he says, *Inasmuch as you did it to one of these my little ones, you have done it to me,* Matt. xxv. 40.

2. Our *zeal* is indispensably necessary to the welfare and happiness of *others.* Do we

we regard our neighbour's eternal interest ?
'Tis *zeal* represses sin, and propagates righteousness ; 'tis *zeal* defends the faith and
suppresses heresy and error; 'tis *zeal* converts the unbeliever, and builds up the be-
liever; 'tis *zeal* that awakens the drowsy,
quickens the lukewarm, strengthens the
weak, and inflames the good with a holy
emulation ; 'tis *zeal* that baffles all objections, refutes all calumnies, and vanquishes
all oppositions raised against religion, and
oppresses its enemies with shame and confusion. 'Tis, in a word, *zeal*, and *zeal*
alone, that can make religion appear lovely
and delightful, and reconcile the world to
it ; for this alone can *adorn the gospel ;* for
it renders virtue more conspicuous, more
taking in life and example than it can be
in the precepts and descriptions of words.
Nor is *zeal* less serviceable to the *temporal,* than *eternal* interest of mankind.
When God laid the foundations of the
world, he laid the foundation of *virtue*
too ; and when he formed *man,* he wove
the necessity of *good works* into his very
nature. How necessary is *justice* to poor
creatures who lie so open to wrongs and
injuries ? How indispensable is *charity,* or
generosity, to these, who are exposed to so
many accidents, to so many wants, to such
a vicissitude of fortune ? And being all subject to so many follies and infirmities, to
so

fo many miftakes and fancies, how ftrong
muft be our obligation to mutual *forbearance*, *patience*, and *gentlenefs* ? In a word,
fin and *mifery* abounds in the world; and
if there were not virtues and good works
to ballance the *one*, and to relieve and fupport us under the *other*, life would be intolerable. So that revealed and natural
religion do neceffarily terminate and center
in a *zeal* for good works, as their ultimate
end, and utmoft perfection in this life ;
and the rule of our Saviour, *Whatfoever ye
would that men fhould do to you, do ye even
fo unto them*, is an abftract, not only of the
law and the prophets, but of the code of
nature too ; and this fingle principle, if
fincerely purfued, will ferment and work
us up to the nobleft heights of *zeal*. I
might here, if it were neceffary, eafily
fhew that *zeal* has as happy an influence
on the *publick* as the *private* ; that *this* muft
animate that juftice and mercy that fupports the throne ; that is the foul of that
honour, integrity, generofity, and religion,
which fupport the ftates and kingdoms of
the world ; and without which all politick
fyftems muft needs tend to a diffolution.
But I have faid enough ; and from what I
have faid, the truth of my *third* confideration naturally appears,

3. *Viz.*

3. *Viz.* That zeal ministers most effectually to the glory of God. For if zeal be in it self thus lovely, thus necessary; if the fruits and effects of it be thus serviceable to the temporal and eternal interest of man; what a lovely, what an agreeable notion of God shall we form from this one consideration of him, that he is the great Author of it? That he is the Origin and Fountain of that light and heat, of that strength and power of which it is compounded and constituted? He commands and exacts it; he excites and encourages to it by the promise of an eternal crown, and the ravishing fruition of himself: he has planted the seeds of it in our nature, and he cherishes them by the blessed and vigorous influences of his Word and Spirit. How gracious is the divine *Nature!* how gracious is the divine *Government!* when the substance of his laws is, that we should love as brethren, that we should cloath the naked, feed the hungry, deliver the captive, instruct the foolish, comfort the afflicted, forgive one another, if need be, seven times a day; and such like. If to do all this be an argument of being *regenerate,* and *born of God;* if this be a proof of his Spirit ruling in us, his Nature communicated to us, and his Image stamped upon us, how amiable must *God* be, when

we

we difcern fo much benefit, and fo much pleafure, and fo much beauty, and fo much lovelinefs in thofe qualities which are but faint and imperfect refemblances of him! in a word, the *holinefs* of *his* children and fervants, is a demonftration of the *holinefs* of *God* himfelf; and in this confifts the very luftre of divine glory. Holinefs is the flower of all his attributes; the moft *perfect*, becaufe the moft *comprehenfive* of all his divine perfections; for *holinefs* includes *wifdom, power*, and *goodnefs*. As to *goodnefs*, the cafe is fo plain, that *holinefs* and *goodnefs* are commonly ufed as terms equivalent. As to *wifdom*, 'tis evident, that no action is commendable and lovely, whatever the matter of it be, unlefs the principle, the motive of it be *wife* and *rational*; therefore *wifdom* cannot be feparated from the notion of *holinefs*. Laftly, As to *power*, this muft needs be comprifed in it too; for *beneficence*, which is at leaft one great branch of *holinefs*, muft unavoidably imply *power* in the *benefactor*, and *impotence* and *want* in the *beneficiary*. And this is the notion wherein *holinefs*, when afcribed to God in fcripture, is generally taken. *Holy, holy, holy, Lord God of hofts; heaven and earth are full of thy glory*, does exprefs the greatnefs and majefty, as well as the rectitude and purity of the divine Nature; and to *fanctify the Lord God in our*

our hearts, is, in the language of the
fcripture, not only to love him for his
goodnefs, but revere and fear him for his
majefty and greatnefs. Need I here add,
that the excellencies of the *creature,* their
fitnefs and fubferviency to the great ends
of their creation, is the glory of the *Creator* ; juft as the beauty, ftrength, and convenience of the *work,* is the honour of the
architect ? If the fun, moon, and ftars,
the irrational and inanimate parts of the
creation, fhew forth the glory of God ;
how much more do fpiritual and rational
beings ? And *virtue* is the perfection of
reafon, and *zeal* of *virtue* ; for this is that
which does directly and immediately advance thofe great ends that are deareft to
God, as I have, I think, abundantly made
out.

C H A P. XI.

Of Humility. *How neceffary it is to*
Perfection.

OUR Saviour has fo often pronounced the *humbleft,* the *greateft* in the
kingdom of heaven ; he has fo often pro-
mifed the *firft* place and the *greateft* ex-
altation to the *loweft* condefcenfions : he was
himfelf fo illuftrious an example of *lowli-
nefs*

ness of heart, of *poverty of spirit*; and the apostle has so expresly asserted his *joy and crown,* to be the reward of his *humility, Phil.* ii. that I can never think, that man can ever rise to a more eminent height, than *that* to which the imitation of this virtue of Christ will advance him. The more *perfect* therefore man is, the more *humble* must he be too: the clearer view, and the more assured hope he has of heaven, the more unconcerned must he be for all those things which the world pays a respect and honour to, the more he must be above them: the more fervent his love of God and his neighbour grows, the more confidently must he place all his glory in this one thing, the conformity of his affections and life to that of the blessed Jesus. Then is he *perfect,* and *the same mind is in him that was in Christ Jesus.* Finally, The more he *knows* God, the nearer he is admitted into *communion* with him; the more plainly will he discern at how infinite distance he stands from the divine Majesty and Purity, and will prostrate himself even into *dust and ashes* before him. The *perfect* man admires, adores, obeys, loves, relies, trusts, and resigns up himself, and all that is dear to him, to God. He is nothing in his own eyes; he pretends to nothing, he lays claim to nothing, or any other title than

that

that of the goodness and bounty of God; whatever virtues he has, he ascribes them to the grace of God; and the glory and immortality he expects, he expects only as the *gift of God through Jesus Christ our Lord.* And whatever he be in *himself,* he compares not himself with *others,* but he proves his *own work,* that *he may have rejoicing in himself alone, and not in another.* Nothing but *zeal* for God, or *charity* for man, can put him upon the asserting his own merit or service; but when he glories, it is like St. *Paul,* in his *infirmities,* that *the power of Christ may rest upon him.*

Need I here insist on the *fruit* of humility? Surely 'tis conspicuous to every one that thinks at all. Great is the peace and rest of the *humble* soul *here;* and great will be his glory *hereafter.* He, who loves not the world nor the things of it, *the lust of the flesh, the lust of the eyes, and the pride of life,* enjoys a perpetual calm and serenity of mind. There is no object that can raise any storm in him; there is nothing that can breed in him uneasy desires and fears. He, that loves the *Father,* is fixed on an immutable and perfect good; and he that *now* quits all for God, shall *one day* participate of the fulness of God, and that for ever.

Need I invite and exhort man to *humi-lity?* Need I guard him againſt ſpiritual *pride?* One would think 'twere altogether uſeleſs to attempt it. Is it poſſible, that the *creature* ſhould think himſelf ſo independent of his *Creator,* that he ſhould be able to pay him more ſervice than were due to him? Is it poſſible, that man ſhould ſet ſuch a rate upon his own righteouſneſs, as to think it capable of deſerving the utmoſt rewards that an infinite God can beſtow upon him? Is it poſſible, in a word, that *man,* poor, frail, ſinful *man; man,* that can do nothing that is good, but by the aſſiſtance of divine grace; *man,* depraved and corrupted in his *nature,* and but a very ill husband of *grace;* is it poſſible, I ſay, that *man* ſhould be *proud* towards *God,* towards that glorious and incomprehenſible Being, who is the Creator and Lord, the Monarch and Patron, the God and Father of heaven and earth? But as abſurd as this is, univerſal experience teaches us, that *humility,* true *humility* is a hard leſſon; and that very excellent perſons are not out of the danger of falling into vicious elations of mind. In order therefore to promote the one, and ſecure us againſt the other, I will propoſe theſe two or three conſiderations.

F f   1. There

1. There never was mere man yet, that did not fall fhort of his duty.

2. *Man* is the creature of *God*, depends upon him, and has received all from him; and therefore let him do the utmoft he can, he does no more than his *duty.*

3. God ftands in no need of our fervice; and 'tis our *own,* not *his* intereft we promote by it.

1. There never was mere man yet, *&c.* For proof of this, I will not fly to original corruption, or fins of infirmity. Alas! I need not. The apoftle, *Rom.* i. and ii. and iii. *ch.* lays the foundation of juftification by faith, in the univerfal defection and depravation of mankind. *They are altogether gone out of the way, there is none that doth good, no not one.* And what *fins* he there charges the world with, the *catalogue* he gives us of them will inform us. But are *we* no better than *they?* I anfwer, the light of the gofpel, and the preventing grace of God has undoubtedly given a great check to the progrefs of fin in the world : but fince no *man* can be juftified, but through faith in the blood of Jefus, 'tis plain that *we* too muft be concluded under fin. And tho' *our* fins may not in the number or fcandal equal *theirs;* yet we

we ought to remember too, that every fin
is the more provoking, the more voluntary it is; and the greater the grace is which
it refifts and defpifes. But what need I
compare our felves with the *Jew* or *Gentile*? What need I prove. by argument and
authority, that no man ever yet lived, or
will live, without fin? I mean mortal fin.
Who ever. yet looked back diligently into
his paft life, and did not meet with ftains
and deformities enough? When I confider
what legions of fins are ranged under thofe
two banners of the devil, the filthinefs of
the *flefh*, and of the *fpirit*; when I call to
mind envy, difcontent, murmuring, dif-
truft, pride, covetoufnefs. ambition, wilfulnefs, contention, frowardnefs, paffion,
diffimulation, falfhood, flattery, and a
thoufand other fins; and when I reflect upon the weakneffes and propenfions of nature, and the almoft innumerable temptations to which we are expofed, I muft confefs I am not at all furprifed to think, that
no flefh can be juftified in the fight of God
by a covenant of works: and when ever I
find any upon a death-bed, as I do fome,
acquitting themfelves from the guilt of
any deliberate wickednefs, I rather admire
their ignorance and partiality, than their
innocence. And yet, after all, a good man
is not to examine himfelf only concerning

F f 2 the

the evil that he has done, but alſo concerning the good which he has omitted. He muſt inquire, how far he has fallen ſhort of that poverty of ſpirit, and purity of heart, which he ought to have come up to: and how far he has been wanting in thoſe duties which a thorough zeal would have puſhed him on to. And when he has done this, let him be proud if he can.

2. *Man* is the creature of *God*, depends upon him, and has received all from him. And therefore let him do the utmoſt he can, he does no more than his duty: and, ſtrictly ſpeaking, cannot merit of *him*. He that will pretend to *merit*, muſt be his own maſter; he muſt have a right over his own actions; he muſt be free to diſpoſe of his affections and ſervices as he pleaſes. For, if he be antecedently bound, if he hath no liberty, no freedom, no right to diſpoſe of himſelf, or any thing he is poſſeſſed of, 'tis plain ſuch an one cannot *merit*. And this is the direct caſe between *God* and *man.* God is the great Lord, the great Proprietor of heaven and earth. He that gives alms, does but reſtore a part of what God lent him: he that takes patiently the loſs of goods, or health, or friends, does but give back what he had no right to retain: he was but tenant at will, and had no right to any thing longer than God thought fit

to continue it. And in all other inftances of duty the cafe will ftill be plainer. If he adore and worfhip God, there is infinite reafon that he fhould; for he depends upon him for his being and prefervation. If he love God never fo much, God has deferved much more than he can pay him: not only the enjoyments of life, but even life it felf, being derived from him. From this argument it will follow, that it is impoffible for a *creature* to *merit* of its *Creator* : *angels* themfelves never could. For might it not be faid with as much truth concerning them, as concerning man, *Who made thee to differ ? Or what haft thou which thou didft not receive? And if thou haft received it, why doft thou boaft as if thou hadft not received it?* 1 Cor. iv. 7. And the fame may be concluded concerning *Adam* in *Paradife.* For I demand, had he kept the covenant of God, had he done this by divine *grace*, or by his *own* ftrength? If by the *grace* of God, as divines generally hold, then may we apply the expreffion of St. *Auftin* to *Adam*, as well as to any one now under the difpenfation of the *gofpel:* that *when God rewards the works of man, he does only crown in him his own gifts.* But fuppofe he had done this by his *own* natural ftrength : were not the endowments of *nature*, as much the gifts of *God*, as

F f 3 the

the endowments of *grace?* The one were *natural,* the other *supernatural* gifts: both *gifts* ftill, tho' of a different kind. If it be here *objected,* if this be fo, how comes St. *Paul* to affirm, *To him that worketh is the reward due, not of grace but of debt?* Rom. iv. 4. I *anfwer, firft,* God feems, when he enters into covenant with man, to fufpend, or lay afide the natural right which he has over him as his creature; and to tranfact with him, as free, and mafter of himself: but this is all infinite condefcenfion. *Secondly,* It feems unfuitable to the infinite goodnefs of God, to bereave man of the life and happinefs he has once conferred upon him, unlefs he forfeits it by fome demerit: *The gifts and calling of God are without repentance;* nor can I think how *death,* which has fo much evil in it, could have entered the world, if *fin* had not entered it firft. In this fenfe, *unfinning* obedience gives a kind of *right* to the *continuance* of thofe good things, which are at *firft* the mere effects of divine grace and bounty. *Laftly,* A covenant of works being once eftablifhed, 'tis plain, that as fin *forfeits* life, fo obedience muft give a *right* to it: and as the penitent could not be reftored, but by an act of grace, fo he that commits no fin, would need no pardon. But then life it felf, and an ability to work righteoufnefs,

teoufnefs, muft be owing to grace antece-
dent to the *covenant:* and fo fuch an one
would have whereof to *boaft* comparatively, with refpect to *others* who fell ; but
not before God. The fum of all is, *man*
has nothing to render to God, but what he
has received from him ; and therefore can
offer him nothing but *his own:* which is no
very good foundation for merit. But fuppofe him abfolute mafter of himfelf ; fuppofe him holding all things independent
of God. Can the fervice of a few days
merit immortality and glory, angelical
perfection, and a crown ? He muft be
made up of vanity and prefumption, that
dares affirm *this.*

3. God ftands in no need of our fervice ;
and 'tis our *own,* not *his* intereft we promote by it. The foundation of merit a-
mongft *men* is *impotence* and *want:* the
prince wants the fervice and tribute of the
fubject ; the fubject the protection of the
prince : the rich needs the miniftry and the
labour of the poor ; the poor fupport and
maintenance from the rich. And it is thus
in imaginary, as well as real wants. The
luxury and pleafure of one, muft be provided for and fupported by the care and vigilance of others : and the pomp and the
pride of one part of the world cannot fub-

fift,

fift, but on the fervitude of the other. **In**
thefe cafes therefore, mutual *wants* create
mutual rights, and mutual merit. **But**
this is not the cafe between *God* and *man.*
God is not fubject to any wants or neceffities : nor is his glory or happinefs capable
of diminution or increafe. *He* is a Monarch, that needs no tribute to fupport his
grandeur, nor any ftrength or power befides
his own, to guard his throne. If *we* re-
volt, or rebel, we cannot injure *him :* if
we be loyal and obedient, we cannot profit *him.* He has all Fulnefs, all Perfection
in himfelf : he is an almighty and all-fufficient God. But on the quite contrary, tho'
God have no *wants, we* have many : and
tho' *his* Majefty and felicity be fubject to
no viciffitude, *we* are fubject to many. Our
fervice to *God* therefore is our *own* intereft ;
and our obedience is defigned to procure
our *own* advantage : we need, we daily
need his fupport and protection ; we depend intirely on his favour and patronage :
In him we live, and move, and have our be-
ing : and from *him,* as from an inexhauftible fountain, we derive all the ftreams of
good, by which we are refrefhed and improved. To know, and love him, is our
wifdom ; to depend upon him, our happinefs and fecurity ; to ferve and worfhip
him, our perfection and liberty ; to enjoy
him

him will be our heaven; and thofe glimp-
fes of his Prefence, which we are vouch-
fafed through the Spirit in this life, are the
pledges and foretafte of it. This is the
conftant voice of fcripture. *Every good
gift, and every perfect gift is from above,
and cometh down from the Father of lights,*
Jam. i. 17. *If I were hungry, I would not
tell thee; for the world is mine, and the fulnefs thereof. Will I eat the flefh of bulls, or
drink the blood of goats? Offer unto God
thankfgiving, and pay thy vows unto the moft
high: and call upon me in the day of trouble;
I will deliver thee, and thou fhalt glorify me,*
Pfal. l. 12, 13, &c. *If thou be righteous,
what giveft thou unto him? Thy wickednefs
may hurt a man, as thou art, and thy righteoufnefs may profit the fon of man,* Job
xxxv. 7, 8.

SECT.

SECT. III.

Of the Impediments *of* Perfection. *Five Impediments reckoned up, and insisted on. 1. Too loose a notion of religion. 2. An opinion that Perfection is not attainable. 3. That religion is an enemy to pleasure. 4. The love of the world. 5. The infirmity of the flesh. The whole concluded with a prayer.*

THO' I have been all along carrying on the *design* of this *section*, that is, the removing the obstacles of *Perfection*; yet I easily foresaw there might be *some* which would not be reduced within the compass of the foregoing *heads* : for *these* therefore I reserved this place ; these are *five*.

§. 1. Some seem to have entertained such a *notion* of *religion*, as if moderation here, were as necessary as any where else. They look upon *zeal* as an *excess* of righteousness ; and can be well enough content to want degrees of glory, if they can but save their souls. To which end they can see no necessity of *Perfection*. Now I would beseech such seriously to lay to heart, that salvation and damnation are things of no *common* importance : and there-

therefore it highly concerns them not to be miſtaken in the *notion* they form to them-ſelves of *religion*. For the nature of things will not be altered by their fancies; nor will God be mocked or impoſed on. If we will deal ſincerely with our ſelves, as in this caſe it certainly behoves us to do, we muſt frame our *idea* of *religion*, not from the opinions, the manners, or the fa-ſhions of the *world*; but from the *ſcrip-tures*. And we muſt not interpret *theſe* by our own inclinations; but we muſt judge of the duties they preſcribe, by thoſe de-ſcriptions of them, by thoſe properties and effects, which we find there. We muſt weigh the *deſign* and *end* of religion; which is to promote the glory of God, and the good of man, and to raiſe us above the world, and the body: and ſee how our platform, or model of religion, *ſuits* with it. And if, after we have done this, we are not fully ſatisfied in the true bounds and limits which part vice and virtue, it cannot but be ſafeſt for us to err on the right-hand. We ought always to remem-ber too, that the repeated exhortations in ſcripture to diligence, and that the moſt earneſt and indefatigable ones, to vigilance, to *fear and trembling*, to patience, to ſted-faſtneſs, and ſuch like, are utterly incon-ſiſtent with an eaſy, lazy, gentile religion. That the *life* of *Jeſus* is the faireſt and ful-

leſt

left comment on his *doctrine* : and, that
we never are to follow the examples of a
corrupt world, but of the best men, and
the best ages. This, this one thing alone,
will convince us, *what* endeavours, *what*
virtues are necessary to gain an incorruptible crown. See with what eagerness the
disciples of *Jesus pressed towards the mark !*
see with what courage, nay joy too, they
took up their cross and followed him ! how
generous were their *alms !* so that the
riches of their liberality were conspicuous
in the very *depth of their poverty.* What
plainness and singleness of heart; what
grace and warmth, what peace and joy
shewed it self in their conversation! what
modesty, what humility in their garb, deportment, and the whole train of life !
how frequent, how fervent, and how long
too, were their prayers and retirements!
In one word ! the spirit and genius of a
disciple of Christ discovered it self in all
they said and did : and the virtues of their
lives did as evidently distinguish a *Christian*
from a *Jew* or *Pagan,* as their *faith.*
How lovely was religion *then !* how full
its joy, how strong its confidence ! *then*
did Christians truly overcome the world :
then did they live above the body; *then*
was the Cross of Christ more delightful,
than the ease or honour, the pride or
pleasure, of a sinful life : *then* did they truly,

ly, through the Spirit, wait for the hope of righteoufnefs by faith. Let us now compare *our* lives with *theirs*, and then fit down content with poor and beggarly attainments if we can. Let us put *our* virtues in the fcales againft *theirs*; and, if we have any modefty, the inequality will put us out of countenance: we fhall blufh at our vanity; and fhall not have the confidence to expect the fame crown, the fame kingdom with them. But as too lax a notion of religion is apt to beget too much indifference and unconcernment; fo will it be faid, too exalted an one is apt to beget *defpair*: which is a *fecond* and no *lefs obftacle* of *Perfection*.

§. 2. Many there are, who, forming their judgment upon the flips and defects of good men, and the corruption of human nature, conceive *Perfection* to be a mere imaginary notion. They believe indeed, that, confidering how apt man is to fall fhort of his duty, 'tis very fit that the rule prefcribed him fhould be exact; and that he fhould be frequently preffed, and exhorted to *Perfection*: but that the thing it *felf* is too difficult for mortal man to attain in this life. But to this *objection* I muft oppofe *thefe* few things, which I believe will be fufficient to remove it.

1. The

1. The *beginning* of virtue is the moſt difficult part of it : the nearer we approach to *Perfection*, the eaſier, as well as pleaſanter, is religion. And therefore, whoever ſtartles at the difficulties, which lie in the way to an exalted virtue, has as much reaſon to be ſtartled at thoſe which will encounter him in his firſt entrance upon religion : and yet *theſe* muſt be conquered. 2. The avoiding the difficulties of religion, does but plunge us into worſe. We are neceſſarily under this *Dilemma* : if we will attain the peace and tranquillity of the *mind*, we muſt mortify and reduce the appetites of the *body* : if, on the other hand, we propoſe to gratify the appetites of the *body*, and enjoy the pleaſure of *ſin*, we cannot do ſo without offering much violence to the *mind*. And if this be ſo; if ſuch be the war and oppoſition between the ſoul and the body, that there is no way to a true and well-ſettled peace and pleaſure, but by the reduction and mortification of the one or the other ; *then* it will be eaſy to reſolve what we are to do. For thoſe appeals which atheiſts themſelves make to reaſon, proclaim the *ſoul* of man to be the ruling and nobler part of him. Beſides, the *ſoul* is the more vital, the more tender and ſenſible part of us : and conſequently the affliction of *this* muſt render us far more miſerable, than any hardſhips or

or difficulties virtues can impofe upon the *body.* 3. Whatever be the difficulties of *virtue*, they will foon vanifh, if we often call to mind, that peace and joy are the *fruit* of *virtue*; but fhame and remorfe, of *fin*: that no man ever yet repented of his refifting and conquering his lufts; but no man ever yet did not repent of following them; unlefs he *died* as much a brute as he *lived*: that heaven is a cheap purchafe, whatever it cofts us; but the pleafure of fin a very dear one, how eafily foever we come by it: and finally, that we are not our own mafters: there is a God to whom we ftand accountable for our actions: and confequently, whether we will, or will not, we muft either undergo the hardfhip and difcipline of virtue, or the eternal plagues and punifhments of fin. Laftly, The truth is, this opinion of the *impoffibility* of *Perfection*, has both been begot and cherifhed by thofe wild *fchemes* of it, which have been drawn by the hands of a flaming, indeed, but an indifcreet zeal. But I have here recommended to the world, no fantaftick, or enthufiaftick *Perfection.* I have advanced no heights of virtue, but what many do, I hope, at this day actually feel and experiment in themfelves: none, I am fure, but what the *followers* of the bleffed *Jefus* actually attained and practifed.

fed. *Be ye followers of us,* faid the apoftle; *as we are of Chrift.* Their lives were as bright a rule as their doctrine: and by their own actions they demonftrated the power of the faith they taught. They did not, like the *Scribes* and *Pharifees, bind heavy burdens upon others, and not move them with their finger*; they did not, like *Plato* and *Ariftotle,* magnify temperance and modefty at the tabernacles and carnavals of princes; nor commend the pleafure of wifdom in the gardens of *Epicurus:* but they *lived* as they *taught,* unfpotted by the pleafures, unbroken by the troubles of the world; modeft, ferene, equal, and heavenly minded, in honour or difhonour, want or abundance, liberty or prifon, life or death. Let us then no longer *object* or *difpute,* but with faith and patience be followers of thofe who have inherited the promifes: being *incompaffed with a cloud of witneffes, let us lay afide every weight, and the fin which doth fo eafily befet us; and let us run with patience the race that is fet before us, looking unto Jefus the author and finifher of our faith; who, for the joy that was fet before him, endured the Crofs, defpifing the fhame, and is fet down at the right hand of the throne of God. For confider him that endured fuch contradiction of finners againft himfelf; left ye be wearied and faint in your mind,* Heb. xii.

xii. 1, 2. I have done with those, who endeavour to *soften* or *shun* the difficulties of religion, not to *conquer* them.

§. 3. There are *others*, who will look upon this setting up the doctrine of *Perfection*, as a design against the *pleasures* of mankind. What, says such a one, shall I let go my present *pleasures* out of my hands, to hunt after I know not what, and I know not where? Shall I quit *pleasures* that are every-where obvious, for such as have no being, it may be, but in speculation? or at least, are never to be enjoyed by any, but some few rare and happy creatures, the favourites of God and nature? *Pleasures*, that have matter and substance in them, for such as I can no more grasp and relish than I can dreams and visions? But to this I answer, This pretty talk is all but stupid ignorance and gross mistakes. For, 1. As to innocent and virtuous *pleasure*, no man needs part with it. I endeavour not to deprive man of *this*; but to refine and purify it. And he, that prefers either silly, or vicious *pleasure* before religion, is wretchedly mistaken. For, 2. *Perfect* religion is full of *pleasure*. Had we but once arrived at true purity of heart, what could be so full of *pleasure* as the business of religion? What can be more delightful, than blessing and praising God, to a grateful soul;

G g

Allelu-

Allelujahs, to a foul fnatched from the
brink of deftruction, into the bofom of
its Mafter? What can be more tranfporting than the melting tendernefles of a holy
contrition, made up, like *Mary Magdalen*'s,
of tears and kifles, forrow and love, humility and glory, confufion and confidence,
fhame and joy? What can be more tranfporting than love, the love of a Chriftian,
when he is all *love, as God is Love*; when
he *defires nothing in heaven nor on earth, but
God*; when *all things are dung and drofs to
him, in comparifon of Jefus*? 4. If the *pleafures* of the *world* be more tranfporting
than thofe of *religion*, 'tis becaufe our faith
is weak, our love imperfect, and our life
unfteady. A conftant and exalted *pleafure*
is, I grant it, the fruit of *Perfection* alone.
The *peace and joy* of the Holy Ghoft reigns
no-where, but where that *zeal and love*,
which is an effect of the fulnefs of the
Spirit, reigns too. I had once propofed
to have infifted on the reafons of this here;
but this labour is prevented, for they are
very obvious to any one who hath read the
chapter of *Zeal* with ferioufnefs and attention. Laftly, What is infinuated in the
objection, that the *pleafures* of the *world* are
more numerous, or obvious, than thofe of
religion, is altogether a falfe and groundlefs fancy. In every place, and in every
ftate, do the pleafures of virtue wait upon
the

the *perfect* man. They depend not, like those of the body, on a thousand things that are not in our power; but only on God, and our own integrity. But this part of the objection I have, I think, for ever baffled, *sect. 1. chap. 4.* These *obstacles* of *Perfection* being thus removed, and the mind of man being fully convinced of the happiness that results from a state of *Perfection*, and of his obligation to surmount the difficulties which obstruct his way to it, there seems to be nothing now left to disappoint the success of this discourse, but somewhat too much fondness for the *world*, or somewhat too much indulgence to the *body*; which I am *next*, tho' but very *briefly*, to consider.

§. 4. There is a *love* of the *world*, which tho' it be not, either for the matter, or degree of it, criminal enough to destroy our sincerity, and our hopes of salvation; yet is it strong enough to abate our vigour, hinder our *Perfection*, and bereave us of many degrees of pleasure at present, and glory hereafter. The *indications* of this kind of love of the world, are too much concern for the pomp and shew of life; too much exactness in the modes and customs of it; too quick a sense of honour and reputation, pre-eminence and praise; too much haste, and too much industry to grow

rich,

rich, to *add house to house, land to land, and to load our selves with thick and heavy clay* ; too brisk a relish of the pleasures of the world ; too great a *gaiety* of mind upon the successes ; too much *dejection* upon the disasters and disappointments of it; too much care, and too much diligence ; an incumbring and embroiling one's self too far in worldly affairs; too much diversion, too much ease. These, I say, are the symptoms of a mind tainted with a love of the world, tho' not so far as to sickness and death. However, it will be enough to check the vigour, and dilute the relish of the mind. Now, the only way to overcome this defect, and to captivate the mind entirely to the love and service of religion and virtue, is to consider frequently and seriously the rewards of *Perfection*, the pleasure that will attend it in another life. Had the *young man* in the *gospel* done this ; had he had as lively a notion, and as true an estimate of the riches of *eternity*, as he had of *temporal* ones, he would never have *gone away sorrowful*, when he was advised to have exchanged the treasures of *earth* for those of *heaven*. Had the soul of *Martha* been as much taken up with the thoughts of *eternity*, as that of *Mary*, she would have made the same *choice* as *she did*. They who often *think*, how soon the fashion, the pomp and grandeur of this world

passes

paffes away, and how much better their *heavenly* country is than their *earthly*; how much more lafting, and how much more glorious the *New Jerufalem*, that *city that has foundations, whofe builder and maker is God*, than this city of ours, which may be overthrown in a moment; will neither weep, nor rejoyce, with too much paffion; neither buy, nor poffefs, with too much application of mind. In one word, he that fo often and devoutly *thinks* of that day, wherein *Chrift, who is our life, fhall appear, and we alfo appear with him in glory*, that he comes to *love* and *long* for it; fuch an one will have no great tafte of the honours, or the pleafures, or the interefts of life; nor will he be flothful or remifs, but *fervent in fpirit, ferving the Lord*: whatever degrees of affection he had for any thing of that nature, they will all vanifh; he will have no emulation, but for good works; no ambition, but for *glory*; I mean, *that* which is *eternal*. In the purfuit of *this* will he lay out the ftrength and vigour of his mind, for *this* he will retrench his profit, for *this* he will deny his pleafure, for *this* he will be content to be obfcure, mean, and laborious; for if the *world* be once crucified to him, *he* will the more eafily bear the being crucified to *it*,

§. 5.

§. 5. After all, there is an *Infirmity* in the *flesh*, against which if we do not guard our selves, if we do not struggle heartily, we shall *miscarry*. *The spirit is willing,* said our Saviour, *but the flesh is weak.* Without much care, and much watchfulness, the vigour of our minds will be relaxed; the exultation of our spirits will flag and droop; and we shall soon lose the relish there is in religion. The more effectual *remedies* against this frailty and fickleness of our nature, are *two*. *First*, Godly *fear*; and *this*, the purity and presence of God, the strictness and the impartiality of a judgment o come, the loss of an eternal crown, the terrors of eternal punishment, the number and strength of temptations, the deplorable falls of the greatest saints, and the conscience of our own weakness, will not fail to work in us. Let us then, not only *begin*, but also *perfect holiness in the fear of God. Blessed is he that feareth always. Secondly,* The stedfastness of *hope*; of hope, that waits and longs for the coming of our Lord. *This* will invite us often to take a view of *Canaan*; *this* will fill the mind often with the beauties and the glories of eternity; *this* will often call to our thoughts, the security, the rest, the transports of another world, the love of God and of Jesus, incorruptible crowns, the hallelujahs of angels, the shouts of victory,

tory, the fruit of the tree of life, the streams that water the paradise of God. And every such object will chide us out of our weakness and cowardise; every such thought will upbraid us out of our laziness and negligence; we shall hear always sounding in our ears the words of *Jesus* to his *disciples, What! can ye not watch with me one hour, and yet do you expect to reign with me for ever?* Or those to the *Church* of *Laodicea, To him that overcometh will I grant to sit with me upon my throne; as I have overcome, and am sat down with my Father on his throne.*

And now, *Reader*, if you find I have done you any service, if you think your self under any obligation to *me*, the *return* I beg from you is, that you will *first* offer praise and thanks unto God; and *next*, whenever you are in the vigour of the spirit, and the ardors of faith and love before God in prayer, put up these, or the like petitions for me, which I now offer up for my self.

O my

O My God, and my Father, increase the knowledge of thy Word, and the grace of thy Spirit in me. Enable me to perfect holiness in thy fear, and to hold fast the stedfastness of my hope unto the end. Pardon all the sins and errors of my life; and accept of my imperfect services through Jesus Christ. And because, tho', after all we can do, we are unprofitable servants, thy infinite bounty will yet certainly recompense our sincere endeavours to promote thy glory; let me find my reward from thee; or rather do thou thy self vouchsafe to be my reward. I should have ever thought my self unworthy to have put up this petition to thee, O thou glorious and incomprehensible Majesty, had not thine own Goodness, thine own Spirit, kindled this ambition in me. Behold! what manner of love is this, that we should be called the sons of GOD! these are the words of thy servant St. John: and now therefore my soul can never be at rest, till I awake at the last day after thy likeness; I can never be satisfied till I behold thy glory: which vouchsafe me, I beseech thee, by thy mercy and thy faithfulness; by the sufferings and intercession of thy dearly beloved Son.

F I N I S.